W9-CDS-518

Your Wife Is Not Your Momma

YOUR WIFE IS NOT YOUR MOMMA

How You Can Have Heaven in Your Home

WELLINGTON BOONE

DOUBLEDAY

New York   London   Toronto   Sydney   Auckland

OVERTON MEMORIAL LIBRARY
HERITAGE CHRISTIAN UNIVERSITY
P.O. Box HCU
Florence, Alabama 35630

PUBLISHED BY DOUBLEDAY
a division of Random House, Inc.
1540 Broadway, New York, New York 10036

DOUBLEDAY and the portrayal of an anchor with a dolphin are trademarks
of Doubleday, a division of Random House, Inc.

BOOK DESIGN BY JOANNE METSCH

Library of Congress Cataloging-in-Publication Data

Boone, Wellington, 1948–
Your wife is not your momma: how you can have heaven in your home
/ Wellington Boone. — 1st Doubleday ed.
p. cm.
Includes bibliographical references.
1. Husbands—Religious life.   2. Marriage—Religious aspects—
Christianity.   I. Title.
BV4528.2.B63   1998
248.8′425—dc21   98-42310
CIP

ISBN 0-385-49416-5
Copyright © 1999 by Wellington Boone
All Rights Reserved
Printed in the United States of America
March 1999
First Edition

1   3   5   7   9   10   8   6   4   2

TO THE THREE WOMEN IN MY LIFE:

My Momma, Rose Taylor
Thank you for praying me through to salvation,
and for calling out my name before heaven even now.

My Wife, Katheryn
You're my first accountability partner.
You've always been there for me.
Thank you for pressing me through to new levels in God.

My Daughter, Nicole
You're my seed. You've allowed me to
take you to the next level, and it's awesome to see
how far you've come to this point.
You're a preacher in the making. Keep going for God.

PREFACE

WHY THERE'S A SELAH AT THE END OF EVERY CHAPTER

At the end of each chapter, there will be a "Selah," a time to pause and meditate on what I've just shared with you from God's Word.

The Bible uses the Hebrew word *selah* most often in the book of Psalms. Although the actual meaning is unknown, it's usually interpreted to mean a pause or an interlude in a song.

After you finish reading each chapter, get alone with God for a "Selah." Look up several of the Scripture references in the footnotes on subjects that interest you to get the original context. Read more in that chapter of the Bible, or search out some related references that you find listed in the margin of your Bible. (If your Bible doesn't give you any cross-references, buy one that does!)

Even if you've fallen far away from God, talk to Him as if Jesus is real again and He's right there with you, and before you know it, you'll know He's real. He'll come to you. Jesus said, "Behold, I stand at the door, and knock: if any man hear my voice, and open the door, I will come in to him, and will sup with him, and he with me."[1]

The Bible also says that if you seek Him with all your heart, you'll find Him.[2] It may take a few false starts, but He wants time with you even more than you want time with Him, so He'll work with you to make it easy.

In your Selah time, ask God for further interpretation and application of what you've read. Meditation is something God encourages us to do on a regular basis, because insight doesn't always come the first time you read something or hear something from His Word. It takes time to stir your consciousness. It takes time to get things from your head to your heart.

Remember that the Lord told Joshua that meditation on the Word was a key to his courage and strength in battle. Moses died before the Israelites entered the Promised Land, and Joshua had to be the leader. God said to Joshua, " '*Be strong and courageous,* because you will lead these people to inherit the land I swore to their forefathers to give them. *Be strong and very courageous.* Be careful to obey all the law my servant Moses gave you; do not turn from it to the right or to the left, that you may be successful wherever you go. *Do not let this Book of the Law depart from your mouth; meditate on it day and night, so that you may be careful to do everything written in it. Then you will be prosperous and successful.*' "[3]

Be strong and courageous as you undertake this journey to make your marriage like heaven. I know you can be prosperous and successful in your marriage. I know you can blow your wife's mind so much that you become the most important and popular person in her life, after Jesus. When that happens, you'll begin to have an impact on many other people's lives, beginning with your children.

Keep at it, and others will grow, too. The way to that kind of success is the way of the Word. That's why the apostle Paul wrote, "Cultivate these things. Immerse yourself in them. The people will all see you mature right before their eyes! Keep a firm grasp on both your character and your teaching. Don't be diverted. Just keep at it. Both you and those who hear you will experience salvation."[4]

$\mathscr{C}$ONTENTS

PERMISSIONS

The following versions of the Bible are used in
Your Wife Is Not Your Momma

KJV *King James Version,* also known as the Authorized Version, originally published in 1611 during the reign of King James I of England. After the king reluctantly accepted a request from a group of Puritans for a new English version, a team of about fifty dedicated Bible scholars worked for nearly three years to complete it. They drew from both the original Hebrew and Greek languages and the work of earlier pioneers, such as William Tyndale, the first major English translator of the Bible.

NASB *The New American Standard Bible,* copyright © The Lockman Foundation, 1960, 1962, 1963, 1968, 1971, 1972, 1973, 1975, 1977, 1994. All rights reserved.

NIV *The Holy Bible, New International Version,* copyright © 1973, 1978, 1984 by the International Bible Society. All rights reserved.

NKJV Scripture taken from the *New King James Version,* copyright © 1979, 1980, 1982 by Thomas Nelson, Inc. Used by permission. All rights reserved.

The Message *The Message, The New Testament in Contemporary Language,* by Eugene H. Peterson. Scripture quotes from *The Message,* copyright © 1993, 1994, 1995. Used by permission of NavPress Publishing Group.

TLB *The Living Bible,* copyright © 1971. Used by permission of Tyndale House Publishers, Inc., Wheaton, Illinois 60189. All rights reserved.

Heaven in Your Home

"Therefore shall ye lay up these my words in your heart and in your soul, and bind them for a sign upon your hand, that they may be as frontlets between your eyes. And ye shall teach them [to] your children, speaking of them when thou sittest in thine house, and when thou walkest by the way, when thou liest down, and when thou risest up. And thou shalt write them upon the door posts of thine house, and upon thy gates: That your days may be multiplied, and the days of your children, in the land which the Lord sware unto your fathers to give them,

as the days of heaven upon the earth."

—Deuteronomy 11:18–21 KJV

Your Wife Is Not Your Momma

1

ℛEALLY LOVE YOUR WIFE

"Husbands, go all out in your love for your wives,
exactly as Christ did for the church."

—Ephesians 5, *The Message*

*Are you exploding with love for your wife? If you aren't, it's because
you haven't believed in the great things God has prepared for you as
a husband.*

*You have a champion inside of you. I'm calling that champion up
to the surface right now.*

*I want you to break free from every bondage that keeps you from
having a great time being your wife's husband.*

*You are absolutely destined for greatness, beginning in your own
home!*

When you get married, you leave your parents' home and enter a
whole new phase of life. Your love for your wife is different from
your love for your momma, and your wife's love for her daddy is
different from her love for you. Your love for your wife should model
how Christ loves the Church. Jesus is your role model for extravagant, joyful love. You are the only church that most people see.

This is a chapter about the great things that happened when I
learned how I could really love my wife as Christ loves the Church.
You can have great things happen in your married life, too, because
you've been ordained to be like Jesus.[1]

You can be a great husband! You know how I know? Because you and I have a great God, and He wants you to experience pure love in your marriage—to have heaven in your home.

HOW TO GET YOUR WIFE TO REALLY LOVE YOU

I saw my wife going off to take a shower, so I looked around to see what she would wear. She hadn't laid out an outfit, so I said to myself, Look, I'm supposed to love her as Christ loves the Church, right? Here's my chance to blow her mind by out-serving her, just as Christ out-serves the Church!

So I looked in the closet, found three outfits, and guess what? I ironed all three of them so she would have something to choose from when she got out. I had finished two and a half outfits when she caught me with the last one.

"What are you doing?" she demanded.

I said, "Honey, I just love you. I didn't see that you had prepared anything to wear and I wanted you to have something." I was humbling myself the whole time, low-looking her, because I really wanted to be a servant to her out of love.

Low-Looking Your Wife

Now, what do I mean by "low-looking her"? We men are so used to dominating people, standing in this certain posture, putting on like we're in control. The Lord says he hates the "high look,"[2] so in order to please God I have had to work on the "low look." I've had to learn to be like Jesus to my wife—"meek and lowly in heart."[3] I've had to go down when I wanted to raise up in my own defense. I had to discover that I was more of a man when I was meek, in the biblical sense, than when I was mighty. I was stronger when I gave in, even knowing I was right, than when I pushed my weight around, telling her to submit. I had to learn that I could show my wife real love only by being kind and by serving her.

My ironing something for my wife was a spontaneous gift of my time from my heart. It was a response to a *kairos*. That is a Greek word used in the New Testament for a divine window of opportunity. It was an opportunity to show my love for her. It came out of the heart God has given me for out-serving her, instead of always expecting her to serve me. It blew my wife's mind! It was great!

My wife was so amazed and embarrassed at my ironing something for her that she started to grab the iron. She said, "No! Give me the iron!" but I said, "No! I have it!" Then she threw down her hands and tears came to her eyes and she said, "This is too much!" It wasn't what I said or what I did that broke her down. It was the attitude of humility and unconditional love that overwhelmed her. She knew beyond a shadow of a doubt that I did it for her because I loved her. I didn't want to dominate her or lord it over her. I wasn't trying to manipulate her to get something for myself. I just wanted to serve her, as Christ serves the Church, and that caused her heart to want to surrender to me. She saw that I really loved her and she wanted to yield. Her heart was so full of joy that it overflowed in tears.

When I finished the ironing, I went into the rest room, where she couldn't see me, and gave God a high five! I said, "Yes! She cried from my loving her so strong!"

Giving Yourself to Your Wife

Strong love. That's what we husbands need these days. The Bible says, "Husbands, love your wives, just as Christ also loved the church and gave Himself for her."[4] Now, that is some kind of strong love! Do you know how much endurance it took to hang on that cross until He could say, "It is finished"[5]? If you've ever done endurance training for running or any other kind of sport, you know how much your muscles scream for relief, but you keep pushing them a little longer, a little harder, past the point of pain.

It's the same way in marriage. When you think you've endured all you can endure, you press on. You embrace the pain. You run the race to win. You stay on your own, personal cross in front of the witnesses in heaven until you're finished and God says, "Well done!"

Why did Jesus stay on the cross? Because He knew it would transform our relationship with His Father. If you stay on your cross, it will transform your wife's relationship with God *and* with you, and in the process, you'll also come closer to God. You'll be able to die to your old way of doing things and be resurrected to a new way of life in Christ-likeness. Jesus did it for you—for the joy set before Him. You can die to your old ways for the sake of your wife, if you become like Him.

JESUS WILL CHANGE YOUR WIFE—AND *YOU*

Take Up Your Cross Every Day

It's like this. On the cross, Jesus was blameless, yet He took on Himself the sins of all mankind. He took on the sins of His Bride so she could be spotless before the Father. In Christ-likeness, you take the blame in a disagreement with your wife, whether you think you're at fault or not. You always admit that you could be wrong. What difference does it make anyway who gets blamed unfairly on earth? God is keeping accounts in heaven. Those are the only accounts that matter. If He says take the wrong and don't get an attitude about it, then I'll take the wrong and keep quiet.

On your cross, you bear your wife's failures for her, as Christ bore our sins for us. Instead of pointing out her flaws to her, you take them before the Father so that He can change her. A man and woman who are married are one flesh. He can't separate himself from her flesh. He is numbered with her as a transgressor,[6] as Jesus is numbered with us. And in the same way as Christ, our High Priest, intercedes for His Bride, the husband—the priest in the home—intercedes for his wife and children.

On your cross of Christ-likeness you say to your wife, "Please forgive me," even if you want *her* to ask forgiveness from *you*.

On your cross, you don't point out your wife's shortcomings by comparing her with your momma. You point out your own faults, and let your wife tell you what to do to get *you* changed! I may speak before tens of thousands of people cheering what I say, but when I get home with my wife she still manages to "adjust" me with her own critique of how I did.

On your cross of Christ-likeness, you appreciate what your wife has sacrificed for you in giving up her single's life to love and serve you—twenty-four hours a day, seven days a week, for the rest of her life.

On your cross, you stop keeping your money for yourself and give it to your wife. You blow your wife's mind by giving her some money and saying, "This is for *you*. Don't tell me how you spend this, and don't spend it on the house or the family. Spend it on *you*." If your wife is working and has her own money, don't even think about it. Give her the money anyway. When her man gives her money under those circumstances, it makes it even sweeter. She knows that he's giving it to her out of extravagant love, not because of circumstances or needs. She sees a love that's beyond measure, and she feels so good! It's a practical application of the biblical truth, "Love your neighbor as you love yourself."[7]

On your cross, you stop doing what *you* want to do all the time and start doing what your wife wants you to do sometimes. If your wife likes to go to the mall, you go to the mall (without a word of fussing about how long she's taking). If she wants to go out with you during the Super Bowl, you go out during the Super Bowl (even if you have to tape it on the VCR until your mind gets really released!).

On your cross, you learn how to cry out to God until you break through to a new awareness of the life and lifestyle of Jesus Christ, who is with you always and will never leave you or forsake you. You face the fact that your life needs to count for something in this world so God can use you in the next.

On your cross, you come face-to-face with the reality of the Judgment Seat of Christ, where God will issue rewards and penalties for all that you have and have not done on this earth. He will judge how you've handled your relationship with your wife and children. Were you saved from hell, but lived like the devil at home? Or did you live each day with an expectation of the joy set before you—the joy of being like Him?

That's what happens on your cross. Anything less than the cross will not be sufficient to show that you love your wife as Christ shows His love for you.

You Can Be Changed

In the first three Gospels, when Jesus talks about our taking up the cross to follow Him, that event is followed by His transfiguration. That's because dying on the cross to your old way of living transfigures you and makes you more like Him. That's what marriage is all about. It's not just a man and woman living together. It's God's people walking out the kingdom lifestyle as a witness to the world.

Jesus said to His disciples, "If anyone desires to come after Me, let him deny himself, and take up his cross daily, and follow Me."[8] Then eight days later He took His inner circle—Peter, James, and John—and went up on the mountain to pray. "And as He prayed, the appearance of His face was altered, and His robe became white and glistening."[9] Even though Moses and Elijah were there as great men of God, God pointed out His Son as the greatest. He said, "This is my beloved Son. Hear him!"[10] Jesus never said, "I'm the greatest," but He lived out the lifestyle of greatness by serving.

Who is the greatest, according to Jesus? The greatest is the one who serves.[11]

Do you hear God calling you to take up your cross and follow Jesus in a life of sacrificial serving? Or do you have your mind volume turned up so high with your own voice that you've drowned Him out?

Do you know why most men really stop loving their wives or even decide to get divorced? Because they are not man enough to stay on the cross. They quit in crunch time. Their team is only one point down, but instead of taking the open shot at the basket, they throw the ball out of bounds. They never allow their marriage to change them as God intended, so God can't use them to bless their wives.

Let your wife be God's instrument of change in your life.

Women, for the most part, are wooed and won over by a husband's sacrificial love. That's the way the Church is toward Christ. If your woman sees you going all out in love for her, giving her gifts, listening to her, taking her places, out-serving her, don't you think she'll love that? Wouldn't you like to make her that happy?

Most men spend their whole married lives thinking they should change their wives to suit them—or trying to get their wives to leave them alone so they can do their own thing—and they never see that their wives were sent to them by God to help change *them*. Positive change is what makes you happy. It's the pruning that makes the vine produce more grapes. You're barren and unfruitful if you run when the pruning woman comes. Your wife can help you live a fruitful life if you'll admit you need to be changed and then give her some liberty to show you how to improve. That takes a real man.

Men fail in loving their wives, or even get divorced, when they stay blind to their own faults but have 20/20 eyesight about their wives' faults. They get divorced because they are stuck on the idea that it's her fault all the time and finally give up thinking that God can change her and save their marriage. "We're just incompatible," they say.

"It's hopeless—irreconcilable differences." What they're really saying is "I'm hopeless. I'm still the same self-centered person I was when she started down the aisle to me."

You can be a winner. You know that? You can beat all the odds and have a great life with your wife. You can stop the divorce rate from climbing if you start admitting your character flaws and asking God to change you, even through your wife.

Your pride tells you, "I'm fine just the way I am. She's the one who's missing it!" That's dumb. Tell her, "Go for it, wife! Tell me my faults! Give me what I need!" You'll probably never have anyone as willing to get in your face as your wife. Let her have input into your change. Yes, *you* need to change!

Have you ever seen someone riding down the highway with a flat tire? Looks pretty strange, doesn't it? Maybe the driver's stuck in traffic and doesn't want all the humiliation of blocking a lane to change it, so he keeps driving on the rim *floppita-floppita-floppita* until he can pull over. At some points in your life, you're like that driver. You won't get out and change the tire, so you jostle around all the passengers inside and in the process wreck the rim and maybe throw off your whole alignment. Stop the car and get out and change the tire! Change everything about yourself that's flawed.

Jesus Can Help

God loves you, flaws and all. That's the way you hope your wife will love you, so she can correct you without crushing you. But even if she doesn't, you can love her the same way that Christ loves you. You may correct her, but you never crush her. You see the beauty in her all the time, just as God sees the beauty in you. That's called seeing with spiritual eyes.

We're on a journey. We haven't arrived. We've got to quit judging our wives all the time and take time to judge ourselves. Real love is wanting God to make *us* better for *them* more than we want God to make *them* better for *us*.

When I catch myself focusing on my wife's faults instead of seeing my own, I have to cry out to God like blind Bartimaeus, "Jesus, Son of David, have mercy on me!"[12] Bartimaeus had to know he was blind before he could cry out to Jesus. When Jesus stopped to call him over he didn't waste any time. "Throwing off his coat, he was on his feet at once, and came to Jesus."[13] What do you need to throw off to show you're serious? When will you run to Jesus to get your eyesight right? What prideful thing is keeping you from "seeing" your wife as Jesus sees her? Are you willing to go to Jesus, or do you want to stay blind?

Recently, I made the decision to get LASIK surgery to correct my eyesight. It was amazing how much a little distortion in the front of my eyeball had kept everything out of focus for years. Two little five-minute cuts with the right instrument (and $5,000!) set me straight.

If my marriage is to be a model of the relationship between Christ and the Church, I have to let Jesus make a few precision cuts—His way. I couldn't in a million years tell the surgeon how to fix my eyes. I had to lie down like a baby and let him go for it. It's the same with us and God. He's the expert. We have to lie down like a lamb sent to the slaughter and let Him use the scalpel of the Word to adjust our vision.

We also need God's help to improve our spiritual vision so that we can see beyond the difficulties of this present world into the world to come. Christ is using our wives as one of His sharp instruments to adjust the way we see things so we can become suited to marry Him and rule with Him in eternity. The Bible says we're being changed "from glory to glory."[14] We've had a veil over our eyes that's kept us from seeing the glory of God, but when we turn to the Lord, the veil is taken away.[15] That's liberating, because "where the Spirit of the Lord is, there is liberty."[16]

We're undergoing a transfiguration that follows taking up our cross. We're changing into His likeness. Come on! We've been pre-destined to be like Him![17] That means all the forces of heaven are in our favor.

God Takes Out the Spots and Wrinkles

Christ loved the Church and gave Himself for her—that's you, and that's your wife. He gave Himself "that He might sanctify and cleanse her with the washing of water by the word, that He might present her to Himself a glorious church, not having spot or wrinkle or any such thing, but that she should be holy and without blemish."[18]

Remember how you hated to get a blemish on your face when you were a teenager? You scrubbed that thing with every cleanser in the drugstore to try to get it to go away. Are you giving that same attention to the blemishes in your marriage? God provides all the cleansers you need. "So husbands ought to love their own wives as their own bodies; he who loves his wife loves himself. For no one ever hated his own flesh, but nourishes and cherishes it, just as the Lord does the church. For we are members of His body, of His flesh and of His bones."[19]

You and your wife are one flesh. In the natural realm, God made Eve from the body of Adam. In the spiritual realm, each wife is a part of the body of her husband. You and your wife are connected both naturally and spiritually. When you bless her, you're blessing yourself. When you hate her (God forbid), you're hating yourself. " 'For this reason a man shall leave his father and mother and be joined to his wife, and the two shall become one flesh.' This is a great mystery, but I speak concerning Christ and the church. Nevertheless let each one of you in particular so love his own wife as himself, and let the wife see that she respects her husband."[20]

HEAVEN ON EARTH—RIGHT NOW

Your House Will Become a Home

When you really love your wife, the atmosphere is so awesome that you aren't just two people living together in a house, which is a physical building, but you are two lovers living to bless each other in a home. A home is a place where people don't just tolerate one another. They have good feelings toward one another. It's a warm and secure haven.

It's a goal of God to help you make your house a home. In a home, the husband represents Christ and the wife represents the Church. The husband has Christ-like love for his wife. He loves her unconditionally. He sees her with the eyes of revelation. She knows that somebody's on her side no matter what she does. Somebody will affirm her and speak over her words of love in the seasons of life. Someone can restore her when her day seems dark or she goes through a long season in the night. Her husband has the words to bring her to the place where she should be, because he carries God's love for her in his heart and gives it away to her as a true expression of his intimacy with God. He's an example for her and the children in humility and a servant lifestyle.

In a home, the wife models out in visible form what the Church is becoming in spiritual form. She brings warmth to the home. She provides receptivity for her husband. She's there for him. She takes care of the house as a good steward. Under her care the house becomes a home, because she carries out her husband's vision to a place that he couldn't take it by himself. She helps fulfill in practical ways the vision for the home that her husband sees spiritually. She keeps excellence in their home and in her heart. She maintains "the level" in her dress, her appearance, and her manner of speaking. She is an expression of beauty—both natural beauty and spiritual beauty—by seeing her husband with the eyes of love.

In a home where the husband and wife have come into a union of spirit, soul, and body, the obvious fruit of their love and intimacy is their children. God said, "Be fruitful, and multiply, and replenish the earth."[21] That is fulfilled when two people who really love each other become one in their children.

In a home, the wife is blessing her husband. The husband is blessing and loving his wife. The children are peaceful and under subjection. The in-laws see that there is always a place for them. Friends and neighbors find the environment so awesome that they want to come and spend time there and be inspired about heaven.

Because God designed your marriage to be like Christ's marriage to the Church, it is simple to fix it whenever anything goes wrong. All you have to do is become more like Christ! And Christ has left the Holy Spirit to help us be like Him in every area of our lives.

You'll Bring a Revival to Your Home

As you read this book, it is my prayer that Jesus Christ Himself will come into your heart in such a new way that you will begin to think like Him, pray like Him, and act like Him. Your heart is the ground the Lord is using to prepare you for the glories of God.

Do you want it? Then ask Him, "Lord, don't let me desire anything more than seeing the reality of heaven operating in my home."

If you want the reality of heaven in your home, first you need a revival in *you*. Most people usually think of revival as being a series of meetings where somebody comes to preach in church services, but revival means new life, a fresh breath from God. Revival breathed into marriages cancels divorces.

> **Heaven in your home begins with revival in your heart.**

Revival comes when you out-serve your wife. The man plays the major role in bringing revival to the home. Revival came to my family when I took the proper position of Christ-likeness in my home—not just in serving, but in every area—because in Him is life.[22] You absolutely will bring a revival to your home if you love and out-serve your wife. It's a game. Get competitive in serving her more than she serves you! You've got to "beat your wife" in doing every task. That takes a little effort, but it will be worth it. You old lazy thing, get up off your behind and do some things around the house!

Revival started in our home when I looked around my house and realized that my wife was doing all the serving. She was the one bringing me a drink while she fixed a meal. Even though she was out working in the marketplace all day, she'd come home and immediately start fixing dinner for the children and me. I'd be sitting down, looking at television or reading the newspaper, being my old lazy self, and she'd be serving me. She'd call us to dinner, be the last one to sit down, then go on and clean up. After that, she would go upstairs and make sure the beds were ready and everything was set for the next day.

When I realized that she was a much greater servant than I was, it hit me that ultimately before the Judgment Bar she would get greater rewards than I would. She would be more qualified in heaven than I was.

The Lord put it like this. She might be bringing me coffee on earth, but I would be taking her tea in heaven. The standard for greatness is not who is being served but who is serving. In every home, the greatest in God's eyes is the one who does the most serving. It has nothing to do with gender or privilege. It has to do with the nature of Christ. We're called the Bride of Christ. We're His woman. Tell me the time that the Church, Christ's woman, has ever out-served Jesus? Jesus, our Husband, always out-serves us. The Great One serves.

Let's make it very practical. Don't just do dignified things. Clean the bathroom, and if it's already clean go under the sink and clean the dusty pipes. Iron her jeans. Sneak in and take her clothes out of the dryer and fold them and put them away, and don't forget to clean the lint filter. Don't let a member of the body of Christ out-serve you right in your house! Don't hold on to your "rights" as head of the house.

You don't have any real authority at all unless it is delegated from someone above you with more authority than you have. In your case, that's God. And He says you qualify for authority in His house if you serve.

You're the leader in your house when you serve. I find that some men marry for two reasons: 1. To get a legalized sex life; 2. To get their wives to serve them—to do things their momma did for them. Many men think because they're the breadwinner and she's described in the Bible as the "weaker vessel," she's supposed to show her submission by serving him. Jesus said just the opposite. He said that the greater one serves.[23] A man doesn't lead by forcing his wife to say yes to everything he sees. You're the leader in your house when you're the servant, not when you're the king—the male. Being a male doesn't necessarily make you a man, either. A man is mature, and maturity comes through serving.

A *home where the woman out-serves the man misrepresents heaven.* God wants our homes to be so full of love that they represent heaven. Because my wife was out-serving me, the model of Christ was being misrepresented in my home. Since the Church cannot out-serve Jesus, a home where the wife is out-serving the husband mismodels the kingdom of God and therefore that model cannot be transferred into heaven. When I realized this, I said it's time for me to take ground: The ground of humility. The ground of a servant spirit. The ground of unconditional love. When I became a Christ-like servant to my wife, revival came to my family. We came to life again.

OVERCOMING THE SPIRIT OF DIVISION IN YOUR HOME

Jesus Had a Unique Way of Handling Disputes Over Power

When you really love your wife, you don't fight with her, even when you disagree. You don't have to "win" every argument to make yourself look like the head of the house.

Jesus had to deal with His disciples at the Last Supper because they were fighting among themselves over power and position. The Bible describes it this way: "Now there was also a dispute among them, as to which of them should be considered the greatest. And He said to them, 'The kings of the Gentiles exercise lordship over them, and those who exercise authority over them are called "benefactors." But not so among you; on the contrary, he who is greatest among you, let him be as the younger, and he who governs as he who serves. For who is greater, he who sits at the table, or he who serves? Is it not he who sits at the table? Yet I am among you as the One who serves.' "24

The spirit of division among Jesus' disciples is the same spirit you find in a marriage. It's the same spirit that divides people into denominations and cultures. When you really love your wife, you do everything you can to understand her position without trying to put her down.

When you aren't ruled by love, you will try to win your case through law or logic (*your* logic, that is). But people disputes can't be resolved by the letter of the Law, as you understand it from the Bible, or the limits of your human logic. They have to be resolved through love—through the heart. The Law is good. God set it up for a purpose. When we're young and immature, God uses the Law to keep our flesh from ruling over us. A season of life under the Law builds in certain controls that eventually become a part of one's character. The Law provides a minimum standard for society, and especially for those who say they are "God's people." It prevents anarchy on earth.

However, people living solely under the Law don't develop close "heart" relationships. Employees of the same company, for example, can be thrown together through the circumstance of working together every day and receiving paychecks from the same source. They have a personnel manual they all follow, and they develop a degree of fellowship, but in most cases nothing lasting develops. A church, unfortunately, can function in the same way. When it happens in a marriage, it's disastrous. It makes your wife think you don't really love her.

Like the disciples, people who don't function at the level of love are always looking for loopholes to get themselves ahead. They relate in love when they're changed in their hearts, not when they're controlled by circumstances and rules.

One of the greatest evidences of a heart relationship, especially a heart toward God, is a willingness to serve. When our homes begin to function by heart relationships characterized by serving, relationships in church and society will follow. The controls that the Law provided on the outside will have been built into a change of character on the inside, done by the Spirit.

Follow the Law of Love

In a marriage, the Lord changes a husband and wife from two separate entities into two aspects of one new entity. The two become one: (1) first by law, in a legal ceremony performed before witnesses by a recognized authority to establish their covenant, then (2) by love, through everyday relationships of serving each other in the home.

Before we became Christians, the Law was there, but we still weren't changed. We needed grace, and grace comes only through Jesus Christ. He comes to us on the inside and changes us from the inside out. The law says you're married, but until you begin to live by the law of love and exercise grace—unmerited favor—toward each other, you're not in a real marriage relationship that represents heaven, on earth.

> Lasting marriages are built on the law of love
> and the gift of grace.

Let God search your heart. Is your heart committed to your wife as Christ's heart is committed to the Church? Or are you relating to her out of the letter of the Law? Maybe you're a good provider and you come home every night, but where is your heart? Are you into duty, or devotion? "Search me, O God, and know my heart: try me, and know my thoughts: And see if there be any wicked way in me, and lead me in the way everlasting."[25]

Real Love Drives You to Keep Praying for Your Wife

Do you ever have moments when it seems impossible to get along with your wife or children? In spite of everything you possibly do to be a Christ-like model in your home, do they still seem to have the wrong attitude toward you at times? If so, you may need to step up the intensity of your prayer life and travail for them in prayer. Love gives you the endurance to PUSH—Pray Until Something Happens.

Women travail and *push* in the birthing process to bring forth children. Men never have to experience the pains of childbirth firsthand, although most men who "coach" their wives through labor and delivery almost feel the pain with them. The apostle Paul spoke of the pain of travail in prayer, which is necessary to bring others into Christ-likeness. He spoke of the church at Galatia, "my little children, of whom I travail in birth again until Christ be formed in you."[26]

Through his prayers, Paul was helping to birth the Galatian church into a new formation of Christ-likeness. It was analogous to their first birth, when they were born again, but the gestation period and labor were accomplished to overcome their childishness and spiritual immaturity. Like a parent, Paul wanted to help. He believed that they could be birthed into a new dimension of their relationship with Christ and with one another if he would travail.

The problem with the Christians in Galatia was that they were reverting to the level of Law when they needed to relate at the level of love. Sometimes that can also happen in the home. If a husband prays his wife and children into spiritual maturity by the pains of intercession and travail, in effect, he carries them. He takes them in prayer to where he sees they're going to go in their spiritual walk. The burden to pray remains inside of him because of his desire coming out of his own intimacy with Christ. He is able to see where his family should go and what they could become, and prays them there, laying tracks for them to go to the place that Christ has for them.

Today, much of the Church doesn't understand travail. Like the women in labor who beg the doctor to use drugs to take away the pains of labor, the Church seems to be anesthetized when it looks at broken marriages and has no grief. The Church looks at America's inner cities and their death rate and has no pain. It looks at rich people who are cheating on their taxes, and insurance companies who drop you when you have one accident after twenty years, and doesn't feel a thing. A husband sees his wife falling short and not meeting his expectations and doesn't care. He leaves her to her misery and goes out to find his satisfaction somewhere else. That is sin. Jesus did it another way, and the witnesses in heaven are watching to see if we follow His example.

"Wherefore seeing we also are compassed about with so great a cloud of witnesses, let us lay aside every weight, and the sin which doth so easily beset us, and let us run with patience the race that is set before us, looking unto Jesus the author and finisher of our faith; who for the joy that was set before him endured the cross, despising the shame, and is set down at the right hand of the throne of God."[27]

Carry Compassion in the Womb of Your Spirit

You can look at your wife and children and get frustrated instead of becoming pregnant with vision for them. Jesus can help you become filled with compassion for them and willing to travail and experience their pain. However, if you use a "hypodermic" of annoyance that dulls the birth pains that should drive you to prayer, you will be doing nothing to bring them to birth. Instead, like a woman travailing to birth a child, ask God for the compassion in prayer to break them through to a different level of life. As the Scripture says, "And of some have compassion, making a difference."[28]

You can think of your spirit as a womb that God impregnates with vision. When you love your wife, you carry her in the womb of your spirit. You become impregnated with the compassion of God for her.

Do you think God is as mad at your wife as you are?

Do you think God's feelings are hurt and He won't talk to her?

Do you think God has so many more important things to do that He never takes time to listen to her?

In the travail of intercessory prayer, immature people come forth into spiritual maturity. God is about to break the water so that your wife can come forth in a new birth, so that your children can experience a breakthrough in their relationships with you and her and especially with God.

Are you going to take the hypodermic and not be identified with their pain?

Or can God impregnate you with vision for them and keep you pregnant, until Christ is formed in all of you?

Spiritual labor pains indicate that something is about to come forth. If you are experiencing pain, something in you is coming to birth, both for yourself and for your wife. A time of fulfillment is near.

"Before she travailed, she brought forth; before her pain came, she was delivered of a man child. Who hath heard such a thing? Who hath seen such things? Shall the earth be made to bring forth in one day? or shall a nation be born at once? for as soon as Zion travailed, she brought forth her children. Shall I bring to the birth, and not cause to bring forth? saith the Lord: shall I cause to bring forth, and shut the womb? saith thy God."[29]

OUR AWESOME MARRIAGE TO CHRIST

Something You Never Thought of on Your Wedding Day

On your wedding day, you had a vision of what an ideal marriage would be like. If you're honest, it probably related first to getting your needs met and second to meeting the needs of your wife, and far down the list was making a marriage that would attract people to God. But that is the highest purpose of a wedding ceremony—to point people to Jesus Christ and the coming great marriage ceremony of Christ and the Church.

> Let us celebrate, let us rejoice,
> let us give him the glory!
> The Marriage of the Lamb has come;
> his Wife has made herself ready.
> She was given a bridal gown
> of bright and shining linen.
> The linen is the righteousness of the saints.[30]

Seeing Your Marriage with Eyes of Revelation

The greatest vision any groom can have for his marriage is that it will someday come to represent the awesome relationship of Christ and the Church. God wants you to "see" your marriage with the eyes of revelation. He knows that if you see something, you'll believe it and work to attain it. That's a principle He used when He gave land to Abram—whatever Abram could see would be his. "And the Lord said to Abram, after Lot had separated from him: 'Lift your eyes now and look from the place where you are—northward, southward, eastward, and westward; for all the land which you see I give to you and your descendants forever.' "[31]

God told Abram to *see* that he and his family for generations to come would own a vast area of land. From that time on, that was it. Abraham, his son Isaac, and his grandson Jacob all kept the faith from what that man saw.

If you can see your marriage as something so awesome that it models the kingdom of God, it doesn't matter what you're going through; you will see the potential and work toward it with all your might. You'll gladly out-serve your wife, even if no one else you know serves his wife, because you've got the revelation.

GOD'S VISITATION FIXES EVERYTHING IN YOUR HOUSE

When you've got the revelation of out-serving your wife, you can get the visitation. A visitation from God takes care of every concern you have about your marriage. Here are some practical steps from the life of Moses to help you get the visitation of God in your home.

Moses could see himself delivering a whole nation just with his anointing because he had such a presence of God operating in his life. Where did he get that anointing? From spending time in the presence of God.

The God of Moses is there with you in your home. He sees the same potential for greatness in you. Can you see it? Just as Moses delivered the children of Israel from worldly Egypt, God sees that you can deliver yourself and your wife from worldly living now. You just have to get the right perspective. It's all about your point of view—whether you see from God's perspective in heaven or man's perspective on earth. The point from which you view a situation determines what you "see."

Don't Let the Devil Make You Blind with Rage

You've heard the term "blind with rage." The devil likes to get you so mad that you can't see straight. When you can't see that *he's* your enemy, and *not* your wife, you won't drive him away. However, when you really love your wife, you can see that your wife and family are being oppressed by the devil, and you can move in there and set them free, just as Moses liberated Israel from the Egyptians.

God said to Moses, " 'Yes, the wail of the people of Israel has risen to me in heaven, and I have seen the heavy tasks the Egyptians have oppressed them with. Now I am going to send you to Pharaoh, to demand that he let you lead my people out of Egypt.'

" 'But I'm not the person for a job like that!' Moses exclaimed.

"Then God told him, 'I will certainly be with you.' "[32]

God was with Moses, and God is with you. Moses had a visitation, and so can you. Do you want it?

Because Moses' heart became good ground, God used him to deliver possibly two to three million people out of 430 years of bondage. Not only did he deliver them out of Egypt and Pharaoh's hand, he also gave them the Word of God, which eventually transformed them and got them ready for the Promised Land.

Moses had to leave Egypt, and so do you. Your wife needs you to be delivered from the world so you can disciple her and get the world out of her. She needs to hear fresh insights from the Word from you, every day. She needs to hear you praying for her. What could be more important than that? That's why your family is waiting for you to get your visitation. That's what He's calling you to seek from Him, right in your own home.

Get the visitation and begin to give out the revelation. Then God can say, "This family is serious! It's becoming like the Marriage Supper of the Lamb!"

Step back and look at what's really happening. Stop getting mad at your wife and start getting mad at the devil. Open your eyes and see past your wife to what is going on in the spirit world that is causing interference in her communication with God. Wrestle against that. Pray hard and fight hard and you will win. God has ordained victory for you. "For we do not wrestle against flesh and blood, but against principalities, against powers, against the rulers of the darkness of this age, against spiritual hosts of wickedness in the heavenly places."[33]

"God is strong, and he wants you strong. So take everything the Master has set out for you, well-made weapons of the best materials. And put them to use so you will be able to stand up to everything the Devil throws your way. This is no afternoon athletic contest that we'll walk away from and forget about in a couple of hours. This is for keeps, a life-or-death fight to the finish against the Devil and all his angels.

"Be prepared. You're up against far more than you can handle on your own. Take all the help you can get, every weapon God has issued, so that when it's all over but the shouting you'll still be on your feet. Truth, righteousness, peace, faith, and salvation are more than words. Learn how to apply them. You'll need them throughout your life. God's Word is an *indispensable* weapon. In the same way, prayer is essential in this ongoing warfare. Pray hard and long. Pray for your brothers and sisters. Keep your eyes open. Keep each other's spirits up so that no one falls behind or drops out."[34]

Make Your Points of Desperation Places of Rededication

Are you saved? Salvation is not a title. Salvation is a transformed life that comes from living in the reality of the face of God. It is having God at work in you, "to will and to do of his good pleasure."[35]

How saved are you? You're no more saved than Christ is real to you. You can quote Scriptures all day long; however, the Bible says the letter kills but the Spirit gives life.[36] Where's your heart? Are you giving your family letter or life? Do you beat them up with legalism or love them in the spirit?

If you're getting desperate, celebrate! Seek God with a new intensity! Every point of desperation is a point of rededication. In every trial, ask God to tell you what it means. And when you get the revelation, offer yourself back up to Him and rededicate yourself on the altar of total surrender.

On that altar, the Lord sanctifies you. He sets you apart from the world so that you don't just walk with rhetoric, you walk with reality. You don't just say the right words, you think the right thoughts and do the right deeds. That's what every family needs.

God said He would be with you. Ultimately, God wants to give you manifestations in your home that show people that your family doesn't just talk denominationalism and religion. You talk the reality of the Lord. You say outwardly what is going on inwardly. God is with you. He is in your heart, and when you speak, you speak out of a heart for God. What did he say to Moses? "Certainly I will be with you."[37]

The thing that hurts Christians the most and stops them from saving the world—the thing that causes more difficulty than anything else—is their lack of the sense that God is with them. Even if you can say, "God is with *us*," you probably can't say, "God is with *me*."

Say it! Say it right now, right out loud, if you're bold.

"God is with me!"

"God is with me!"

You know why you don't really believe that sometimes? Because you're not sanctified on the altar of total surrender. You haven't given yourself totally over to God, so the Spirit doesn't bear witness to the offering. Make yourself into an offering and lay yourself on the altar of God. Paul said, "I am crucified with Christ."[38] The Spirit gives life only to that which is dead. Die daily—to your own selfish thoughts, your criticisms of others that are stinking up the place, your self-defeating, self-pitying attitudes. Grow up and become a man! And then get in there and win your wife. She's probably way ahead of you, waiting for you to catch up.

Your wife may still try to out-serve you. Ever since I started out-serving my wife, she's been trying to beat me in serving. Sometimes she'll sneak in and do something more than I did for her and leave me a note that says, "BAM!" That stands for "By A Mile"—she beat me by a mile!

My wife has also been wild about making sure I have a good time—with or without her. It was my wife who got me going in golf. She said, "Honey, go ahead. Enjoy yourself. Take your clubs. You're going to play golf today."

I said, "Honey, that takes four hours!"

She said, "I don't mind, darlin'. As a matter of fact, would you like for me to ride along with you?"

Why does she want me to have a good time? Because she's seeing me. Why is she seeing me? Because I saw her.

But we are still in competition. She knows I refuse to let her beat me in Christ-like service.

PRAYER FOR WHAT I WILL HAVE TO FACE NEXT

Jesus, I thank You for all that You've done for me. I know I can't say it with enough desire, but I trust You by the Holy Spirit to cause me to have heaven's appreciation for what You're doing to my heart.

I need Your power for what I must face in the days ahead. Thank You for the release of power so that I will not walk with pride. I will not let my emotions rule me when people do me wrong. I'll be able to stand when I see the weakness of others, and God, when necessary, even allow myself to be defrauded.

Give me that level of power where I will not use Your power for revenge, but I'll use it for healing, for revival, for reconciliation, so that the glory of God might be seen.

Thank You that You've given me the power to receive the change that has come to my heart today. Thank You for grace to forgive everyone who has sinned against me, whether they have repented or not.

Thank You for every backslider I know whom You will help me to love, even as You love me when I do not stay as close to You as I should.

Thank You that I am not afraid of what the future will bring, because I know that Your power will be released in me, and is even now being released.

In Jesus' name I pray. Amen.

SELAH

The number 50 in the Bible has a special significance. It stands for the Lord's release. In Leviticus 25 and Deuteronomy 15, God called the people to release all their debtors every 50 years. He told them they would not need to plant crops on the fiftieth year, because He would feed them. As you try to come up with 50 items for each of the categories below, may the Lord release His blessing to you, and bring heaven to your home.

1. List 50 reasons why you love your wife.
2. List 50 reasons why your wife loves you.
3. List 50 things that you can change about yourself and your household that will help bring revival to your wife and your home. Make a prayer list out of them and PUSH (Pray Until Something Happens).
4. Read 1 Corinthians 13 in five different versions of the Bible. If you have a Greek dictionary, look up key words there.
5. Look up *love* in a standard dictionary. Write down 50 important points you want to remember about God's definition of love and how you can be more Christ-like in your love for your wife.
6. Look up the words *wedding* and *marriage* in a Bible concordance. Describe the themes you find in the relationships between husbands and wives and their parents.

2

BECOMING BLENDED: MAKING THE TRANSITION FROM BEING SINGLE TO BEING MARRIED

"Can two walk together, except they be agreed?"

—Amos 3:3 KJV

A few years ago, with little advance notice, our ministry announced that we were having an all-day Saturday seminar for singles on the subject of marriage. No married couples could attend.

The morning of the seminar, which we called "One Love Marriage Seminar for Singles Only," single men and women from as far away as Michigan were lined up in the hotel lobby in Richmond, Virginia, waiting to register. Some had driven all night to be there.

The response to the conference demonstrated that most Christian singles want to leave their momma and daddy and get married. They also want to beat the odds against divorce and build successful, Jesus-centered marriages that last.

These young people knew about the successful marriages of our ministry's leadership team and so they said, "I want to get me some of that!" The reason the singles came to that conference is the same reason they need to read this chapter.

In the years since that conference and the conferences that have followed in other states, many of those singles have gone on to get married. Many have told us that the conference was a turning point in their understanding of the importance of marriage as a proving ground for their relationship with Jesus, and a training process for their success in all of life. Those who were part of one of our churches, and spent time with our successfully married pastors and leaders, have especially benefited over the years. I know that they would recommend that you read this chapter and the rest of this book as well.

GOD AND THE FUNCTIONAL FAMILY

You Can Build a Functional Family

Godly marriages and families are the only stable building blocks for a successful society. When families in America are restored, the whole culture will feel the positive effects, beginning with the Church. One of the reasons the Church is dysfunctional in society right now is that families *within* the Church are dysfunctional. Even pastors and missionaries in many Christian denominations can't make their marriages work. Something must be done. Something *can* be done.

Married people need to read this chapter on singles to discover that some of the reasons they don't get along with their mates are related to unresolved problems they had as singles. Once they resolve these problems, their married life will change. Then, as they move on through this book, they will learn how to build on that restored foundation a successful marriage that lasts for life.

Singles need to read this chapter to learn how they can make the transition from the single life to being blended together into a life of permanent marriage. Then they can read the rest of the book to learn how to keep their marriages awesome.

Previously married people need to read this chapter to identify the key elements to making their home like heaven the next time around.

Parents need to read this chapter to help their sons and daughters create a godly single's lifestyle so that they will not carry over problems into their future married life.

> The best way to prepare for marriage and to stay married is to get to know your First Husband, Jesus, and then apply what you learn in intimacy with Him to your human marriage.

Singles Are Already Married to Jesus

Keep Jesus as your first love. The best way to prepare for marriage and to stay married is to get to know your First Husband, Jesus, and then apply what you learn in intimacy with Him to your human marriage. Go after Him until you have the substance of God formed within you. Go after Him until you understand His nature so well that you become like Him. Make no mistake about it! Your home will become a proving ground that exposes just how much of the life of God is working in you and through you.

The Bible says that our Maker is our Husband.[1] It also says that the Church is God's woman. He's our First Love, or at least He should be if we're paying attention to the nudging of the Holy Spirit. When Jesus is your First Love, you hear Him calling you to a holy life. If you deny Him and sin, it proves you've never truly yielded your affections to Him. He's not your First Love.

Loving Jesus is the best preparation for marriage anyone can have. When you love Jesus as He loves you, you're not just loving Him for what He can do for you, but learning to wait on Him, and learning the satisfaction and fulfillment of a life that pleases Him.

Stay with Him in fasting and prayer until you get results. As a single, go places in prayer you can't manage after your time is dedicated to your wife. Give God your passionate dedication. Learn to live the fasted lifestyle, because once you're married, the Bible says you have to ask permission from your mate for long fasts.[2]

Do "knee work" for your future mate. The most useful thing you can do in the transition from singlehood to marriage is pray. Mrs. Boone will tell women that one of the greatest gifts they can give their man is "knee work." When he drives you up the wall, get on the floor. Get on your knees, she says, "so God can fix your husband instead of you fixing him."

> **The most useful thing you can do in the transition from singlehood to marriage is pray.**

"I don't know how to fix a car," she says, "so wouldn't I look silly taking my car to the repair shop and telling the mechanic, 'This is where you put the oil and this is where you put the battery,' and he would look at me and think, 'This lady is crazy!' because I wouldn't know what I was talking about. Well, I don't know how to fix my husband, either. I can't tell God what to do. I just take my husband to God and say, 'Here! You fix him!' "

That sets up what we call "The Squeeze Play." She's praying from up under me and God is working from up over me, and I get squeezed into the will of God.

The same thing works for me in reverse. Sometimes my wife is so upset with me that I can't get her reconciled. I try saying I'm sorry. I go down low. Nothing makes any difference. So I say, "My God! My God! HELP!" And in just a little while she comes to me and she's my little sweetness again and neither one of us can imagine what was the problem. It's out of here. The solutions may not always come that easily, but things get a lot easier to handle when you give up and let God take control.

Be faithful by going to church together regularly. Let everybody know that you love and respect the saints, and respect their walk with the Lord. The Bible says, "Let us not neglect our church meetings, as some people do, but encourage and warn each other, especially now that the day of his coming back again is drawing near."[3] The fellowship of believers shows your love relationship with your brothers and sisters. It says, "I want to be around you. I want to be around the saints."

Learn to think like a pioneer, and teach your mate to think that way, too. As a single person, while the opportunity is there, cultivate a pioneer spirit. If you do something daring for God while you're single, then when you're married it won't be so difficult to boldly serve Him again.

Be persistent in making time for Jesus. In the book of Revelation, Jesus tells the church at Ephesus, "I know your persistence, your courage in my cause, that you never wear out.

"But you walked away from your first love—why? What's going on with you, anyway? Do you have any idea how far you've fallen? A Lucifer fall!

"Turn back! Recover your dear early love."[4]

If people are messing up, and even if they are putting "that certain someone" before Jesus, they are doing Lucifer's work and denying their Lord.

When you've got Lucifer kicked to the curb and you're making time to get to know Jesus and become more like Him as a single person, your marriage can't help but benefit. Even if the other person acts up, you've got enough of the love of Jesus in you to stay focused on Him.

If your courtship was characterized more by *struggling* to spend time with God than by passionately pursuing Him, you've laid a shaky foundation for your marriage, which needs to be rebuilt.

HOW TO SEEK GOD FOR A MATE

- Learn how to make Jesus the First Love of your life. Give Him first place as your Husband.
- Pray secretly every day.
- Immerse yourself in the purposes of God. Don't look for a mate. Look for a mission, and God will surprise you with a life partner who will help you to fulfill it.
- Consider carefully what kind of spouse you want God to bring to you.
- Study the Bible and Bible-based books on marriage.
- Learn whatever practical things you need to know to be able to serve another person.
- When you find someone who seems to be "the one," submit yourself and your relationship to the will of God.
- Spend time together with your family. Listen for God's voice through them.
- Go to church. Listen with your spiritual ears open.
- Seek mature, proven advisors who demonstrate Christ-likeness in their own relationships.
- Love the other person as Jesus loves you. Discern the difference between lust and love.
- Maintain a high moral standard during courtship. Avoid potentially compromising situations. Keep touching to a minimum.
- Be real. Don't lie. Don't try to fake it to impress the other person.

Courtship Is God's Divine Delay

In most relationships that seem to be leading to marriage, there is a divine delay while the two seek God's will and also seek to find out all the ways they are different and how they can become one.

Courtship is the time to be talking to both sets of parents often and at great length about how they view marriage. Even if their marriage isn't that hot, they probably know some principles that are right, and they definitely have a right as your parents to be asked. Don't miss it. Talk to them and other members of your extended family, like grandparents.

Courtship is the time to read the Bible and biblically based books on marriage. The Bible is a book of courtship, and we are in the espousal period for the greatest marriage of all—Jesus marrying the Church at that great feast, the Marriage Supper of the Lamb. Study everything you can about God's view of marriage, both in the Bible and in books by modern Christian authors like James Dobson, John Trent, Gary Smalley, Dennis Rainey, and others.

Courtship is the time to get several weeks of premarital counseling from your pastor and/or others in the body of Christ whose marriages you deeply respect. "Study to show yourself approved unto God, a workman that needeth not to be ashamed, rightly dividing the word of truth."[5]

Courtship is the time to discuss your opinions on vital issues. If you're single, you've never married or you're divorced or widowed. Each state represents its own particular needs. If you have children that you are bringing into a new marriage situation, that adds other factors of blending.

Sometimes we think only of young singles getting married, but there are many people now who wait until they're thirty or more before they even start considering marriage. When that happens, they may have many strong habits that are already set and have to be adjusted to a mate.

Courting couples and newlyweds need time out together. God knows it takes time to make the adjustment to a mate, regardless of the circumstances of your singlehood. That's why He gave young husbands in ancient Israel a full year off from military service so they could establish their relationship with their wives. "If a man has recently married, he must not be sent to war or have any other duty laid on him. For one year he is to be free to stay at home and bring happiness to the wife he has married."[6] That means you shouldn't expect to get married one day and go back to work the next as if nothing significant has happened to change your life.

Goals to Reach Together

Whatever the specific circumstances surrounding the couple to be married, they should use the courtship season to lay on the table all of their expectations, then come to an agreement of how they will define heaven in their home. In the presence of their parents, mature pastors, and other mentors who know what it takes to stay married, the couple should seek these goals together.

If you are single, the steps listed below will help you reach the goal of a good adjustment to marriage. If you are already married, you can make sure you are taking these steps, and also teach them to your children.

- Develop spiritual intensity.
- Develop sensitivity and share thoughts freely.
- Settle anything outstanding from the past.
- Honor each other's parents.
- Respect each other's friends and godly advisors.
- Establish shared concepts about a "home."
- Plan how both will help around the house.
- Discuss money matters openly.
- Come to an agreement about working outside the home.
- Discuss future education for spouse and children.
- Prepare for purchasing clothes and clothing care.
- Find common interests in restaurants and entertainment.
- Plan for future vacations and time for renewal.

Goal	How to Reach the Goal
Develop Spiritual Intensity	• Pray and study the Bible together as a couple and with others. • Attend church and participate in group activities. • Start to develop your new family's vision for ministry, even if it is part-time because of your work schedule.
Develop Sensitivity and Share Thoughts Freely	• Husbands: Plan ahead to give her time, money, a listening ear, and say-so in your affairs when she is your wife. (See Chapter 4, "Blow Your Wife's Mind.") • Husbands: When your wife says, "Let's do family things together," she may really mean she doesn't think you're doing enough things together that meet her interests. • Start sharing information about your work and your dreams for the future. • Decide how often you will eat together without distractions like TV and phone calls. • Learn to share everything, even a favorite cup or the last piece of your favorite cake. It's good for your soul. • Examine how you spend your evenings and weekends, and decide how you *should* spend them. • Discuss how you will handle disagreements in a positive way. Get input from happily married couples on how they handle disputes and keep loving each other in the process. • Decide how you will develop your family decision-making process. Who will have the final word? • Talk about sleeping and waking times so you can always provide for private time together,

Goal	How to Reach the Goal
	especially after you have children. Sometimes you may have to sacrifice sleep or activities to which you are accustomed to fulfill your marriage vows. · Learn about each other's interests so you can be companions in as many areas as possible. Learn about sports interests, movies, favorite books.
Settle Anything Outstanding from the Past	· Don't carry old offenses against your future mate or others. Unforgiveness is unlike Jesus. · Don't keep secrets you need to expose, and don't expose what you need to keep secret.
Honor Each Other's Parents	· If you're still single, make a commitment to ask your girlfriend's father for permission to marry her. If you're already married and didn't do it, go back to him and repent, and teach your children what is right. · Speak well of the parents to each other and to others. · Have good attitudes toward them. · Get to know each other's parents by spending time with them in an attitude of respect. · Don't degrade them by putting them down and refusing their advice. · Follow their standards of decency in your relationship.
Respect Each Other's Friends and Godly Advisors	· Don't cut off your friends or expect the other person to cut off theirs. Men still need brothers even after they get married, and women still need sisters. No one can get all his fellowship needs met by one person. · Spend time with successfully married couples. You'd be surprised how many people have

Goal	How to Reach the Goal
	experienced the same kind of adjustments you're facing, and can tell you what you need to do.
Establish Shared Concepts About a "Home"	· Decide if you will have an apartment, town house, or house. · Will you rent, lease, or buy? · Look at various furniture styles and decide how you want to decorate your house.
Plan How Both Will Help Around the House	· Get your momma to teach you how to clean house and wash clothes. You also need to go up a level in keeping yourself clean and neat for your spouse. · Learn to cook. Get a few specialties you can whip up. Shop for the food! And don't pay too much for it, either. · When you use the bathroom, be considerate of your spouse coming in after you. Put down the toilet seat. Wipe off the sink (if that's important). Did you use up all the toilet paper? · Learn preventive maintenance for the car and the house. · Decide who will do which household chores, and what to do if one of you slacks off.
Discuss Money Matters Openly	· Agree that your family will tithe to the church and make offerings as often as possible. All your money belongs to God. " 'The silver is mine, and the gold is mine,' saith the Lord of hosts."[7] He just lets you keep most of it. · Start a savings account and contribute regularly. · Make a decision not to get into debt. Pay cash or wait. If either of you has outstanding debts, discuss how these will be paid off as soon as possible. · Open a personal checking account and savings

Goal	How to Reach the Goal
	account. You may want to hold off on a joint account until after you are married. · Determine who will handle the money, and how the other person will get the money they need. · Set up a family budget. Decide how much you can afford to spend weekly on cars, clothes, furniture, housing, phone and utilities, entertainment, etc. · Plan your finances so that you can provide for your family if your wife becomes pregnant and unable to work. · Discuss if you want to be bargain hunters or shop in expensive stores.
Come to an Agreement About Working Outside the Home	· Will you work on Sundays or always request Sundays off for church? · Agree whether or not the wife will work, how much she will work, and what additional responsibilities she will have around the house. · How will you handle overtime? · What about bringing work home from the office? · Will you need equipment like computers, fax machines, and cellular phones? · Discuss what hours each of you will work, and how you will arrange for quantities of time together every day. If you want to stay married, you have to plan to spend time together.
Discuss Future Education for Spouse and Children	· If either of you desires additional education, plan strategically for money, time away from the family, a place to study at home, and the end results that you want to achieve. · Be sensitive to the potential for division as this process proceeds, and head off anything that could cause problems.

Goal	How to Reach the Goal
	· Discuss if you will send your children to public school, private school, Christian school, or if you will home school.
Prepare for Purchasing Clothes and Clothing Care	· Go to the best clothing stores and let the clerks teach you about quality. Husbands, learn how to buy women's clothes for your future wife, and the wife for the husband. Even if you don't have the money yet, you need the vision. · Get a handle on how to use that iron and ironing board, even the clothes that you have to sprinkle or spray with starch. Don't complain! Just do it. · Find out how to talk to the people at the cleaner's so you can get your clothes back the way that you want.
Find Common Interests in Restaurants and Entertainment	· Learn about quality restaurants where you can go for a quiet evening alone. · Learn how to practice social graces, and how to eat in quality restaurants and use the proper silverware. · Men: Sacrifice worldly habits like drinking beer and smoking cigars, listening to secular music and dancing. · Plan out the best ways to still spend time with friends after you're married, without sacrificing important times with your spouse.
Plan for Future Vacations and Times of Renewal	· Practice doing strategic planning for vacations that you can take together. · Visit some travel agencies. · Read the Classified ads.

WORKING ON YOUR ATTITUDES

For both men and women, in God, your attitude determines your altitude. If you want to rate highly in the eyes of God and your wife, humility is more important than pride. Here are some ways that singles can check out their attitudes, which will also help married couples to evaluate themselves.

Do What God Wants You to Do

Be God-conscious, not people-conscious. Don't be afraid of what people think. Be afraid of what God thinks. Learn what He thinks through spending time with Him in prayer and reading His Word. If you always do what other people want you to do, you'll never be happy. If you always do what God wants you to do, you'll be blessed, and you'll have the endurance you need for any trial. The people who have the greatest, most lasting self-esteem are the ones who know that God is with them.

"The Lord says: 'Cursed is the man who puts his trust in mortal man and turns his heart away from God. He is like a stunted shrub in the desert, with no hope for the future; he lives on the salt-encrusted plains in the barren wilderness; good times pass him by forever. But blessed is the man who trusts in the Lord and has made the Lord his hope and confidence. He is like a tree planted along a riverbank, with its roots reaching deep into the water—a tree not bothered by the heat nor worried by long months of drought. Its leaves stay green, and it goes right on producing all its luscious fruit.' "[8]

> One of the keys to finding the right marriage partner is understanding the difference between lust and love—the kind of love we learn about through Jesus.

Learn the Difference Between Lust and Love

Jesus said, "I always do those things that please [My Father]."[9] Most singles who say they have "love" relationships with the opposite sex are usually talking more about lust than love. Love is a God-pleasing quality of character, not an emotional attachment or self-centered demands. If you've been lusting after someone the whole time you're single, it's hard to start suddenly loving them in the quality way that Jesus loves as soon as you get married, especially if you've given in to the lust and done things in secret that your momma and daddy wouldn't approve.

Lust doesn't just apply to sexual lust. It also means a craving for anything that drives you from intimacy with God. If you're always trying to get your own needs met first, you're living in lust. If you don't grow up before you get married, you'll be miserable and you'll make your wife miserable, too. "The person who plants selfishness, ignoring the needs of others—ignoring God!—harvests a crop of weeds. All he'll have to show for his life is weeds!"[10] As long as all you can talk about is "me, me, me," God won't be backing you. You need to learn the basic Christian lesson of putting others' needs before your own.

The Bible says that all of the self-centered sins we commit ultimately come from these three sources: "the lust of the flesh, and the lust of the eyes, and the pride of life." It says that these things are not of the Father, but of the world. "And the world passeth away, and the lust thereof: but he that doeth the will of God abideth for ever."[11]

When people have a stronger drive to meet their own needs through sex and a spouse than a yearning to know the Lord, you know that Jesus is not real enough in their lives. Something is missing in their relationship with the Father, and weaknesses will show up sooner or later after they're married. However, where Jesus is the First Love of both the husband and the wife, the marriage will be founded on the rock of commitment to the Lord.

> **Learn from the nature of God how to love your spouse with unconditional love.**

Love Unconditionally

When single people get married, one of the hardest lessons to learn is how to have unconditional love for their mate. They have basically been living for themselves all their lives. They have often spoken of love without really understanding its true, sacrificial nature. Marriage is a testing ground of mature love, and most people have never faced anything like it before.

Christians sometimes struggle with whether God loves them just the way they are, so they have trouble loving others that way. They are performance-conscious, not conscious of being "accepted in the beloved,"[12] being accepted in the family of God just for who they are. If you blow it with God, you still qualify for His love. When you understand God's love for you, then you understand more about how to love Him, and you also understand better how to love your wife unconditionally, without qualifications.

You couldn't qualify for God's love if you wanted to. You couldn't be good enough. You couldn't pray long enough. You couldn't read the Bible long enough. You couldn't fast long enough. You couldn't come to church enough times. You couldn't do anything to qualify for His love. He just decided to love you. God is love, and He loves you even when you're wrong and when you're mean. When you were in sin, God in His love and mercy sent His Son. You couldn't save yourself. You had to rest in His love. Love your wife that way.

Love Your Wife, Even When She Has a Bad Day

If I really love my wife, I don't change my level of love based on how she acts or what she does. My love is constant. I understand if she's having a bad day. I go the extra mile for her. That's a hard adjustment for singles coming into marriage—putting up with someone moody in the house. There's no escape and no running home to Momma. It's just something you have to do.

God loves me that way, and He has given me enough love both to love Him and to be loving and kind to others. As the first letter of John says, "But if a person isn't loving and kind, it shows that he doesn't know God—for God is love. God showed how much he loved us by sending his only Son into this wicked world to bring us eternal life through his death. In this act we see what real love is: It is not our love for God, but his love for us when he sent his Son to satisfy God's anger against our sins. Dear friends, since God loved us as much as that, we surely ought to love each other too. For though we have never yet seen God, when we love each other God lives in us and his love within us grows ever stronger."[13]

In Matthew 5, there's a portion of Scripture many people would love to take out of the Bible. Jesus said, "I'm telling you to love your enemies. Let them bring out the best in you, not the worst. When someone gives you a hard time, respond with the energies of prayer, for then you are working out of your true selves, your God-created selves. This is what God does. He gives his best—the sun to warm and the rain to nourish—to everyone, regardless."[14]

Be a Winner, Not a Whiner

Look at life from God's point of view. Do you think God whines and complains when things don't go right? Do you think the Father, Son, and Holy Spirit get stressed out and irritable toward one another? Well, then, get some of their substance and you won't get stressed out either.

"In a word, what I'm saying is, *Grow up*. You're kingdom subjects. Now live like it. Live out your God-created identity. Live generously and graciously toward others, the way God lives toward you."[15] Ideally, marriage should not be the first place you learn to love unconditionally as a Christian, but it may be the most intense.

When people get on your nerves, you have to check out if *you're* living in a love relationship with your First Love. If you put people in your family in the dog house and don't let them come out unless they grovel on the ground and wag their tails the right way, then you don't understand God. God never holds back from having fellowship with us. He always wants to be with us. He says, "I'll never leave you or forsake you."[16] He's not like the wives and husbands who try to get away from their mates every night of the week, filling their lives with "busy-ness." Not God. He loves us. He never needs a rest from us. You could always go to Him and He'd always be there. That's the nature of His love.

Since God Himself set up these requirements for the quality of your love, God, not your wife, will supply you with the power you need to do it.

Watch Your Attitude Toward Annoyances

Adjustment from being single to the daily routine of marriage doesn't come automatically. It takes work. Toothpaste companies try to help you out by telling you on the label how to squeeze the toothpaste tube, but it takes a little more than that. It takes God to chase away what the Bible calls the "little foxes that spoil the vine"[17]—things you never thought about before you said "I do" that drive you nuts after you start living together.

Sometimes when you're single and looking for a mate, you think all you have to do is find that one "somebody" and fall in love and you'll live happily ever after. But you forget that two people who have lived private, somewhat self-centered lives since they were born have a hard time sharing their time and possessions and exposing everything about themselves to another person. It's not easy to give up the mysteries.

When someone is single by reason of divorce, there is an additional, deep-rooted problem. They have exposed their innermost selves to a spouse and become vulnerable to them, only to be rejected and betrayed. It's even harder for them to develop the trust needed to again share their secret selves.

Every person has certain things that bug them about other people, and of course some of those things show up in their mate! Maybe he waits until his clothes pile up for a week in the bathroom before he puts them in the wash. Maybe she vacuums only when her momma comes to visit. What if he leaves a ring around the tub, and crumbs and cans around the chair where he watches TV? Little foxes. Who cares, anyway? If one person cares, the other one is going to have to care. Couples have to make seemingly silly adjustments to keep a marriage sound. Real love says, "If it's important to you, it's important to me."

Get Rid of Anything That People Use to Make You Mad

Get rid of your "hot buttons"—things that people know they can say that will always make you mad just as fast as pushing a button. Refuse to get angry when people mistreat you or insult you. Maybe your "hot buttons" are something about how you look. Your skin is too dark. You're too short or too tall. Your nose is too long. Your lips are too big. Who says? God made you one way. If they don't like it, they'll have to deal with Him. Laugh when people provoke you. If you don't fight back, provoking you won't be any fun anymore. Eventually people will leave you alone if they have no power to get you out of the character of Christ.

Give Instead of Taking

We tend to think of love as an emotion. I "feel good" because somebody loves me. That's what you usually hear about love on TV—what this person does or doesn't do for my emotions. Soap operas justify adultery and every other kind of sin based on how people feel, and whether they believe they've been treated fairly (in their own minds). That's because most people go into marriage thinking about what the other person can do for them, not what they can do for the other person. If the husband expects his wife to be his momma at her best—cooking, cleaning house, ironing clothes, and being there every time he shows up—and also expects that she should always be ready to jump in bed with him, he doesn't love her. He lusts after her. He's just looking for what he can get.

God doesn't love like that. God isn't a taker. He's a giver. He initiated a relationship with us by giving. "For God so loved the world, that he gave."[18] He gave His best. He gave His Son. When you love the way God loves, you give your best. The quicker you begin to want your wife to get what's best for her more than you want to get what's best for yourself, the smoother your transition from being single to being married will be.

Learn to "Take the L"—the Low Road

"Take the L"—the low road. Look for ways to meet others' needs more than your own. Learn the blessings of self-sacrifice. Jesus said, "This is my commandment, That ye love one another, as I have loved you. Greater love hath no man than this, that a man lay down his life for his friends."[19] And Paul wrote, "Let this mind be in you which was also in Christ Jesus, who, being in the form of God, did not consider it robbery to be equal with God, but made Himself of no reputation, taking the form of a bondservant, and coming in the likeness of men. And being found in appearance as a man, He humbled Himself and became obedient to the point of death, even the death of the cross."[20]

To be like Jesus, you have to humble yourself and go down when you would rather raise up and make demands. That's what the Bible means when it says to submit one to another in the fear of God.[21] You take the low road.

Be quick to say "I'm sorry," because you should always be sorry when things aren't right between you and your woman. Even if you think you're right, be quick to say "I was wrong," because you know you have only limited understanding of what is right. What did Jesus ever do that was wrong? He was always 100 percent right, but he humbled himself for our sakes.

Don't defend yourself when you're criticized. Be grateful for correction. If they're missing it, God isn't. "Humble yourselves in the sight of the Lord, and He will lift you up."[22]

Learn how to be a worm instead of a snake. A snake strikes back when it's stepped on, but a worm is easily crushed. When you're a worm, you take wrong even when you think you're right.

Forgive your woman for putting you down, even before she asks you to forgive her. If you get walked on, stay down. Be a reconciler. See yourself as her bridge to God, and remember that bridges always get walked on.

Don't lord it over people. Become like the Lord Jesus Christ. If you want to feel good about yourself, don't go looking for a conquest. Go looking for Jesus. Are you a bully? Do you make your woman do things to feed your ego? Someone said that "ego" is "Easing God Out." God wouldn't be a bully to your wife. Quit misrepresenting Him and excusing the way you throw your weight around by saying you're only teaching her authority and submission.

Tell the Truth in Love

Stop lying and covering up your faults to win people over. Let's face it. Most of us will do anything to look good to other people, even lying, or at least leaving out vital information that would hurt our image. God is truth. God is in you. Stop hiding out like Adam in the Garden. Learn to be open. Learn to be truthful and holy in thought, word, and deed. Others' lives are affected by your truth and your lies.

Remember that others are affected by your truthfulness. A famous hymn written by a single young man named Howard A. Walter [1883–1918] says,

> I would be true, for there are those who trust me;
> I would be pure, for there are those who care.[23]

Your lies hurt you and hurt others and they especially hurt God. It's better to take your punishment by telling the truth about yourself than to put all that effort into trying to cover your own back and fake it about your faults.

> A key question about the words that husbands and wives say to each other: Do the things you say *to* your spouse—and *about* your spouse—have a sweet savor to God, or do they stink up the place?

Speak with Kindness, Never Cursing

Learn how to communicate in a spirit of love and mercy, not judgmentalism. When you "speak the truth in love,"[24] don't use that as an excuse for being harsh or domineering. Be merciful. Temper your words with kindness, gentleness, and affirmation. Jesus said it is a blessing to be merciful.[25] When you have to bring a word of correction, use the "plus-minus-plus" formula: Say at least two positive things for every negative one. Don't throw the pie in the other person's face; serve the pie a slice at a time. If you keep in mind your own need for God's mercy, you will be a lot more merciful toward others. "For judgment [will be] merciless to one who has shown no mercy; mercy triumphs over judgment."[26]

Criticizing is the same as cursing. Your words have the power to lift your wife and family to a new level in their walk with the Lord, or to put them down into the territory of the devil. Words can bring a blessing, or words can bring a curse. Usually we think of cursing as four-letter words that nice people don't say, but cursing is also criticizing. It is saying things that don't bring out the nature of God in another person. It's saying the worst about what you see with your natural eyes instead of the best about what you see with your spiritual eyes. When you speak life-giving words of blessing, they are like a sweet perfume. When you criticize, your words are like bad breath. You're putting out a bad odor with your mouth.

Don't get careless with your words when you're angry. When you're single, you may get careless and let words fly in the heat of a disagreement. You speak whatever comes to your mind, just to relieve your emotional distress, not realizing your words are cursing and damaging the other person. That's doing the devil's work!

You curse when you cut someone down by speaking about their shortcomings, rather than building them up for their strengths. You curse when you use your mouth as a weapon of revenge against someone, putting them down, not raising them up.

Do Your Words Smell Good to God?

God doesn't curse under His breath. He doesn't cut people up. He heals them. Our words should be just like the Word. It works inside like a laser beam, making adjustments, but never smelling bad and never leaving a scar.

Watch your words. Ask God to help you smell the odor of your words, and to make your words smell pleasing to Him. That's one sure way you can bring heaven to your home.

Check out how your words to one another compare with this biblical standard:

> "Now thanks be unto God, which always causeth us to triumph in Christ, and maketh manifest the savour of his knowledge by us in every place. For we are unto God a sweet savour of Christ, in them that are saved, and in them that perish."[27]

FINANCIAL MANAGEMENT AND INTEGRITY

No Finance, No Romance

In the transition between being single to being married there are certain financial principles to consider. Money may not be able to buy happiness, but the way you and your wife handle money together has a definite effect on the health of your relationship.

My friend O. T. Lockett pastors a large number of college students at his church, Evangel Fellowship in Greensboro, North Carolina. He always tells the students who are considering marriage that if they are considering marriage to any of the young ladies in his church they have to pass this test from their spiritual father: "No finance, no romance."

Every young man, preferably long before marriage, has to work out the practical elements of creating a financial base. He should look at how he manages his checking account. Does he do budgeting and forecasting future expenses? Has he been provident enough to save the money for a house before he gets married? He may be the kind of industrious young person who has already bought a house and has a house or two and an apartment as investment property before he marries. It's good to think that way.

Women go to school and they understand financial management, too. Some of them may be astute businesswomen and have money in savings and investments. They may be very successful and progressive in their mentality about money.

Maybe you want to invest in insurance. Study several options so you won't just depend on one company. You may want to invest in annuities. You also need to prepare your will. Having those things worked out before you ever get married adds soundness to the relationship and helps lay a good foundation.

God doesn't require that every man who wants to marry one of His daughters be rich, just responsible. The more quickly you learn to be responsible, the more headaches you'll avoid as you provide for your family's future.

Plan as though you're going to live a thousand years, but live as though you're going to meet God at any moment.

A Reputation for Integrity

Would you want your daughter to marry a man who was an unreliable employee with a questionable testimony? Of course not. Being a man of integrity in the workplace, not just in the church, is a key to your ability to make the transition into your role as spiritual leader and provider for your family. Before you marry, you may learn some principles of management and become a successful businessman, but do you have the restraint to practice principles of Christ-likeness in your business? Being in a competitive world, when you're behind the scenes do you manipulate, dominate, deceive, and even lie? Does it seem so necessary to you in order to succeed that you separate those business practices from your Christianity?

Maybe you're an employee and in competition with the person next to you, so you promote yourself rather than being like Christ to him, and as a result you advance your career at his expense.

You may be a politician who is more into the influence of man than having God's favor, so you love positioning yourself where you receive honor. Jesus said, "I receive not honor from men."[28] He doesn't receive honor from men, and neither should you. Check out what God thinks instead. "For promotion cometh neither from the east, nor from the west, nor from the south. But God is the judge: he putteth down one, and setteth up another."[29]

In order to remain promotable in God's sight, you must have a right heart. So you've got to make a distinction between heart qualities of Christ-like character and the world's management and business and political methods. You may be successful on earth but never be approved when you get before the Judgment Bar because of all the "dead bodies" left behind—the people you've hurt, things you've said, actions you've taken that would never be acceptable in God's sight but you justified on your rise to the top.

God wouldn't run that company the way you run it or win business that way. He wouldn't justify sin by saying, "You just don't understand that this is a hard world. This is a cold world. It's dog eat dog."

"No," God would say, "you don't understand. You have to maintain a certain godly standard of righteousness, even with the potential of being rejected by your customers or your peers, or even losing your whole business. The Holy Spirit is witnessing down inside of you, and your conscience is accusing or excusing you[30] through words that the Holy Spirit brings to your mind and heart."

We have to be standard bearers for God. The Lord says, "Lift up a standard for the people."[31] If I compromise on the standard, then at the time of judgment those people will look at me with reproach and say, "I thought you were a Christian. What happened?" Of course, that won't be a justification for their sin, because they knew better and besides, those principles are in the Bible. But God will still hold me accountable for not telling them what I know and warning them of His judgment.[32]

When you keep your work life blameless before God, you will be delighted to share it with your wife, not ashamed.

HONORING HER PARENTS AND YOURS

Merging Two Families

When you marry a woman, it's not just the two of you. You actually merge your family with hers. That's why it's so important to go through all the proper steps of this merger with the people involved. One of the keys to making the transition from singlehood to marriage successfully is to leave your father and mother, and for your wife to leave hers, but you should never stop honoring them.

Ask her father's permission to marry his daughter. God says to honor your father and mother. The most important thing a young man does to honor his girlfriend's parents is to ask her father for permission to marry her. That's almost unheard of today, but it shows that you have enough character to qualify for that girl. You don't just get a free ride by going after her emotions and making it sound as if you'll live happily ever after. You have to face her father.

Answer all her father's questions about your intentions. Her daddy needs several meetings with you to ask you some hard questions and to get to know you. He should do it in a spirit of meekness, but nevertheless with the strength of a father under the authority of God. Remember this when your children are the age of marriage, and be sure they understand this protocol.

If she doesn't have a daddy, or she has more than one set of parents through multiple marriages, ask her who she considers to be in the role of father. Who will give her away when she gets married? There's always someone who is a father figure, or there should be. It may be a stepfather, an uncle, a brother, or a pastor. Your responsibility is to honor *everyone* in authority over that woman, even if there are several people, in the same way that we give honor to God before He marries Jesus to the Church, His Bride.

Don't degrade your parents and her parents by putting them down and refusing their advice and standards of decency. Don't curse your roots. In-laws are not outlaws. Don't just tolerate them. Honor them. They prepared their daughter to be your wife.

Examine your attitudes toward your in-laws and your parents. Are they like Jesus' attitudes toward His Father? One reason that most singles have a hard time adjusting to marriage is that they have spent too many years being rebels—against their parents' standards and against God. They wanted to date and stay out as late as they felt like it. They wanted to kiss and have sex as singles. They didn't want any rules. Well, I can tell you that the kind of lifestyle those singles have is a terrible preparation for marriage. The single years are supposed to be a time when you consecrate yourself. You cultivate a sense of spiritual reality when you establish standards pleasing to God and find out God's plan for your life.

Use any delays in your marriage plans to get to know your future mate and her family. Don't see her parents as appendages that you can ignore 99 percent of the time. When you marry her, you also make a lifetime connection to them. You can benefit from their experiences in raising her. They know her as no one else does.

Win the favor of your future mother-in-law. Be sincere. Always speak to her. Say nice things about how she looks or how the house looks or something she has done professionally. Compliment her for the way she raised her daughter to be like her.

Get to know your future wife's daddy. Every daughter's daddy has questions for the man who is seeing his child. How do you handle money? Do you have a savings account? Do you have a problem with anger? Do you ever lose your temper? Have you ever slapped a girlfriend? Do you tell the truth? Ask the girl's father for permission to marry her. In some traditions, the father chooses his daughter's husband, often when she is still a child. He sets her apart for her future groom. It is still the biblical model for the father to approve his daughter's husband. A man still needs to ask a woman's father for her hand.

If you've struggled with your in-laws during your courtship and marriage, repent to them and set things right. If you don't, you may find you have some unpleasant experiences when your own children prepare to marry and it's suddenly *you* who are the in-law.

We are restoring right relationships that have been lost in society. In some circles, respect for each other's parents has almost ceased to exist. So much of our culture just doesn't think that way, but God says it is right.

QUESTIONS A GIRL'S FATHER CAN ASK A PROSPECTIVE HUSBAND

· Are you a Christian?
· What are your intentions?
· Will you take the good seed that we have sown into her and continue to make it grow?
· Will you be faithful to her, knowing that God is your witness?
· Will you see her as beautiful—both on the inside and the outside—and help her to become more beautiful with your love?
· What kind of a commitment are you willing to make—for life? Are you willing to grow old together with my daughter?
· What if she gets sick and can't do the same things for you anymore? Will you still love her?
· Will you commit to me not to have sex with her before marriage? Will you promise never to commit adultery?
· Will you have children and raise them up in the nurture and admonition of the Lord? Will you commit yourself to their upbringing and not leave it to others? Will you love them as you wanted to be loved when you were a child?
· Will you provide a godly example of Christ in your home?
· Will you pray with her often and study the Scriptures with her and the children to come?
· Tell me about your parents. I want to get to know them. Will you allow this process of acquaintance to take place and continue over the years?
· Do you have any money in the bank?
· Do you have a steady job to be able to support my daughter?

- What kind of a track record do you have in getting and keeping jobs?
- What kind of education do you have? Do you want to pursue more? Why?

STAYING PURE

Jesus Blessed the Pure

When Jesus said in the Sermon on the Mount, "Blessed are the pure in heart: for they shall see God,"[33] He was speaking about everybody, including couples who are dating. Purity is a blessing, not a curse to spoil all your fun.

Singles can stay pure. The best preparation for finding a one-man woman for a wife and being a one-woman man for her is keeping your virginity while you're single. That's true because the Bible calls for singles to be virgins and it's also been proved over and over again in life. Even sinners think it's great when two virgins marry. In our ministry, when two people marry they haven't even kissed before they take their wedding vows!

The risk of adultery *after* marriage is directly related to the promiscuity *before* marriage. When a man and woman become engaged, or "espoused," they make a pledge that they will marry. When they marry, they make a covenant committing themselves to one another for life. Here's a familiar statement from the *Book of Common Prayer:*

> "[T]o have and to hold from this day forward, for better for worse, for richer for poorer, in sickness and in health, to love and to cherish, until we are parted by death. This is my solemn vow."[34]

Marriage Is a Blood Covenant Under God

The breaking of the hymen seals the marriage covenant. While a man and woman are still single, their covenant has not been sealed, so he doesn't touch her sexually. When a single woman is a virgin, that means that the hymen—the part of her anatomy leading to her internal reproductive organs—remains unbroken. The first time she has sexual intercourse, it will be broken and bleed. The breaking of the hymen is the culmination of a blood covenant, just like other blood covenants in the Bible, such as the convenant God made with us through Jesus' blood on the cross.

The blood on the marriage bed sheets was the Old Testament proof of a daughter's virginity that the father of the bride would keep. It proved that the hymen was broken only by her husband, the man to whom she had committed herself to be faithful for the rest of her life.

The father of the bride was the protector of his virgin daughter's integrity, even after marriage.

> "If a man marries a girl, then after sleeping with her accuses her of having had premarital intercourse with another man, saying, 'She was not a virgin when I married her,' then the girl's father and mother shall bring the proof of her virginity to the city judges. Her father shall tell them, 'I gave my daughter to this man to be his wife, and now he despises her, and has accused her of shameful things, claiming that she was not a virgin when she married; yet here is the proof.' And they shall spread the garment before the judges [the bloodstained sheet from her marriage bed]. The judges shall sentence the man to be whipped, and fine him one hundred dollars to be given to the girl's father, for he has falsely accused a virgin of Israel. She shall remain his wife and he may never divorce her."[35]

Legal Protection of a Woman's Virginity

Virginity was so important in the Law that severe punishments—even death—were listed for the men who raped some father's daughter. "But if a man finds a betrothed young woman in the countryside, and the man forces her and lies with her, then . . . the man who lay with her shall die."[36]

Today, some sexually transmitted diseases still carry a death sentence even after all these centuries of scientific advancement. When you have sex with someone who is not a virgin, you take into your body the diseases caught at every previous sexual encounter that person has had.

God takes sexual sin very seriously. He doesn't care if everybody in the world is "doing it." It's still wrong. He says, "Do you not know that you are the temple of God and that the Spirit of God dwells in you? If anyone defiles the temple of God, God will destroy him. For the temple of God is holy, which temple you are."[37]

God is the author of sex. He wants your sexual intimacy with your mate to be unifying and fruitful. If you violated your wife by touching her (or another woman) before you were married, make sure you stop and repent and allow the Lord to cleanse you and your defiled marriage bed. God says, "Marriage is honorable among all, and the bed undefiled; but fornicators and adulterers God will judge."[38]

Intimacy Means Knowing

Intimacy is giving yourself to another—first to God, and then to your mate. It comes about in the context of a covenant, and it results in the conception of a vision that you both share. The idea of sex as an end in itself isn't a biblical concept. It's a result of our American way of thinking. Think about how you go into the prayer closet to be alone with God. You want to *know* Him. That's also the highest purpose of marriage—not to use each other's bodies for self-gratification but to come to know that other person in a wonderful way that no one else will ever know them. Just as you don't go into prayer just to get goose bumps, you don't go into sexual union just to get high. God gave us feelings so we would be attracted to one another, but living on the basis of feelings never yields good fruit. Giving is much more blessed than receiving,[39] especially in your intimate relationship with your mate. Emotional highs don't last, but the fruit of giving lasts for eternity.

Men Can Stay Pure

Becoming a one-woman man. Even though I had fooled around with a number of women before my wife and I were married, she got me to rise up to a level of faithfulness to her that was just like that of Jesus. She made me want to become a one-woman man.

When I was young, I wasn't the kind who would stick with one woman. However, my wife didn't have that vision for me. She said I had to raise my standard and just see her! By loving me unconditionally, she really did cause me to rise up and be faithful to her. Her standard of devotion made me rise up and be a one-woman man, because she was a one-man woman.

"My beloved said to me, 'Rise up, my love, my fair one, and come away. For the winter is past, the rain is over and gone. The flowers are springing up and the time of the singing of birds has come.' "[40]

Sir, you need to come away from those dogs whose filthy attitudes about women bring out the worst in you. None of those dogs ever think about how they are lusting after some daddy's virgin daughter or some man's woman. They keep your brain operating at the level of a dog, where your lusts rule instead of your character.

My wife said, "Come away," and I walked away from the low-down dogs ruled by the flesh to a woman—a one-man woman. That woman had enough devotedness and loyalty to me to drive me into a new level of character.

Get to know her without involving sex. When the sex experience is set aside until after marriage, you can come to know that other person's real nature before the sexual intimacy. Is she "the one" by all the other standards? Then she will be "the one" on the marriage bed as well. It doesn't work in reverse—if sex works, everything else will work—because all the physical attributes that relate to sex are going to change with age, and you better have something else left to fall back on when that time is past.

Jesus Proved a Man Could Be Pure

Commit to making your relationship a reflection of Jesus in you. When people see you with your girlfriend or your wife, they should see Jesus in both of you. Everything you do with each other should come from a motivation to honor the Lord. God deals with motivations, and He expects us to deal the same way.

At every stage of your relationship you should be conscious of questions like these:

· Why are we doing this?
· Does this glorify God or are we just trying to fulfill our needs?
· Could others model their relationships with the opposite sex after what they see us doing?

· Should we be doing this in church? I don't see any necessity for even husbands and wives sitting in church with their hands all over each other. Save that stuff for when you're alone, not when you have a whole lot of people behind you getting distracted from the Word.

Jesus was a single man and never had physical sex on the earth. Because a man is becoming like Jesus Christ, he can remain a virgin, and a married man can remain faithful to his wife. Jesus was a virgin, and if we want to be like Him we have to be virgins, because God has predestined us to be like Him. We are also destined to be His Bride. At the Marriage Supper of the Lamb He will marry the Church, and by the time He finishes perfecting her, she will be a sinless virgin. There isn't one person on earth who has never sinned, so Christ Himself by His sinless virginity is perfecting His woman, the Church. He makes her like Him. He removes her sin. He imparts a virgin spirit. He sows into the woman what He is. He cleans up the woman and makes her one with Him. He is a perfect example in every way.

Define happiness God's way. Some people defend premarital and extramarital sex by saying, "I enjoy being with this person, and I know God wants me to be happy." My questions to them would be:

· Are you happy because you are embracing the purposes of God or because you are suppressing the truth?[41]
· Can you honestly say that your study of the Word and your sense of the holiness of His Spirit confirm the rightness of your actions?
· Is your heart pure and do you have a sense of blessedness when you participate in and defend your extramarital sexual relationship, even to yourself? Jesus said, "Blessed are the pure in heart, for they shall see God."[42]

When you get before God at the Judgment Seat of Christ, what will He say? I do not believe He will say, "I understand that you cared for this person and I want to make you happy, so everything is OK, including sex outside of marriage." That isn't consistent with the Bible, including the passage in Revelation 22:15 that says all sexually immoral people will be kept out of heaven. Why does He bar you from heaven? Because you would defile up the place with your filthy sin.

Women Can Stay Pure

Stay faithful to God's vision for your life. Often when God speaks of His people's unfaithfulness to Him, He uses the analogy of the promiscuous woman. He calls people "harlots" who are supposed to love Him and serve Him but are running after other gods and their own lusts. All that the word *harlot* means is a woman who has sex outside of marriage. Are you a harlot? If that's such an awful thing to God, why would you want to be one voluntarily, if you say that you know God?

Submit your body to God alone. If you're a single woman, there's only one Person to whom you should submit your body, and that is God, because He will respect your body as a holy sacrifice. "I urge you therefore, brethren, by the mercies of God, to present your bodies a living and holy sacrifice, acceptable to God, which is your spiritual service of worship."[43]

Save your virginity, and your dignity. God wants you to wait as a virgin for someone He sends as a husband, someone with the character of Christ. As you wait on God and refuse to yield to peer pressures to date and lose your virginity, you will not only protect yourself but will also be growing closer to Jesus and increasing in Christ-like character.

In the inner city, dudes have a name for the young virgins they persuade to have sex with them for the first time. They call them "lambs." After these young girls lose their virginity, they will follow those evil guys anywhere.

Girls who lose their virginity almost invariably lose their dignity as well. They become some braggart's locker-room story. If the girls keep it up, they can become hardened to the warning voice of God. They will go to bed with someone without a conscience of good and evil. But all the time, that adultery against their divine Husband is exacting a terrible price on their soul. It will also affect their future in many devastating ways.

Don't become used merchandise. Most men who have sex outside of marriage will tell you they love you, or you're good in bed, but all the time they think you're too easy for them and you're not right for a wife. When the time comes for them to marry, they'll go looking for a virgin. They will defile somebody else's future wife—some father's daughter—and cause her not to be a virgin, but then reject her when it is time to marry. He has messed you up, but he wants to find a bride who is not messed up. He wants a woman cleaner than he is and cleaner than he has made you. Girl, which would you rather be—the used merchandise or the sought-after wife?

When a single woman allows someone other than her husband to have sex with her, she loses not only her virginity but also that sense of specialness God meant her to have with her husband, the man to whom she is related by covenant for life. People don't talk much about covenants anymore, even in the Church, but we should, because a covenant is the way God relates to us and the way He expects us to relate to one another, if we're serious.

If you read women's magazines, you've probably seen the term "dress for success." Real success in life means only one thing: finding the will of God and doing it. Do you think your heavenly Father wants His daughter defiled by some dirty old man? Do you think He wants her to dress seductively or even carelessly so that some dirty old man is attracted by her? The guy who comes after your flesh may look like Mr. Nice Guy, but inside he's unclean.

Men are all the same when they're looking for a conquest. Some just aren't as obvious about it as others. He may sweet-talk you and take you to nice places all the time and give you beautiful gifts and tell you you're wonderful, but he's got the devil in him. He may tell you he's a Christian and go to church with you and still be after your body. The Bible says the devil looks like an angel of light.[44] Have you met any of those angels recently?

"They're a sorry bunch—pseudo-apostles, lying preachers, crooked workers—posing as Christ's agents but sham to the core. And no wonder! Satan does it all the time, dressing up as a beautiful angel of light. So it shouldn't surprise us when his servants masquerade as servants of God. But they're not getting by with anything. They'll pay for it in the end."[45]

Even one compromise can make you sick for life. When you have sex outside of marriage, you get dirty. You not only get that guy's semen all over you but you also get a dose of whatever he got from his previous sex partners. That could be any one of a number of diseases, with symptoms you don't even want to think about, that can make you sick, sometimes for life. Did you know that some sexually transmitted diseases cause you to lose your mind? You literally go insane if they are untreated, or if the treatment doesn't work. You get sores on your body that hurt and won't heal. You can even die a slow, painful death. Isn't there some divine message God is trying to tell us here? His message is be pure so you'll be blessed.

Preventing Sex Outside of Marriage

Here are some practical ways to prevent involvement in sexual encounters outside of marriage.

If you're single, don't be motivated to seek a woman just so you can get sex and service, and if you're married, don't see your wife in that light, either. That's not of God. He wants you to have a woman as your mate who will help you fulfill His purposes for your life. You have to change your focus. A relationship based on the provision of sex and service won't carry you through the tough times of blending from singleness into marriage. Sex and service won't appeal very long to your woman, either, no matter what enticements you offer her. And they definitely won't last into your old age. You will grow old someday, you know.

Consecrate yourself daily for strength against the enemies of your soul. Before Joshua crossed the Jordan and faced the enemies of Israel, he told the people, "Sanctify yourselves: for tomorrow the Lord will do wonders among you."[46] You *will* be challenged daily by the enemies of your soul. *Before* you get sexual desires that could overwhelm you, ask God to strengthen your inner man with His holiness. Ask Him daily to *make* you holy, as He is holy. Ask Him to *cause* you to walk in His ways,[47] and He will do it. Yield your will to Him totally. Hunger and thirst after righteousness, and He will fill you.[48] "For I am the Lord your God: ye shall therefore consecrate yourselves, and ye shall be holy, for I am holy."[49]

Clothe yourself in holiness every day. Start out the day committed to living the Christ-like lifestyle of chastity. Don't dress seductively. Don't draw attention to your flesh. Clothe yourself in holiness, both spiritually and naturally.

The Israelites literally wore robes that represented the character and commandments of God.[50] You need that mentality, both spiritually and naturally. There are laws against adultery and fornication both in the Bible and in society. It's wrong. It's a crime against God and the woman, her family, and society. It's Evil with a capital *E*. It's the devil's scheme to undermine the purposes of God.

When Jesus prayed what we call the Lord's Prayer, He said, "Deliver us from evil" [or "the evil one"].[51] Before you get tempted, if you can't think of anything else to pray, or even if you can, pray the Lord's Prayer. Those are powerful words to clothe yourself with daily.

Just how holy are you anyway? What kind of nonverbal messages do you put out? Whether you are married or single, women should definitely not feel comfortable making suggestive or even "playful" comments around you because they sense the holiness of Jesus. If such ungodly attention flatters you or feeds your ego, you need to plead with God to make you holy.

Recognize what is evil and pray against those things. Yell a loud no to the devil! The Bible says, "Submit . . . to God. Resist the devil."[52] In *The Message* it says, "So let God work his will in you. Yell a loud *no* to the Devil and watch him scamper. Say a quiet *yes* to God and he'll be there in no time. Quit dabbling in sin. Purify your inner life."[53] Don't even pretend to accept the ridiculous attitudes some of your peers have about sex and women.

Don't allow your mind to be dulled and confused by the fact that sexual sin is so prevalent, but instead allow God to raise you up as His standard. Don't let television or office gossip be your standard. *You* set the standard, based on God's Word.

Let virtue flow from you, as it flowed from Jesus when the unclean woman touched Him.[54] "Virtue" is *dunamis* in Greek, and *virtus* in Latin. It means intrinsic power, strength, and the ability to accomplish something—even miracles.[55] It is a quality of a man of character, like Jesus. The opposite of virtue is being incapable, incompetent, or driven by lust. Are you a man of virtue or are you a sorry excuse for a man? Are you a man or a mouse? You need to place as much value on virtue and purity as God does, even if you weren't raised that way. Ask God to renew your mind.

Don't dwell on sexually related thoughts. Even your thoughts are subject to Jesus' standard. "But I say to you that whoever looks at a woman to lust for her has already committed adultery with her in his heart."[56] Capture your thoughts. Make your mind obey Christ.[57] Get in the holiness habit when you're single, and it won't be such a fight when you're married.

Keep your heart pure. Don't be plotting unclean things. Remember, Jesus said, "Blessed are the pure in heart: for they shall see God."[58] When you're held captive to your sexual drives, either in premarital sex or adultery, your mind perverts something that God ordained to be a sacred marriage relationship that would help sustain your exclusive intimacy with your wife for the rest of your lives together, and also produce your children.

Impurity during singlehood undermines your marriage before you've said "I do." Even if you never act on a thought, it will infect your marriage and your children if you don't kill it off. You can't defeat the devil in the world if he's having his way in your heart.

Live in the fear that you will be judged by God for what you do, including what you do with your wandering eyes. "If your right eye causes you to sin, pluck it out and cast it from you; for it is more profitable for you that one of your members perish, than for your whole body to be cast into hell."[59] Sex is a seal on a lifetime marriage covenant, not a recreational pastime. If you have had sex outside of marriage, or if you still fantasize about it, you need to have the fear of God come upon you. You are dabbling with spiritual death.

When you sin repeatedly, God eventually stops warning you, it says in the first chapter of Romans, and lets you go into all kinds of degraded behavior, with dire consequences. That's what has happened when people don't feel any shame about premarital and extramarital sex. It's not that such behavior has become acceptable to God. It's just that they can't hear Him anymore. What an awful price to pay for a few minutes' visit to sin's palace—separation from God! The Bible says, "Since they didn't bother to acknowledge God, God quit bothering them and let them run loose. And then all hell broke loose."[60] Keep a constant, divine awareness that you will answer to God for everything you do. That sensitivity will keep you from the sick behavior so characteristic of sin.

"Flee fornication,"[61] *the Bible says.* Many godly men in the Bible fell into sexual sin because they didn't obey the command to FLEE. They felt they were strong enough or spiritual enough to resist, but even heroes like Samson, David, and Solomon all fell when they didn't flee. Joseph, the favored son of Jacob, is an example of a man of God who fled fornication and was vindicated by God. Decide in your heart that you will physically leave any situation where there is potential for sexual sin.

The Bible says that all fornicators will find themselves in the Lake of Fire.[62] If you are having sex outside of marriage, either you are not a Christian and you are going to hell, or you are a Christian and you have greatly sinned. When you fall back into unrepentant sin, you are walking away from God's will.

Remember that God is blessed when you hold on to your virtue, and He'll reward you. He blesses you, and you bless others when they see you continue in well doing, which includes sexual fidelity. "And let us not grow weary while doing good, for in due season we shall reap if we do not lose heart. Therefore, as we have opportunity, let us do good to all, especially to those who are of the household of faith."[63] Don't let the devil deceive you into thinking you are actually missing out on something worthwhile by living for God. When you throw away all that garbage thinking, you'll wonder what took you so long to get the stinky stuff out of your house.

Get rid of all your pornography. It's sin. That includes X-rated videotapes you can rent at your friendly video club and things you wander into on the Internet or TV. It includes "soft porn" like soap operas, romance novels, and a lot of R-rated movies. Don't watch anything if you think Jesus wouldn't enjoy it. Leave it alone.

Don't masturbate. It's of the devil. When you masturbate, you are having sex with demons. You have to trick your body to get a climax by using your imagination to feed your lust. That is not of God. Whatever is not of God is sin. "In this the children of God and the children of the devil are manifest: Whoever does not practice righteousness is not of God."[64]

If you're not married, what are you kissing her for? I often provoke teenagers by telling them that any form of premarital sexual arousal is wrong. I ask them, "Do you kiss?" Then I ask them, "Do you tongue kiss? How do you feel when you tongue kiss? How does that make you feel inside? Why don't you ask the girl you're kissing to spit in a glass, and when she gets it half full, ask her to give it to you to drink. And then you go ahead and spit in one and hock up and get her to drink it."

When I say that they go ballistic on me and shout "Ugh! Ugh!" And I say, "Well, when you're tongue kissing, you're sucking spit. If she has flu symptoms and a runny nose, you're kissing snot. Sucking snot. If you're sexually aroused by that, your defiled soul is blinding you to the filth of each other." They get all over the floor "yuk-ing" and laughing. It's funny, but it's also not funny. They get my point. Outside of marriage, intimacy makes no sense to an enlightened mind.

Let's face it. The sexual arousal brought about by kissing can entice the body into the sex act. To initiate even the first step of such things outside of the marriage covenant is a violation of virtue. One of the best ways you can show honor to your future wife is to restrain yourself throughout courtship, despite your physical desires for each other. A good guideline is never to do anything to a woman to whom you are not married that you wouldn't want some man to do to your daughter.

Save touching stuff until after you're married. There is no Scripture that says, "Thou shalt not hold hands before marriage." Personally, however, I believe that the more you can save until after the covenant is sealed, the more significant it will be. It's also best to save conversations about most personal things until marriage, unless you are in the presence of a minister in premarital counseling.

Never place yourself in a compromising position. Don't put yourself in a place where the devil could tempt your flesh. Set a curfew during courtship to avoid the temptation of the late-night hours. After you're married, don't get into situations where anyone could even accuse you of adultery, no matter how hard they tried. Stay out of trouble by staying in His presence.

Ask yourself, "What would Jesus do in a situation like this?" Jesus was around prostitutes all the time and He was never tempted by their flesh. He knew they were sinners, and He had come to save them, not to make them fall farther into sin.

Sexual Sin Affects the Marriage Bed

"Satanically active" lifestyle. A "sexually active" lifestyle outside of marriage is a satanically active lifestyle. It's a life-destroying lifestyle. Marriage is ordained to be two virgins coming together to become one after the formal lifelong covenant is made at the wedding ceremony. The Judgment Bar is real. Jesus is real. God the Father is real. The Holy Spirit is real. You have to order your life on earth to be perfectly suited for the realm of heaven. You have to restrict sex and sexual arousal to marriage.

When a man and woman marry who have previously had sex with others, they bring comparisons of others into the marriage bed. If you have hurt others in the process of your sinful sex lives—lied, deceived, pretended love, and otherwise taken advantage of others to get sexual fulfilment—that is seeded into your marriage unless God intervenes on your behalf. That's why you need to recognize what you have done as sin, repent, and take on that virgin spirit of Christ. Everybody would rather marry a virgin and be the other's "first one." You can't change your history, but you can be transformed by the power and virtue of God.

A wounded spirit. There is an old saying that "virtue is its own reward." Virtue is a blessing. Sin is a curse. You can take pills sometimes to get rid of some of the symptoms of sexually transmitted diseases, but there is no pill for a wounded spirit.

The most lasting damage done by extramarital sex is to your spirit. When you have exposed yourselves to one another in the face of God, who forbids fornication, you have mocked Jesus and driven fresh nails into the hands of the One who should be your only True Love. "You cannot bring yourself to repent again if you have nailed the Son of God to the cross again by rejecting him, holding him up to mocking and to public shame."[65] That's why you need the help of the Holy Ghost—first, to see what you have done, and next, to help you get it undone.

You can repent and begin again. Maybe you'll realize after reading this chapter that you have greatly sinned by having sex outside of marriage. If so, you must repent now, if you have not already done so. This is not an issue that will just go away if you try to avoid it. Even if you are already married, and even if you had premarital sex only with that person, it was still wrong. You don't necessarily have to make an open confession. Just get alone in your prayer closet and tell your Father what you did. Ask Him to forgive and cleanse you.

There is hope in Jesus Christ for every sinner who repents, who brings into the light of day the sin that he or she has been hiding in the darkness. The Bible says, "But if we walk in the light as He is in the light, we have fellowship with one another, and the blood of Jesus Christ His Son cleanses us from all sin. If we say that we have no sin, we deceive ourselves, and the truth is not in us. If we confess our sins, He is faithful and just to forgive us our sins and to cleanse us from all unrighteousness."[66]

Even if you don't tell anyone what you've done, you'll notice a new freshness in your relationships with others. That burden of sin is gone. That constant necessity of hiding something from your past has disappeared. Even if the facts become known at some future time, you will know that you are not condemned because God has forgiven you through Jesus Christ. Then, take the advice Jesus gave the woman caught in adultery: "Go and sin no more."[67]

When you are born again, because of the cleansing of Christ's blood, Christ's virginity comes on you and you become a "virtuous woman"—whether you are male or female, whether or not you have had sex outside of marriage. Even though you were unclean before you were born again, you become clean. He purifies you forever.

If you are born again and you backslide into sin, that's a terrible thing, but God will take you back if you sincerely repent and get His help to turn your life around. You can receive a virgin spirit from Christ and live a holy lifestyle from now on.

Now that you're clean, don't violate your virgin spirit. You need to keep that virtue.

Giving Chastity Rings to Sons and Daughters

If you are reading this and you are a father, you are a man of God whose children will watch your life to see what is an acceptable way for a man to treat a woman. Don't let them learn this from movies or their friends. You set a godly standard. They'll love you for it.

A few years ago, a movement started where single young people wore chastity rings or signed pledges to stay pure until marriage. This is especially meaningful when the parents are involved. The father takes his son or daughter out to dinner or does some other special thing and presents a ring to them to show his personal commitment to their purity. This becomes a seal on something sacred. The conversation that follows can build the moment into an opportunity for practical guidelines like the ones in this book.

All too often parents make jokes about sex or in the worst case buy their children contraceptives. That's like saying, "I give up!" Don't you ever give up on raising your children to be righteous. Would God the Father give us contraceptives, or would He give us chastity rings?

It's time for parents to make a more aggressive stand for righteousness in training their children for life. The world would like to make it seem as if parents who take a stand for godly living are abusive fun-spoilers, but that is a lie of the devil. Don't listen to them. Listen to God.

Is Dating of the Devil?

Each year, chapters of our campus ministry hold seminars on controversial subjects that are so provocative they draw students from the

university at large. One of the subjects that is guaranteed to bring
the crowds and keep them on the edge of their seats is dating, and
specifically, "Is Dating of the Devil?"

Dating is a practice taken for granted on almost every campus in
America. Hardly anyone dares question its validity. In fact, judging
by how they spend their time at college, most students seem to have
more interest in dating, sex, drinking, partying, and sororities and
fraternities than they do in preparing their minds for a future career.
I want to challenge that mind-set.

Is dating of the devil, or is it of God?

In light of God's plan and purpose for the lives of our youth, parents have to bring their children to a level of maturity where dating
is being evaluated by what is right in heaven's eyes—not on the basis
of what their body says, or their friends say, or even what a moderate
pastor says, but on the basis of what the Bible says. They may be
dulled into dating now, but they will have to answer for it at the
Judgment Seat of Christ, if they are Christians, and the Great White
Throne Judgment if they are not. When your children are judged,
you will be judged also. If you have not confronted them with their
sins, their blood is on your hands, too.[68]

Most people enjoy dating because they like the feelings they get
when they are with someone who makes them feel they have worth.
They like to be able to tell their girlfriends and boyfriends that they
have a date, because they feel a need for their approval.

Can one immature person truly give another immature person the
sense of self-worth they need, or is every one of them just as needy
as the other? The only one who can give you a true sense of value is
God Himself. His love is the only unselfish love. Jesus' life is the only
model of life we should follow.

The only way to get a true sense of self-worth is to know God and
do His will. That's what Jesus was trying to tell us. He held to a
perfect standard of holiness and He was the happiest man who ever
lived. He knew what it was to have true joy. The Bible says we should
always be "Looking unto Jesus the author and finisher of our faith;
who for the joy that was set before him endured the cross, despising
the shame, and is set down at the right hand of the throne of God."[69]
There is only one worthwhile theme for chastity programs, sex education programs, and discussions of dating. Ask yourself, "What
would Jesus do?" Study His life to see how He made decisions. Get

your excitement from running with God, not from running with sexually immoral people.

"Keep your eyes on *Jesus,* who both began and finished this race we're in. Study how he did it. Because he never lost sight of where he was headed—that exhilarating finish in and with God—he could put up with anything along the way: cross, shame, whatever. And now he's *there,* in the place of honor, right alongside God. When you find yourselves flagging in your faith, go over that story again, item by item, that long litany of hostility he plowed through. *That* will shoot adrenaline into your souls!"[70]

BECOMING BLENDED UNDER GOD

God's Vision for Your Home

Men have the responsibility of finding God's vision for the home. Women have the responsibility of seeking God's help to come into agreement with that vision, and together they both help bring it to pass.

God's vision for your home is that it would resemble heaven. He expects the single man to consider carefully how he will bring that to pass *before* he ever gets married. God will hold the husband accountable for the atmosphere of his home. He will also hold him accountable for the sense of vision and purpose for his family that is created within that atmosphere.

With his words and his lifestyle, the man sets the atmosphere in his house, so that it becomes a place where God dwells. When you're single, your momma and daddy set the atmosphere of your home. When you're married, the responsibility is up to you. Jesus said, "In My Father's house are many mansions: if it were not so, I would have told you. I go to prepare a place for you. And if I go and prepare a place for you, I will come again and receive you unto Myself, that where I am, there ye may be also."[71] If Jesus took the responsibility for preparing the home, you know He expects you to do the same.

In communication, the man is the initiator. Until this past generation, it was always improper for a single woman to initiate a male-female relationship. It was even embarrassing—because in the heavenly model God Himself initiated the relationship with us. Christ initiates the relationship with the Church. He's the Man. He opened up the way to the Father. He's the one doing most of the talking, ever living to make intercession for us.[72] He's the one who speaks a word to us in season. If he doesn't initiate communication, we can't get to Him. He says, "Before you call I am there." As the Bible says, "It shall come to pass that before they call, I will answer; and while they are still speaking, I will hear."[73]

That should carry over into the home. Just like in the sexual union, where the man gives and the woman receives because their bodies are made that way, give your wife the benefit of your communication first. Call her often. Every time you see your wife after you have been apart, even briefly, take time to say hello, give her some love, and ask about her day.

The man creates an environment where sex ia a normal part of the love relationship that has existed all day. Because he has been initiating communion with his wife, before any actual union on the marriage bed takes place they are one. Sex is not something couples do as one act. The sexual encounter only crescendos the environment that has been created all day because God is there.

The environment that the man has created is the atmosphere for conception, both spiritual and natural. Conception occurs in both the natural and the spiritual realms.

Physical conception of children is a natural expression of physical intimacy. Marriages are expected to produce children.

Spiritual conception occurs when the Word comes forth from the husband to his wife, after He has spent time in an intimate relationship with God. A spiritual union takes place that makes her pregnant with God's intentions and vision for their family.

Your Family's Potential for Greatness

In making the transition from the single life to the blended life, you have to broaden your thinking beyond having faith in God just for yourself. Now you need faith for your wife and children also. Your faith is expressed not only in expecting new blessings to come in the future but also in seeing the blessings that are already there—inside the person who is your wife or child.

When you find a mate, at first your attraction to her may blind you to her faults. But when you start seeing those faults, remember what God did when He saw yours. He covered for you. He made a way for you to look better in His eyes. If you remember that none of us—including yourself—was able to qualify for God's love, that should take all the critical spirit out of you. If you see that He knew in His mind that you were a sinner, and He knew you were in such a bad state that you couldn't save yourself, then you can have mercy on someone else who is in tough shape, too. That's what makes God so great, and that's what will make you great, when you embrace it. Mercy makes you great! You are entering into your glorification when you are a person of mercy!

God knew us, and He knew our weak frame, yet He still planned a glorious future for us. He knew that ultimately we would be glorified. Can you see a glorious future ahead for yourself, your wife, and children? Can you visualize it and bring it to pass with your love and mercy?

God knows our potential for greatness because He predestined Christians to be like Christ. The Bible says, "For whom He foreknew, He also predestined to be conformed to the image of His Son."[74]

After we're saved, He starts at the end—where He wants us to be, in the image and likeness of Christ—and then He works backward to bring it to pass. "Moreover whom He predestined, these He also called; whom He called, these He also justified; and whom He justified, these He also glorified."[75] That verse means this:

First, He called us to Himself. Then He justified us—cleansed us from our guilt. And when we were cleansed, He glorified us—put us on track to be like His Son. "So, what do you think? With God on our side like this, how can we lose? If God didn't hesitate to put everything on the line for us, embracing our condition and exposing himself to the worst by sending his own Son, is there anything else he wouldn't gladly and freely do for us?"[76]

Remember that God doesn't call the qualified. He qualifies the called. He called you when you were unqualified. Then He qualified you Himself so you would be accepted in the beloved.[77] That's exactly how you should be toward other people. Be like Christ! You don't condemn anybody, especially your wife. You love her and stick up for her, even if nobody else is seeing her.

"Who is he who condemns? It is Christ who died, and furthermore is also risen, who is even at the right hand of God, who also makes intercession for us."[78] "And who would dare tangle with God by messing with one of God's chosen? Who would dare even to point a finger? The One who died for us—who was raised to life for us!—is in the presence of God at this very moment sticking up for us."[79] God—loving us, providing for us, sticking up for us forever—that should make you extravagant in your faith and extravagant in your love and mercy, just as extravagant as God is. That should carry you and all your house to the next level in God.

Ask God to expand your vision, to help you see your wife beyond her faults, so you can bring out the greatness in her.

Every church has certain sayings that they repeat at the end of their church services. One of the things we say is this: "It's time to depart from this service, but not from His presence. Depart to serve."

That's what I would like you to do, now that you have read this chapter. Depart from reading this having gained new knowledge that will not only help you in your own personal relationships, but also help the generation to be changed by what you know. God be with you as you depart to serve.

PRAYER FOR BECOMING A UNIFIED FAMILY

O, Jesus, we love You so much! Create a hunger in our hearts to do Your will. You loved us and treated us like a wife before we ever came to Your marriage feast. Help us to love others like that, even before they earn our love.

Thank You for the way that You're healing us, You're restoring us, You're returning us back to the Shepherd and Bishop of our souls. We're in Your sheepfold, and we're learning to be like You. Please bless us with more of Your wisdom and knowledge.

O God, thank You for the men who are learning to be godly husbands, and the women who are reaping the benefits. Thank You for teaching us how to treat each other as our relationships grow, so that we love being together. Thank You for keeping us clean and holy and taking away all the guilt on the inside so we're looking better and better on the outside all the time.

Thank You for the deep level of repentance that You have given to those who have closed themselves off from Your holiness and as a result have lost the benefits of Your love. Thank You that You are destroying every work of darkness by the power of the Holy Spirit. They will come back now, and remarry You in ways that they've never experienced before.

We honor You and bless You. In Jesus' name. Amen.

SELAH

1. Read Genesis 1–3. Adam was the first single man. God had to change Adam's single's mentality before he could adjust to his mate. List some of the adjustments that you imagine Adam had to make. How do you think he could have avoided the Fall?
2. Study the subject of covenants. When you have a covenant with someone for life, what does that mean about your responsibilities?

I told you in Chapter 1 that the number 50 in the Bible represents the year of Jubilee, when God instructed the Israelites to release all their debtors from what they owed them.[80] He called it "the Lord's Release" because that level of giving releases the person who gives even more than the person whose debts are forgiven. To get the Lord's release for yourself, once again make lists of 50.

3. List 50 things you saw in your wife, her family, and her friends *when you were single* that made you want to marry her.
4. List 50 adjectives to describe Jesus, especially His purity and holiness.

3

$\mathcal{W}$OMEN SHOULD MARRY ONLY GROWN-UP MEN

"Yet your fellow citizens say, 'The way of the Lord is not right,'
when it is their own way that is not right."

—Ezekiel 33:17 NASB

After I finished my conference message in a certain city, several people made their way to the front of the church and got in line to speak to me.

A few brought copies of my book for me to autograph.

Some had a look of excitement, and I knew that probably something I had said agreed with what they had been thinking but had not heard expressed quite that way before. Some were ready with business cards, because they wanted me either to buy something or to participate in ministry with them in some way.

But there was one man who was crying. I could tell it wasn't because he had been particularly moved by the message. This man was in grief.

When he reached the front of the line, he told me what was breaking his heart. His daughter's husband had committed adultery. His son-in-law, to whom he had entrusted his daughter on her wedding day, had betrayed them. He had not been man enough to stay faithful. This husband was a child.

Potential adultery is only one of many reasons that women should marry only grown-up men. Grown-up men are faithful to their wives.

They cherish them. They are covenant partners with their wives in all things for life. They don't expect their wives to take care of them as a boy is taken care of by his momma. Instead, they expect to take care of their wives.

In this chapter, I describe what a grown-up man looks like in God's eyes. Also, I tell you my own growing-up story and how my wife had sense enough not to marry me until I matured in certain areas in life.

I still need more growth, and I assume you sense that you need to grow, too, because you are reading this book. If you are single, this chapter will show you certain character qualities you need to develop before you ask a woman to marry you. If you're already married, you can use this as a chart for your change, and also as a measuring rod for your daughter's future husband.

The greatest biblical standard I know of for a godly, grown-up man—other than Jesus Himself—is found in Job 29. The standard for a grown-up woman is in Proverbs 31. You can read those chapters and keep them in mind as you work through this chapter.

GOD WAS KEEPING ME

I Needed to Grow Up

I am an example of someone who needed to grow up before God could approve my getting married. In 1964, when I was sixteen, my stepfather was assigned to an army base in Germany. He and my mother sent me off to an American boarding school there, Bremerhaven High School.

In those days, if you were a black student in a foreign country, especially a star basketball player, everybody knew your name. I was the only black basketball player on the team, and there was one black cheerleader. Guess who? My future wife. It was a setup. She was fine. I went after her then, and I've been after her ever since.

We were physically attracted to each other right away, but we did have a little trouble getting our relationship off the ground. Her father wasn't seeing me too strongly.

I was the son of a sergeant and I lived in the third-floor maid's quarters of somebody's house. Her father was a colonel. They *had* a maid. They were wealthy and had a nice house that could accommodate their every need. They had their own chauffeured Cadillac. Her father, Colonel Watley, was director of logistics for all of Europe. He was definitely not seeing me.

Katheryn loved me from the very first. She especially liked my big legs. It had to be God. He had mercy on me by keeping her for me for the next several years when I went off and did some wild things that could have lost her for me forever. Thank Him!

I became a Christian at the age of ten by seeing my mother get instantly saved and healed from heart trouble. Everything about her lifestyle changed as well. It was one of the most spectacular miracles of God I have ever seen. I became a child preacher almost as soon as I got saved, but when I went to that boarding school I began to act like a real pagan.

I was coming out of a protected, holiness-church background, and when I had the chance to be on my own, I went wild. When I got away from my mother and the old mothers in my church who had kept their eyes on me, I didn't have enough of the substance of God in me to hold me back from sin.

After high school, the future Mrs. Boone went away to college at Morgan State. I was still in love with her, and all I was thinking about was marrying her, but we weren't spending much time together because I had to go to Vietnam. That's where at age eighteen I had my first taste of alcohol. Somebody turned me on to rum because I was depressed, and from then on until Christ Himself broke through to me a few years later I was in and out of alcohol and drugs.

I don't know how I kept functioning, other than that God was keeping me. I got so high one time that I saw milk cartons floating around in the air. I saw snakes flying. I called the future Mrs. Boone and said in this real weird voice, "If I die or I get put into an insane asylum I want you to know that the last thing I said was 'I love you.' " That is called tripping! Then I messed around with women for years, and all the time I was married to Jesus and didn't even know it. Talk about patience! How did He ever put up with me! It was all grace. He was saving me to love and serve Him and to love and serve my wife.

Looking back at myself, I see how desperately I needed to grow up. I was still acting like a child, only my means of acting out my rebellion against authority had become more complex and dangerous. Most young people think sex and taking drugs and drinking are signs of adulthood, but they're not at all. They are signs of immaturity and the need to grow up. People like that are definitely not ready to get married.

Praise God for Two Praying Women in My Life

My momma gave me life and brought me into the kingdom of God, and my wife, Katheryn, brought me back into the kingdom. During the time that I was backsliding and acting like a rebellious child, they were both not too happy with me, but, praise God, they kept on praying.

Along the way, Katheryn had become a Christian, so I tried to trick her into thinking that I, too, was right with God. Actually, I had joined a church, but it was only for the sake of getting more clients. My uncle in Kinston, North Carolina, had said he would give me an opportunity in the real estate business. We joined two different churches there so we could get more sales.

I called Katheryn and told her that I was going to church. I told her I wanted her back, and I even told her I was saved. When she got to town, I took her to her room in the hotel, and as soon as I got her in private I started to kiss her and tried to get her down on the bed. She fought back and shouted at me, "You can't be saved! I'm not staying here with you!" She got in her car and turned right around and went back home to Richmond, Virginia.

I was totally rejected! I thought, She just thinks she's better than me. But in my heart I knew it was because she was saved and I was not. I was just seeing her on the basis of the lusts of my own flesh, and she had enough sense to know that a flesh-walker is no candidate for a husband. I was not qualified in the eyes of God to marry anybody. I still had to grow up and be a man. My wife was not about to be my momma.

God Himself Set Me Straight

The turning point in my life came when I got set straight with a divine visitation. That's the only way I can explain it. I was in one more bar with one more girl when I suddenly couldn't concentrate on what she was saying to me anymore. I staggered up to my room and got alone with God.

When I cried out to Him that time, He came in so real and His Shekinah glory—like the glory in the Holy of Holies—came in so strongly that it was a greater high than I ever got off mescaline. It was more joy than I could ever have imagined. It was unspeakable. It was real! All that other stuff I did as a kid in church was a preparation, because it sowed the Word into me all those years, but my old stubborn self needed more than that. I needed that incredible presence of Jesus Himself. I needed His substance. I needed to be able to touch His reality.

After that, I drove everybody crazy with my zeal. I mean, I went out on the streets and called everybody to account for their souls. I married my wife and became a minister as fast as I could. Some of the other ministers thought I was wrong to be so wild about Jesus. Some of them were still messing around with sin. They told me, "You'll get over it." But I never did. I couldn't settle for anything false anymore. I'm still crazy about Jesus!

MARRIAGE IS FOR THE MATURE

Don't Focus on Her Looks

I'm not only crazy about Jesus. I also want to be like Him. God always shows us a natural picture of a spiritual reality. The natural picture of marriage represents a spiritual reality of Christ and His Bride.

When a man finds the woman he wants to marry, he better forget about being so immature as to focus only on her physical appearance. He needs to start thinking about being like Jesus. If a lot more women were like my wife, insisting on a God-centered relationship and praying to that end, a lot more men would be driven to the face of God.

When you become a husband, your calling is to represent Christ, and your wife's calling is to represent His Bride, the Church. That's the standard. That doesn't take away from your desire for each other. It just keeps everything in the right perspective. Feelings come and go like the weather. A marriage that grows strong—rain or shine—is for the mature.

Focus on Your Wife's Inner Beauty

Look for the inner beauty in your wife that God alone sees, then speak it out. Tell your woman she's beautiful. Feed the hunger she has for a sense of being beautiful with a meal of your pure love. Solomon's woman said, "He brings me to the banquet hall and everyone can see how much he loves me. Oh, feed me with your love."[1]

If your wife has character weaknesses, bear those infirmities as Christ bears yours. In every relationship there is usually one who is stronger than the other in character. When two people are in union with each other, someone will probably have more substance than the other. When you marry Jesus in eternity, He will be the strong one. You will come into union with His mind, heart, and will, and will come into oneness with who He is. Marriage on earth is a picture of the stronger bearing the infirmities of the weaker so that the two become one. The weaker person may not be a giver or server, but once they are overtaken by the stronger person's character, they can be changed.

As a grown-up groom, you can get a vision for what your wife is becoming as you sow your life into her. Put your wife's name in the place of "love" in 1 Corinthians 13 and read it all over again. And then commit yourself to make that woman happy so she acts just like this.

I'll show you how 1 Corinthians 13 reads with my wife's name inserted. After you read it, put your wife's name on that line. Then keep that in your Bible and read it aloud to yourself every day until you believe it, and then keep repeating it until you see the manifestation in your life and hers:

> *Katheryn* is very patient and kind, never jealous or envious, never boastful or proud, never haughty or selfish or rude.
>
> *Katheryn* does not demand her own way. She is not irritable or touchy. She does not hold grudges and will hardly even notice when others do her wrong.
>
> *Katheryn* is never glad about injustice, but rejoices whenever truth wins out.

If *Katheryn* loves someone, she is loyal to him no matter what the cost. She always believes in him, always expects the best of him, and always stands her ground in defending him.

Yes! That's my woman! That's Mrs. Boone!

THE MARRIAGE COVENANT

Your Covenant with Your Wife

The agreement that a mature bride and groom enter into is called a covenant, because it is a model of the type of agreement that God makes with His people.

A contract and a covenant are different. A contract usually covers just part of a person's life, such as a skill, something he can do. You make a contract with someone to fix your plumbing or to build your house, but you don't own his life. A contract has a beginning and an end. When the job is finished, the contract is fulfilled.

In a covenant, in the biblical sense, there is no limit on your relationship to the other person. It involves your whole being. God makes covenants. He doesn't make contracts. And His covenants are a model for ours.

God made a covenant with Noah never again to destroy the earth with a flood.

He made a covenant with David that his heirs would always sit on the throne of Israel. He fulfilled it a thousand years later as the coming of Jesus, the Messiah, a descendant of David.

Your covenant with your wife involves her whole being. You leave your daddy and momma and are joined to your wife, and the two of you become one flesh. This is no contract. This is no partnership. No prenuptial agreement with escape clauses applies. This is a merging of two individuals into one new family for life.

You know what keeps your marriage from getting stale? Constantly looking for ways to take your wife to the next level. Seeing the potential in her that you personally can develop because she has your commitment to her, your unconditional love and attention for life. That takes a grown-up man.

Husbands and Wives Need to Pull Together

Marriage partners intertwine like a rope. Have you ever looked up the word "marry" in the dictionary? In addition to all the usual meanings, there is this one: "to join (two ropes) end to end by inter-weaving their strands."[2] That's quite a picture of a husband-and-wife team—two ropes becoming one! You can put all the tension you want on one end of the "married rope" and the other end will stay attached. That's what you see in a mature marriage—not two people pulling against each other but two pulling together.

God has a covenant with each one of us, even though He knows that we are so flaky that we're always going to let Him down. But the awesome thing about God is that even in the face of our sins and imperfections, He keeps His Word. When we start pulling against His purposes, He doesn't abandon us. He woos us to repentance and sets us straight, because His purposes are not only for this life. They are also for the life to come. He has made an eternal covenant for an eternal kingdom.

God wants to use lifetime marriage covenants to prepare us for a realm that will last forever. He has created the eternal Word, eternal life, and an eternal kingdom. So in this life we have to prepare our-selves for the life to come. There will be no divorce in heaven, so we shouldn't be divorcing each other now. A grown-up man learns how to stay with his wife by covenant, even in the toughest times.

Why God Hates Divorce

There's no such thing as a friendly divorce. How friendly is it to cut a piece of rope in half? Divorce is the ultimate proof that someone was not grown-up enough to get married, and was unwilling to change after the fact. Do you ever think about divorce as an option when you get upset with your wife? It's not an option. Get that out of your mind. Grow up and recognize your challenges as character-building opportunities. Jesus and Paul mentioned a few extreme examples of acceptable divorces, but hardly anybody these days qualifies. Even if you do, God's preference is your mercy and long-suffering with your wife, because that's how you develop the character of Christ. God even instructed the prophet Hosea to marry a prostitute, someone whom he knew would be unfaithful, just so he could use Hosea's life to demonstrate His own mercy and forgiveness.[3]

God hates divorce because marriage is supposed to represent His permanent love relationship to us and Jesus' marriage to us in the future. Do you think God gets into inner conflicts over our bad attitudes toward Him? Would you want God to divorce you every time you got to be too much for Him?

Hosea had to be a man of character to stay married to his wandering wife. In fact, any marriage takes a man of character. That's why God wouldn't let my wife marry me until I grew up and got saved. The Bible says that "the Lord has seen your treachery in divorcing your wives who have been faithful to you through the years, the companions you promised to care for and keep. You were united to your wife by the Lord. In God's wise plan, when you married, the two of you became one person in His sight. And what does he want? Godly children from your union. Therefore guard your passions! Keep faith with the wife of your youth. For the Lord, the God of Israel, says he hates divorce and cruel men. Therefore control your passions—let there be no divorcing of your wives."[4]

It is the ultimate goal of God that everyone who gets married stays married, because marriage represents the Marriage Supper of the Lamb.

However, there seems to be a mark on divorce in the Church that says divorce is an unpardonable sin. The Bible says God hates divorce, but it doesn't say that Jesus' blood doesn't cover the sin of divorce. If a divorce has already occurred, there is power of forgiveness in the blood. The only sin that the Bible says is unforgivable is blasphemy against the Holy Ghost.[5]

Are You Man Enough to Love Her?

Lots of people like to read at their weddings the portion of 1 Corinthians 13 that speaks about love. Even if they're not saved, it gives them a warm, fuzzy feeling that the two of them will live happily ever after in marital bliss. However, if you look closely, the "love chapter" tells you to grow up in the way you love. It is not a promise that love comes without effort. It's saying that you are no longer to think as a child. You can't leave your wife and run home to Momma when your wife hasn't been nice to you! Be a man! Stick it out! Love your wife even when she's acting unlovable. After all, that's what God does for you.

Do you have a grown-up attitude of love toward your wife? Or when you say "I love you" do you mean more "I lust for you"?

This is how the Bible describes mature love:

"Love is very patient and kind, never jealous or envious, never boastful or proud, never haughty or selfish or rude. Love does not demand its own way. It is not irritable or touchy. It does not hold grudges and will hardly even notice when others do it wrong. It is never glad about injustice, but rejoices whenever truth wins out. If you love someone, you will be loyal to him no matter what the cost. You will always believe in him, always expect the best of him, and always stand your ground in defending him.

". . . When I was a child I spoke and thought and reasoned as a child does. But when I became a man my thoughts grew far beyond those of my childhood, and now I have put away the childish things."[6]

Mature love is far more than an emotion. It is the fruit of a grown-up man living a grown-up life.

Being Holy—Not Holier Than Thou—Qualifies You for Your Heavenly Marriage

Most people who marry, at least for the first time, are still young and inexperienced. God knows all about that. He isn't concerned, because over a period of time He can transform the young groom and bride into a mature man and woman of God. In the same way, a transformation process is occurring in Christ's Church.

When older people marry, they sometimes know more about life. They still have areas where they need to change, but they are more godly, more mature, and able to appreciate their children—to be selfless instead of selfish. They regard the time commitment it takes to be a spouse and parent as a joy instead of a burden.

Many times divorced people can look back on a previous marriage and understand how they can do better this time around. They should make a resolve to learn how to serve instead of looking for the other person to serve them, and to meet the other person's needs instead of wanting the spouse to meet theirs. They should think of this not as a second marriage, but as a last marriage.

Because the Husband is holy, therefore the Bible must be holy, without spot or wrinkle. This takes a transformation process of separation from worldly things and an embrace of heavenly things. The Church as Christ's body here on earth is becoming holy—not "holier than thou," which usually means a large does of judgmentalism.

WHEN A FATHER REMAINS HIS DAUGHTER'S PROTECTOR

A Daughter Leaves Her Father's House, but Not His Heart

Let's go back to that father I mentioned at the beginning of the chapter, the one whose son-in-law had commited adultery.

When a man gives away his daughter, she leaves her father's house, but not his heart. This man was crying for his daughter's grief and humiliation, but also for her honor. He wanted to go and grab that sucker by the collar and say, "Hey! You promised me to take care of her! That's why I gave her to you!"

Under extreme conditions like this, the father-in-law has the right to hold his irresponsible son-in-law accountable for his actions. He may not have any legal right, but he has a parental right. He will always be her father.

When circumstances like this occur, he has to step in. If his daughter's life had been threatened, he would have made his home a place of refuge.

The father-in-law has every right to confront his son-in-law for that convenant-breaking act of adultery, and every witness who attended that wedding also has that right. They "stood up" with the bride and groom. They stood in agreement with what was sworn at the marriage ceremony. They were witnesses to those vows. When he broke the vows, he should have to face the witnesses. It doesn't matter how public opinion changes about adultery. God in His Law says it's always sin. "Yet your fellow citizens say, 'The way of the Lord is not right,' when it is their own way that is not right."[7]

Accountability in Cases of Adultery

There are several levels of accountability involved that give the father-in-law the right and responsibility to confront the adulterous husband, and that should provoke us to be far more diligent with adultery whenever it shows up.

The father-in-law speaks authoritatively from within these roles:

1. *As her father holding him to his promise.* The son-in-law personally promised him to take care of his daughter, and he broke his promise.

2. *As a witness.* At the wedding, the bride's father heard the son-in-law promise faithfulness in front of himself and the other witnesses—parents, bridal party, minister, and guests. These witnesses swore to stand in agreement with the groom's vows.

3. *As a brother responsible to bring the word of the Lord to a man in sin.* God said to the prophet Ezekiel, " 'Now as for you, son of man, I have appointed you a watchman for the house of Israel; so you will hear a message from My mouth, and give them warning from Me. When I say to the wicked, "O wicked man, you shall surely die," and you do not speak to warn the wicked from his way, that wicked man shall die in his iniquity, but his blood I will require from your hand.' "[8]

What a Father-in-Law Can Say at a Confrontation

What would the father-in-law accomplish with a confrontation?

1. *Confront him with his lack of integrity.* He made the initial commitment to the daughter and her father at the time of the espousal. Adultery is a lie—to the wife and her father, not to mention the "other woman."

2. *Remind him of his agreement at the wedding ceremony to fulfill the marriage covenant.* Vows were exchanged between a man and a woman before witnesses, including the parents. In the case of adultery, the father must bear witness to the marriage vows.

3. *Recall the Scriptures he has violated.* Adultery is a sin against God, specifically mentioned in the Ten Commandments. God hates adultery and divorce.

4. *Instill a sense of ultimate accountability before God.* We must all appear before the Judgment Seat of Christ.[9] This is not a threat to bring him back through fear, but an impetus to his changing from within, because his current lifestyle leads to ultimate death.

What Do You Do When Your Accountability Group Is Not Around?

Before a man ever gets to the point of committing adultery, he has started down that road with his thought-life. Then he has taken steps in the direction of another woman. There is a movement going on now for people to become better Christians by being mentored or held accountable to others for their right behavior. That helps in the early stages of growth, but none of your friends can do your growing up for you. You can learn all the right things to do and have Bible studies in your home and pray over your wife and have a mentor to pray for you and still not have real intimacy with God. All you've got is information. Information gives knowledge, but it won't necessarily change you on the inside. It won't make you sanctified.

God wants to come upon you with His glory. His glory is what changes you. Jesus demonstrated that principle at the Mount of Transfiguration when God overtook Him and even His clothes began to glisten.[10] That was something real that happened to Jesus when the glory of God came upon Him. Something just as real can happen to you, too, with or without the visible manifestation, when God comes on you with His glory.

When you have a real relationship with God, that's when you're changed. That's also when you can change others. As a discipler of your wife, your children, and your friends, you can pass down the reality of your intimacy with God, and they will become changed. You can give that away. They catch the glory of God through you. That's what changes people.

If you know Jesus in a real way, He teaches you how to order your lifestyle priorities by getting your heart priorities right. He helps you to grow up and stop putting yourself first. He helps you to honor your wife. He gives you a heart for your children's needs. That reality of the consciousness of God orders your life so that what you do with your life every day comes out of what's happened in your heart. It's not a performance for your accountability person based on information he has put into your mind, but an internal change and a new lifestyle that comes from the reality of God inside of you.

Only Jesus can change a heart. Ask your Father to keep your heart tender, and cause you to come to Him, so you can be changed in His presence. Grow up in God.

LEADERSHIP LIFESTYLES OF GROWN-UP MEN

The following section gives examples of how men demonstrate by their actions whether they are leaders or losers. A goal of God is that a husband would be mature enough to lead his family as a grown-up man.

A Leader's Relationship with God

Leadership Lifestyle	Loser's Lifestyle
1. Be a Christian who studies and lives the Word and knows and follows God. Get everything you can out of a message from a man of God.	Look at your watch constantly during a sermon. When the minister goes over his time, frown at him disapprovingly. Be a christianette, who only likes to hear sermonettes.
2. Find out what God wants you to do from prayer and consultation with godly people, and make changes graciously.	Be independent. Do your own thing. And don't let your wife and friends give you significant input into your decisions.
3. Be as Christ-like as you can. Remember that there are witnesses in heaven watching your life.	Do sinful things in secret like watching X-rated movies, gambling, and lusting after women you see. Figure what you do doesn't hurt anybody else.

A Leader's Relationships with All People

Leadership Lifestyle	Loser's Lifestyle
1. Love according to 1 Corinthians 13.	Put yourself first and assume that others are just as self-centered as you are.

Leadership Lifestyle	Loser's Lifestyle
2. Put the needs of others first.	Always put your own needs first. Don't look around to discover others' needs.
3. Try to base all your words and actions on a motivation of love.	Choose words and actions that will cover up your faults and feed your need for self-esteem.
4. Exhibit the fruit of the Spirit (Galatians 5:22-23).	Exhibit the fruit of the flesh (Galatians 5:19–21).
5. Have a merry heart. Be somebody everybody likes to hang out with. "A merry heart does good, like medicine, but a broken spirit dries the bones."[11]	Speak gloomily about your problems. Be moody. Make everybody sick of having you around.
6. When you see someone else's faults, remember your own, and help the other person to overcome theirs.	When you see someone's faults, secretly put them down and put yourself up. When you get a chance to say something, use their faults to make yourself look better by comparison.
7. When you see someone's physical flaws, be gracious enough not to mention them.	When you see someone's physical flaws, tease them about them in public.
8. Tell the whole story, including the places where you blew it.	Tell a partial story, making yourself look good and blaming others.

Leadership Lifestyle	Loser's Lifestyle
9. *When someone treats you badly, take a leadership role in treating him well and resolving the hostility.*	*When someone treats you badly, think about ways you can get even. Treat him just as badly for spite.*
10. *In tense situations, try to speak in calm and embracing tones. Be a peacemaker.*	*When things get tense, get tense yourself and holler at people. Make things worse.*
11. *Tell the truth even when you know someone else is deceiving you, and always try to keep your heart pure.*	*If someone is lying to you, make up your own lies to match. Distort the details of an event for your own advantage. Squelch your conscience.*
12. *Maintain a high level of integrity in dealing with people, both on a personal level and in business.*	*Always be on the lookout for a quick break that will help you promote yourself, whether or not it is morally sound.*
13. *Always put the best interpretation on what someone says to you.*	*Always put the worst interpretation on what someone says to you.*
14. *Don't give in on matters of personal commitment, but compromise when it is possible for the sake of harmony.*	*Hold to a few self-righteous standards you create yourself and criticize others who don't have the same perspective.*
15. *Assume other people have got some things right, even if you disagree with most of what they say.*	*Assume you are all right and other people are all wrong.*

Leadership Lifestyle	Loser's Lifestyle
16. *Be quick to admit you're wrong.*	*Always say, "It's not my fault!" Be quick to blame others. Don't apologize until the other person apologizes first. If you say "I'm sorry," always keep a proud attitude and qualify your words by adding ". . . if I've done anything to offend you."*
17. *Balance emotions with reason.*	*Be ruled by your emotional outbursts.*
18. *Have a low look and "take the L"—the Low Road— whenever necessary. "Humble yourselves in the sight of the Lord, and he shall lift you up."*[12]	*Be proud. Never go down. Always maintain a haughty, high look.*
19. *Be a servant. When you see a need, and it is within your ability and God's will, fill it.*	*Keep yourself detached. Make everyone else do all the work.*

A Leader's Relationships with His Wife and Children

Leadership Lifestyle	Loser's Lifestyle
1. *Love and respect your wife as your wife and be a mature husband to her.*	*Expect your wife to be your momma, to take care of you like a child who wants his needs met first.*

Leadership Lifestyle	**Loser's Lifestyle**
2. Keep family secrets in the family.	Be a gossip and a tattletale. Tell people outside your family things they don't need to know.
3. Consider carefully your wife's input on decisions.	Listen superficially, then over-rule your wife's opinions and tell her to submit.
4. Never strike or push your wife in any way at any time.	When you get angry, give your wife a push if you feel like it.
5. Be considerate. Tell your wife what time you will be getting home and, if late, why.	Get home when you please and get mad if your wife asks where you were.
6. Look for things that you can do around the house and do them.	Leave household chores to others. Develop a blindness to overflowing trash and un-washed dishes.
7. Treat your parents and your wife's parents equally and with respect.	Favor your parents over your wife's parents, but don't really treat either of them with true respect.
8. Nurture your children. Bring out the best in them. Help them find God's will for their lives. Discipline them when they rebel, but be patient with their imma-turity.	Get your children to fulfill things you wanted to do but never could. Boss them around. Criticize all grades less than A+. Punish them for everything not done as an adult would do it.

How a Leader Deals with Adversity and Opposition

Leadership Lifestyle	Loser's Lifestyle
1. *Even when people refuse to discuss something with you, try to get their input before making decisions that affect them.*	*If you can't get people to have a calm discussion with you, kick them to the curb and make their decisions for them.*
2. *When someone tries to force you into some decision or action, quietly resist the pressure until you have time to think.*	*When someone pushes you to do things their way, give in and do what they want to shut them up.*
3. *Be open to being changed.*	*Be closed to change.*
4. *If someone rejects you, don't reject them. Keep a good attitude toward them, expecting them to change and not exalting yourself too highly.*	*When you get rejected, reject the other person too, and hold hostility in your heart and mind toward him.*
5. *Try to learn from everybody, even people who put you down or insult your intelligence.*	*Don't let anybody put you down.*
6. *Even if someone misunderstands you, try to understand them.*	*If you are misunderstood, get disgusted and walk off. Be easily offended. Look for reasons to complain about someone's treatment of you.*
7. *When you are criticized, never respond with cutting words.*	*Use words as a weapon to get back at someone who criticizes you.*

Leadership Lifestyle	Loser's Lifestyle
8. When you have something difficult to say to someone, speak the truth in love.[13]	Don't mince words. Tell it like it is, even if the person winces when you speak.

WOMEN CAN IDENTIFY A GROWN-UP MAN

Key Steps a Woman Can Take

The following are some key steps for a single woman to take, in consultation with her father, in order to confirm if a man is grown-up enough to enter into marriage. There is also a checklist for evaluating a man's maturity. Husbands can use these to evaluate themselves and also the future mates of their daughters.

Seek God's approval. The more secure she is in knowing God and His will for her life, the easier it will be for her to recognize if a potential husband will lead her into His will, or away from it.

Obtain the confirmation of her father. Because earthly marriage represents the marriage of Christ and the Church, the woman's father has to approve her future mate just as God the Father has to approve the Bride of Christ. Every woman has a God-given protector—first her father and then her husband. Her husband can legitimately take over only when she is formally released to him by her father.

Refuse to yield to external pressure. She needs a witness within, regardless of how much pressure there is from without. She should not get married just because she's pregnant. She and the father of her child both violated the chastity standard, but marriage isn't the only option. It could be compounding their mistake. People get married for lots of other external reasons: lust of the flesh, family desires, her personal needs, her advancing age. External pressures should yield to ultimate accountability. She will have to stand before God someday and justify her actions, and whoever is pressuring her will also have to stand before God on that great day.

Ask the right questions. Below is a partial checklist for evaluating whether the husband or husband-to-be is a grown-up man. (See also Chapter 2.)

Checklist for Evaluating a Grown-Up Man

- ❏ Has a strong relationship with God that is a model for the woman's own life
    - ❏ Initiates times of prayer with her and is comfortable praying
    - ❏ Shares with her what he is learning from the Bible in personal study
    - ❏ Has shown a pattern of attending church regularly
- ❏ Considerate and respectful, not critical and controlling
- ❏ Faithful in the following areas:[14]
    - ❏ Personal life
    - ❏ Parents and siblings
    - ❏ Extended family (grandparents, aunts, uncles, etc.)
    - ❏ Employment
    - ❏ Church
    - ❏ Relationship with the woman
        - ❏ Being on time
        - ❏ Keeping his word
        - ❏ Never gossiping about her to others
- ❏ Mature attitudes in disagreements:
    - ❏ Doesn't pressure her to do things his way
    - ❏ Always listens to her point of view
    - ❏ Doesn't pout
    - ❏ Never strikes her in any way
    - ❏ Doesn't get angry without a cause, and doesn't stay angry
    - ❏ Doesn't punish her with silence after a disagreement
    - ❏ Is quick to repent, quick to forgive
    - ❏ Looks at the best side of everything
    - ❏ Not easily offended
    - ❏ Makes the first move to restore a broken relationship
- ❏ Doesn't make her do things that cause her distress, including sexual compromises
- ❏ Doesn't force her to keep secrets that she needs to discuss with others

❏ Has become responsible by finding a spiritual father, either his natural father or a mature Christian man he has sought out
❏ Financial maturity (spiritual as well as natural aspects):
  ❏ Tithing
  ❏ Money in savings
  ❏ Employment with a reasonable income for the needs of a family
    ❏ Has the money needed to get married
    ❏ Will be making enough money to stay married
  ❏ If in college, timetable for completion and means for paying expenses
❏ No record of financial irresponsibility, or if so, has reformed
❏ Cultivates relationships with the in-laws, regardless of their receptivity:
  ❏ Asked the father for his daughter's hand or understands why he should
  ❏ Maintains a respectful attitude
  ❏ Encourages frequent, positive contact
❏ Walks in reconciliation
❏ Has wholesome friends who have been close to him for many years

How God Helps Us When We Feel Like a Loser

The Lord looked at His woman, the Church, and said, "You're a loser, but I'm going to make you a winner. The more of a loser you are, the more my qualities are brought out in your change." Maybe you are a man who is not grown-up yet, but God sees your potential. Just put your future and your past in His hands, and expect a miracle to happen.

PRAYER FOR A SENSE OF DIVINE CONFIDENCE

Lord Jesus, I pray that by Your mighty power You would forgive the people for every sin in their hearts and minds. Lord, in Your forgiving grace, I'm asking for Your mercy. I'm asking You to give them grace to live a Christian life that's approved in Your sight.

Bless Your people, Father, that they may have a sense of divine

*confidence in living and that they will not want to die until the full-
ness of what You've determined is accomplished in their hearts and
minds.*

*I pray, Jesus, for the sin-sick. I'm asking that from this hour,
through Your Word, that they will be healed. If there are those who
are oppressed by demonic influences, You said You would cast out
those spirits with Your Word. I pray, Lord Jesus, that the devil's
power over the people will be loosed and driven away, and that they
will have a divine sense of healing and holiness.*

*Give them a sense of Your presence, Lord Jesus, that they may
walk as the blessed of heaven. Thank You so much, Lord.*

*Now open their eyes that they will see. O Lord, speak as an oracle
to them. Open their ears that they will hear. Cause their hearts to be
so tender and ready to be changed.*

Thank you, Lord Jesus. I bless You.

In Jesus' name I pray. Amen.

SELAH

1. Read and study the differences between the fruit of the flesh and
   the fruit of the Spirit in Galatians 5:13–6:18.
2. Read several other Scripture references listed in the footnotes to get
   the deeper meaning behind them.
3. Think about your own process of growing up, from the time you
   were a child. Which people influenced you the most positively as
   you were coming into maturity? How could you make your lifestyle
   more like theirs?
4. What do you need to change in your marriage so that your wife
   and others will see that you are becoming more grown-up?
5. Apply the message of this chapter to the TV shows and movies you
   see over the next few days. Also the newspaper and magazine articles you read. How many examples do you find of men who are
   not grown-up, according to these guidelines?

4

*B*LOW YOUR WIFE'S MIND

"When you do something for someone else, don't
call attention to yourself."
"[T]he God who made you won't be applauding."
—Matthew 6, *The Message*

*What would you think if you went into a church rest room and found
money draped over the toilet paper? The person who left it there
didn't know who would get it, and they hadn't even left their name.
Come on. Wouldn't that make you think?*

*That's what happened at the church we founded in Richmond,
Virginia—Manna Christian Fellowship—after we had started something we called "secret giving."*

*Most of us, if we admit it, give gifts to get thanked. Not God. He
gives in secret because it's His nature to give. Most of the time we
don't even know it's from Him. That's what you need to do for your
wife. It will blow her mind!*

I had gotten the idea for secret giving in the church from the women's
ministry founded by my wife—Network of Christian Women. Every
year, each woman was assigned to be a secret pal to another woman.
All year long, the secret pal gave the other woman anonymous, unexpected gifts that would blow her mind.

When I heard about that I said, "That's the Bible!" And then I
started figuring out how the rest of the church could get in on it. I
didn't assign people to one another. I just told them to start giving
secret gifts. Pretty soon we had an epidemic. It was wild. It was a

tidal wave of love! And nobody was getting credit on earth, only in heaven.

One woman was given a sewing machine. She needed it for the volunteer work she did for the church and some other projects. It was worth several hundred dollars. She didn't know who paid for it. It blew her mind because she didn't have the money to pay for it herself. Why would anyone do that, and not want to be recognized for it? It had to be God.

Bibles, books, clothing, small appliances—all kinds of things started turning up in cars, the parking lot, hallways, desks, or the seat beside you. People were finding envelopes with their name on it and money inside, but the envelope never said who it was from. Only one person thought about using the toilet paper roll. As soon as the young woman who found that money told about it in the church service, everybody broke out laughing—then broke for the rest room! But lightning didn't strike twice in the same place.

If you want to get a special blessing from God, you've got to try secret giving. Who could get thanked for money in toilet paper? No one except heaven would know you were the one who put it there. You wouldn't even know who received it until you heard them tell about it. That's awesome.

BLOW YOUR WIFE'S MIND WITH SECRET GIVING

You need to find some secret, hilarious, unpredictable ways to give to your wife so much and so often that you blow her mind. You don't have to keep it a secret all the time. She'll probably figure it out sometimes anyway, but keep her off guard. Keep a private checklist of how often she doesn't know what you did.

Jesus didn't play around about how much we need to give secret gifts. He gave it to us straight. We just haven't been paying attention because we have always wanted the credit or we have wanted to get something back. That's especially true with the way we give to our wives.

Now, if you're like most men, you gave your fine young thing lots of gifts when you were first seeing her. That's because you were showing her only your best side. You knew you were not going to get her by dogging her out during that introduction time, so you held back on any criticisms and tried to win her with gifts. Sometimes you gave her gifts just to be nice, but deep down inside you gave because you wanted her to like you. You were giving to get something back for yourself.

As soon as you got your girl locked into marriage, you suddenly got absentminded. You hardly ever thought about giving her things. Maybe you even had to ask your secretary to remind you about her birthday and your anniversary because you never gave her gifts any other time. You old lazy thing! You showed your good side during courtship, but you changed when you got married.

The Lord has only one side. It's always the best. It's awesome. Every way you look He is turning you on, doing something so incredible you want to marry Him yesterday.

"LOOK-AT-ME" GIVING

If you want to be like God and get your rewards in heaven instead of on earth, give secret gifts to your wife. Giving is supposed to be something good, but when we give to feed our pride we're turning it into something bad.

Listen to Jesus' warning: "Be especially careful when you are trying to be good so that you don't make a performance out of it. It might be good theater, but the God who made you won't be applauding.

"When you do something for someone else, don't call attention to yourself. You've seen them in action, I'm sure—'playactors' I call them—treating prayer meeting and street corner alike as a stage, acting compassionate as long as someone is watching, playing to the crowds. They get applause, true, but that's all they get. When you help someone out, don't think about how it looks. Just do it—quietly and unobtrusively. That is the way your God, who conceived you in love, working behind the scenes, helps you out."[1]

In the older versions of this Scripture from Matthew 6 it says essentially, "Don't have a trumpeter calling the people to attention every time you give gifts." Jesus specifically mentioned the deeds of charity that we do. He said that if you give in public, that temporary recognition it brings you is the only reward you'll ever get. But if you give in secret "your Father who sees in secret will repay you."[2] Now, that's what I'm talking about.

Ask God to enlarge your capacity to give to your wife without expecting anything back. Secret giving and serving are the only deeds for which you'll receive rewards in heaven. If you're getting credit for anything now, you're using up the rewards your heavenly Father would have given you later. When I do good deeds for my wife and nobody knows about it but God, I know He stores up the rewards in a treasure chest in heaven with my name on it.

In most of our gift giving we're like children saying, "Watch me, Momma! Look what I did!" People actually get mad if they don't get thanked, or if the thanks they get isn't exactly what they were expecting. If they get a thank-you note they examine every word. Maybe they read it four or five times. That's pretty pitiful. Where's the blessing in that? Sometimes gift-giving becomes an excuse to fight. Entire branches of families have become alienated from other branches because one person didn't properly acknowledge a wedding gift. Isn't that ridiculous? Talk about the devil's work!

Some men even feel they deserve to be thanked just for providing a paycheck to cover the basic needs of the household. That isn't thankworthy. That's expected. God commands husbands to provide and says that any man who doesn't is worse than an unbeliever. "But if anyone does not provide for his own, and especially for those of his household, he has denied the faith and is worse than an unbeliever."[3]

God doesn't pat us on the back for just meeting the requirement. Jesus said, "So you also, when you have done everything you were told to do, should say, 'We are unworthy servants; we have only done our duty.' "[4] It's good for you to give without getting one scrap of credit. God gives to you that way every day. You can't even breathe without having Him give you air. He doesn't let you in on half of what He's doing for you. He keeps it His secret. Why don't you become like Him? If you do, He'll give you credit eventually, in heaven. That's worth a lot more than a few thank you's on this old earth.

What do you think would happen to your wife if you started blowing her mind with secret giving? What if every time she turned around there was some flimsy new thing under her pillow or a dozen red roses arriving at the front door? What if she found a new car in the driveway and you never even said a word?

Jesus said, "Do not lay up for yourselves treasures on earth, where moth and rust destroy and where thieves break in and steal; but lay up for yourselves treasures in heaven, where neither moth nor rust destroys and where thieves do not break in and steal. For where your treasure is, there your heart will be also."⁵ Lay up treasures in heaven for what you do in your marriage on earth. Make the bond God created between the two of you count for something in eternity!

It's easier to give secretly if you've spent secret time with God.

Do you want to know how you can get so creative and so generous that you can blow your wife's mind with your sensitivity and generosity? Get in there more deeply with God. Love is the motivating factor that drives Him. Sure, He's a God of Law. He is holy and He has a standard, but the motivating force of God is love. Before He's anything else, He's a God of love.

The way to give freely is to become close to the God of love, who gives freely. Let Him give you so much in those secret times together that there is a richness about you that overflows and releases people when they come around you. Put out a spirit that gives a sense of sufficiency and a sense of abundance that draws your wife to you when she's down. Give yourself to her. That's what she really wants. She wants you to love her in ways that she can see, and the best way to do that is to love her in ways she can't see.

When God was trying to get Israel to see how much He loved her, He used the analogy of a husband showering his wife with gifts. He said, " 'Then, when the marriage had taken place, I gave you beautiful clothes of linens and silk, embroidered, and sandals made of dolphin hide. I gave you lovely ornaments, bracelets, and beautiful necklaces, a ring for your nose and two more for your ears, and a lovely tiara for your head. And so you were made beautiful with gold and silver, and your clothes were silk and linen and beautifully embroidered. You ate the finest foods and became more beautiful than ever. You looked like a queen, and so you were! Your reputation was great among the nations for your beauty; it was perfect because of all the gifts I gave you,' says the Lord God."⁶

God doesn't just give to us to win us. He gives to us because He enjoys giving! Then He tells us to give and keep on giving to others so we will be as blessed by giving as He is when He gives. "This is how God showed his love for us: God sent his only Son into the world so we might live through him. This is the kind of love we are talking about—not that we once upon a time loved God, but that he loved us and sent his Son as a sacrifice to clear away our sins and the damage they've done to our relationship with God."[7]

One of the most life-changing things you can do is to give, especially to your wife, because you represent Christ and she represents the Church. God is always giving to the Church, whether we deserve it or not.

GIVE YOUR ALL TO GOD

If your wife is not "seeing you" all the time, get the strength you need to love her anyway by spending time with God. God is always seeing you. Let Him love you and value you. If you seek after Him, you're only responding to His wooing. He's always after you. He's wild about you. He wants you to listen to Him. He wants you to tithe and give offerings. He wants to have the most important say-so in your affairs. But remember that He'll use your wife again and again as His mouthpiece, whether you like what she says or not.

The goodness of God leads us to repentance.[8] He's always looking for ways to bless us, even in our sinfulness. He understands how much we're moved by His goodness when we're sinners, so you can show your wife that you're like Him by being merciful when she's mean. How could you be more attractive to your wife than by being good to her all the time? Won't that blow her mind?

FOUR THINGS YOU SHOULD GIVE YOUR WIFE

In addition to personal gifts, there are four things every serious man of God should give his wife, and I don't mean just giving her crumbs of these things, either. Give her the whole loaf! That's what she deserves for having such an awesome man as you for her husband. Let some of your giving be in secret, and let some of your giving be at times when she knows you can't be trying to buy sex, such as that time of the month.

GIVE YOUR WIFE
- TIME
- MONEY
- A LISTENING EAR
- SAY-SO IN YOUR AFFAIRS

How to Give Your Wife Time

It's hard for your wife to live with you when she doesn't feel loved. And she won't feel loved if you are always too busy for her, if you are always disappearing out the door or coming home late at night or you're all tied up on weekends. If I look at my wife and see a love deficit, I know I haven't been spending time with her.

My wife came home one day and caught me cleaning the floor in the kitchen, going into the corner with a toothbrush.

She looked at me with the most peculiar expression and she said, "Honey, what are you doing? Come on, you're down on your knees. You're not cleaning the floor, are you? Don't you have somewhere you're supposed to be going?"

I said, "Yes! I want to do it. Look, girl, go on to the nail parlor and get your nails done. You have no business getting your nails messed up on this floor. Go on outta here. Look in my wallet, get out some money for yourself, and go ahead."

Taking time to serve other people is always going to bless them.

Most men wouldn't think of doing such a thing, and there was a time in my life when I wouldn't have either. When God changed me, He showed me that my time is not my own. He gave it to me, and He wants me to bless my wife by giving "my" time to her.

God makes time for us. If you really want to be like Him, make her need for time with you a priority in your life.

PRACTICAL WAYS TO GIVE YOUR WIFE TIME

· Time to pray together every day
· Time to study the Word together

- Time to go to church and sit together and talk about what you heard—together
- Time to go for walks together when you won't be interrupted
- Time to go for drives to places you both like—the woods, the hills, the mountains, or the beach
- Time to go to bed together and talk without being distracted by the television
- Time to help with grocery shopping and carrying in the groceries
- Time to go out for dinner with her when you were planning to watch the Super Bowl. (That's a great way to beat the crowds at your favorite restaurant!)
- Time to open doors for her
- Time to help her on with her coat
- Time to fix breakfast for her and the children on weekends

How to Give Your Wife Money

Most men feel that if they earn the money, it's rightfully theirs to control. They don't realize that one of the reasons God allows them to earn money is so they can give it to their wives to bless them. One day I found out that my wife wasn't carrying enough money on her, even though she handles the checking account in our house. Most women are so humble that they'd never take money and spend it on themselves. It's always for the family. I couldn't even *make* her take it.

I saw my wife as good ground, so I sowed "seeds" of cash into her myself. When I gave her the money I had to say, "I command you now, don't tell me what you do with it. Don't spend it on the house, or me, or the children. It's only for you. Take this thousand-dollar check and put it in your private account." (You can fill in your own amount.)

Why should you sow money into your wife, even if she has plenty of her own? Because she will just fill all up with love when she sees how you're giving her money as one of your highest priorities. Don't even worry about whether she's going to waste it. Give it to her, no strings attached. It's your release even more than hers.

You know how the black folks say, "You gotta empower us!"

When they talk about the white man, they say, "The white man has to empower us. He needs to get behind us." What are they talking about? Money! When they give us black folks money, it empowers us. It means they're really seeing us. Well, that's the same deal in your house. When you give your wife money, you're empowering her. You're seeing her. You're affirming her value. Don't snivel about how much you give her, either. And don't use your giving as an excuse not to pay your bills. Put it all in the budget first.

How to Give Your Wife a Listening Ear

When I was a child, because of unstable circumstances I didn't start school until I was eight years old, and then I didn't do well for the first two years, until my mother was born again and I made a commitment to the Lord myself at the age of ten. After that, we went to church so much that I had to take my homework to church. In that environment, where the old mothers were praying over me, I began to do so well in school that I started to skip grades. It wasn't that I started memorizing things better. It was that God gave me a listening ear.

I hear men say, "No matter what I do, I just can't seem to understand my wife. It must be that time of the month or something, I just can't seem to understand her." That's because *you* don't have a listening ear.

Sir, the Bible says, "Husbands, love your wives, even as Christ also loved the Church, and gave himself for it."[9] So the issue is this:

Does Christ understand the Church? Because if Christ doesn't understand the Church, then you ought not to understand the woman.

But if Christ does understand the Church, then you should understand the woman.

The problem is not that you don't understand her. The problem is that you are ignoring her. You don't have a listening ear. It's sin to ignore someone God has told you to cherish. It's not that hard to understand your wife if you stop ignoring her. The woman came out of the man, so that means your wife is like you.

Here's the description again of the way woman was created. "And the Lord God caused a deep sleep to fall upon Adam, and he slept: and he took one of his ribs [the Hebrew actually says "sides"], and closed up the flesh instead thereof; and the rib which the Lord God had taken from man, made he a woman, and brought her unto the man. And Adam said, This is now bone of my bones, and flesh of my flesh."[10]

I said to one brother, That's why I know what color Adam was. You know he had to be a brother, right? You know that. Why? Because you know all brothers like ribs. You know that. Ain't no question.

But look what else it says: "She shall be called Woman, because she was taken out of man."[11] Eve didn't get her name until after the Fall. Previous to the Fall, she was called *woman*, or "man with a womb."

The Bible says, "Therefore, shall a man leave his father and his mother, and cleave unto his wife: and they shall be one flesh."[12]

Now, look at this. He named her, therefore he defined her. He defined her, therefore he understood her. You could also say you don't understand the Lord, but the Bible says we are to seek Him to know Him. We need to follow on to know the Lord.[13] *You can understand her. You just have to make the effort to focus in on her and listen to what she says.*

Women open themselves up and become vulnerable to men. If you don't understand your wife, your sin is the sin of ignoring the woman you love. Stop ignoring her and stop hiding your own true feelings when she's exposing hers. Get your clues from God. He showed you His heart first. God exposed Himself and we took advantage of Him. Your wife will expose herself and talk to you out of her heart, but you don't want to hear it and you won't expose yourself in return. That's not God. God understands your wife. Get with Him, and He'll let you in on what He knows about your wife.

PRACTICAL WAYS TO LISTEN TO YOUR WIFE

· Listen lovingly.
· Listen until she finishes talking and respond in love to what she says.
· Listen without waiting for your own opportunity to say what you want to say. If she wants you to respond, first show sensitivity in your remarks to what she's been saying. Say, "This is

what I hear you saying." Don't rush in with whatever point you've been waiting to get across.

- Listen the way you expect God to listen to your prayers, whether you let Him say anything back to you or not.
- Listen by turning off the TV or radio, or putting down the newspaper or your favorite book.
- Listen by saving your computer document and laying the project aside.
- Listen when she comes in the door.
- Listen when a thousand other things are vying for your attention. Give her your total attention.
- Listen to her when the phone rings insistently but she needs you more than whoever is on the other end of the line. Let it ring. They'll call back.
- Listen when she tells you all the things that went wrong with her day, even if they don't seem that earth-shaking to you. Give her enough respect to acknowledge that those things are important to her.
- Listen by looking her in the eyes.
- Listen by holding her hand.
- Listen by putting your arm around her and holding her, without even thinking about sex.
- Listen when she seems to be unhappy or hurt.
- Listen by sitting down to meals with her and waiting around afterward long enough to talk and help her clean up.
- Listen by helping her prepare meals.
- Listen by going to bed the same time she goes to bed.
- Listen when she talks about the things that make her happy, then do them.

Here are a few more examples that will be described in detail below:

- Listen by sharing meals.
- Listen when she complains you don't mean it when you say "I'm sorry."
- Listen as a ministry of reconciliation.

God knows how little people really listen to one another, and how much they ought to listen. The Bible says, "Let every man be swift to hear, slow to speak, slow to wrath."[14] Or as *The Message* puts it, "Post this at all the intersections, dear friends: Lead with your ears, follow up with your tongue, and let anger straggle along in the rear."[15]

Here are a few special cases to consider.

Listen by sharing meals. The early Christian Church practiced a powerful kind of fellowship that helped them keep listening to one another. They ate together, and while they were there they also prayed. (I don't think they said, "God is great. God is good. Let us thank Him for our food. Amen," either.)

In his commentary on Acts 2:42, Dr. Craig Keener explained the significance of mealtime fellowship in the early Church. The Bible says, "And they continued steadfastly in the apostles' doctrine and fellowship, and in breaking of bread, and in prayers."[16] Keener says, "Most special groups in antiquity ate together. . . . Many Greek associations met for communal meals only once a month. . . . This earliest Christian practice of daily meals (later reduced to weekly) is thus noteworthy.

"Table fellowship denoted intimacy, and discussions or even lectures at meals were common. Given the topic of discussion recommended by Jewish pietists and what this text says about teaching and prayer (possibly including participation in the temple prayers—[Acts] 3:1), early Christian fellowship undoubtedly centered more on intimate worship, sharing and learning the Scriptures than its modern Western counterpart tends to do."[17]

Listen when she complains you don't mean it when you say "I'm sorry." The more you say "I'm sorry" the greater is your wife's expectation that you will change. The "I'm sorry's" don't work after a while if they are not followed by a change. Your wife should accept your genuine confession and repentance, but after seventy times she won't want to hear it anymore. She just wants you to do something about it. Usually that's when the breakdown of a relationship comes in. Someone finally says, "I'm through. You don't want to change, you don't mean it, you didn't hear me in the first place. Saying 'I'm sorry' is too easy. You're not willing to make the sacrifice to respond to my need."

When she gets that desperate, you have to recognize within yourself your own inabilities. First cry out to God. Repent. Ask the Lord's forgiveness. Ask God to help you change. Don't try to blame your wife, saying she is the source of your problem, and if she will change you will not be like this. Just say, "I've sinned, I'm wrong. I need to change. God help me. I'm sorry. Change me!"

Listen as a ministry of reconciliation. The Bible says that God has given us a ministry of reconciliation in the same way that He was in Christ reconciling the world to Himself.[18] God's reconciliation effort is what you call in international negotiations a "unilateral" effort. God alone did everything necessary to provide the means of our coming into harmony with Him. That's what happens in your marriage when you give your wife a listening ear and you make an internal decision to carefully consider everything she says without prejudging it or trying to make yourself come out on top.

How to Give Your Wife a Say-So in Your Affairs

Men often believe that "their world" is far too complicated or sophisticated for their wives to understand. Some don't want their wives to know anything about their jobs or investments or anything else they do outside the house. When I tell them they're wrong they say, "But they don't understand anything about thermonuclear dynamics!" Maybe she knows more than you think. Do you ever really listen to her? Do you teach her anything you know so she can be more of a helpmate?

Your wife is a God-given helper to you, and when two people tackle a situation, it's better than one. Besides, while you're sleeping, she's thinking. She can probably solve that problem you have at work faster than you can. Women have intuition that men don't have. You need the benefit of her wisdom.

Admit it. The main issue isn't whether or not she would give you valuable input. It's whether or not you really share your life with her, whether you value her voice of reason and respect her mind.

Give her an opportunity to speak into your life by telling her what you're dealing with. God declared that wives would be a help to their husbands. She's a help to you. She's the capable wife God gave you so that she could have input in your affairs.

Sometimes she's His messenger. Don't dismiss lightly what she says. Even if you take ultimate responsibility for a final decision, don't let any big decisions go by without consulting and praying with your wife. You might be directly rejecting the Lord's counsel.

If she wants to know what you're doing, tell her. Say, "Honey, I'm an open book. What do you want to know?"

THE RELEASE OF UNEARNED GIFTS—JUBILEE!

Maybe you can visualize listening and giving to your wife during times when your relationship is great and you're excited about going home to her every night. But what about when she's ticked off at you? What about when you get the cold shoulder? That's when you can really go into action!

Some men might say, "You don't know my wife. She's lazy. She doesn't take care of the children or the house most of the time. She's more interested in watching soap operas than caring about the well-being of her family. How can I convince myself to serve her and give her my time and money when I have to be the one to keep the family together?"

Most people don't see that giving is gaining. Investing in people is the best investment we can make. In order to give to your wife, you must see her through the eyes of Jesus. See her as a good investment. See what she can become as you model out Jesus in front of her. Bless her. Encourage her. Love her with God's unconditional love. *Give to her* and watch her grow.

Giving is obedience to the Word of God, especially when you give to those who are undeserving. That's your Jubilee.[19] God told Israel to make some major sacrifices to give to others and forgive people's debts, but He called it the *Lord's* release.

When God presented Israel with the principle of the Jubilee, He told them, in effect, "Every fifty years I want you to give people back their land. They have sold it to you, but they really still want it and need it. Release them from all their debts. Set them free in My name. I'm using you as an instrument for their release. It's not *your* release to them. It's *My* release." Then He challenged them to obey Him:

"Can I use you to set them free? You don't need to be stingy with their possessions. You've got me, and I don't have any shortages."

Don't be stingy with your time, money, listening ear, and opportunities for your wife to have a say-so in your affairs, regardless of her moods or her abilities. It's the Lord's release for you to give to her.

Release her from the old unsettled accounts you've been carrying around against her. Maybe you think she wasn't nice enough to you, or she squandered some of your money. Are you going to hang on to those things, or release them?

What would Jesus do? God doesn't need your rationalizing, and your logic, and your reasoning to determine whether or not you're going to release her from debts or spend money on her or bless her in some other way. He knows you need to be released into generosity because your generosity will set *you* free while you're setting *her* free, so God says, "Set her free!"

The Jubilee—extravagant giving, often in secret—releases you into God's ways. You're to be God's instrument of blessing, even when she seems temporarily ill-deserving of your blessings, because *you* need the release to be like Him.

PRAYER OF COMMITMENT TO MEET YOUR WIFE'S NEEDS

O God, it's so blessed to know You! I love You so much.

I'm so glad You dwell among us in our family, Lord Jesus. I see how You treat us like a much-loved wife. Before we ever came to the marriage feast, You were loving us and sacrificing Yourself for us.

Thank You that You're teaching my wife and me how to treat each other kindly and to love being together. Thank You for keeping us clean and holy and taking away all the sin and guilt. Thank You for sowing good seeds inside of us and for keeping those seeds growing. We're looking better on the outside all the time because of the work that You're doing on the inside. Thank You for it, Lord!

O God, thank You that by the power of the Holy Spirit You are showing me all my sins in this relationship. I destroy every work of darkness. I thank You for a deep level of repentance in myself. I have not stayed as close to You as I should. Lord Jesus, I have not been committed enough to Your ways in my life. Help me to read and understand Your Word so that I can become more like You in this marriage and in every area of my life.

I bless my wife now, Lord Jesus, that she may have an abundance of wisdom and knowledge. I thank You that I am learning to dwell with my wife according to the knowledge that You are placing in me. I bless my children. I thank You for the wisdom to train them for life in Your eternal kingdom.

I commit myself to You now, to honor and serve the woman You have called to be my wife. I commit myself to give her time, money, a listening ear, and say-so in my affairs, because that is our release.

I bless You! I love You! In Jesus' name. Amen.

SELAH

1. Make a secret list of things you can give your wife that you know she would like. Give some little thing to her every day, if you can. And find some expensive things to give her from time to time.
2. Start setting aside money you can give your wife to blow her mind.
3. Schedule times to be with your wife when you know she'll be home, but don't tell her you've done it. Just be there for her. If something comes up and she's away, don't get disappointed. Just keep trying. God will help you.
4. Go through your affairs and find important subjects that the two of you need to discuss. Get organized and then find some convenient times when you know you can talk in private and you won't be interrupted.
5. Look at your weekend, morning, and evening schedules for the next week. Which times do you know that the two of you will be together?
6. What TV shows or movies does you wife like to watch? Which ones could you watch together?
7. What music does she like? Does she have tapes or CD's? Does she have a decent system for playing them? Does she need earphones?
8. Drop love notes to her in unexpected places.
9. Order flowers to be sent to her at home or work—and not just once!

5

*H*AVE THE HOME-COURT
ADVANTAGE ALL THE TIME

"Even when we are too weak to have any faith left,
he remains faithful to us and will help us."
—2 Timothy 2:13 TLB

"Hey, bro', who's got the home-court advantage?" That's the big barber-shop question when it's NBA play-off time. Every team needs the home-court fans cheering them on at crunch time.

In fact, that's true about your wife. She needs your cheers as much as a basketball team. She needs them even more!

She needs you cheering her on when she's not scoring as much as usual, and you need her cheering you on. If you work it right, your marriage can have the home-court advantage all the time.

YOUR WIFE IS EVERYTHING YOU HAVE MADE HER

Unconditional Love Wins in Crunch Time

The greatest home-court power God gives you is unconditional love. With unconditional love comes a lifetime commitment to your team-mates: your wife and children. Do you love your wife without conditions? Can she still count on you in crunch time, or have the years and the tight games you didn't always win dimmed your enthusiasm for cheering her on?

If She's Not Awesome, Maybe You're Not Awesome

When you first got your wife, she was a fine woman. You wanted to be seen with her everywhere. But now that you've been married some time, she's, you know, she's not fixing her hair so well anymore, maybe she even has a few gray hairs, a few wrinkles. She may have a little extra "love"—you understand, a little extra weight. Maybe it seems like she's made her job more of a priority than the family, and she doesn't cook too much anymore and she doesn't keep house and take care of the family the way your momma did. And what ever happened to all those nice things she once whispered in your ear? Everything has changed.

> **When you married her, she was the product of her momma and daddy's upbringing, but now that you've been married a few years, she's the fruit of what *you've* sown into her.**

So now if she's not that gorgeous thing you saw and heard at first, guess what? When you married her, she was the product of her momma and daddy's upbringing, but now that you've been married a few years, she's the fruit of what *you've* sown into her.

As Captain of the Team, Build Her Up

Your wife is the public picture of what you're like in private. If she's not awesome, it's because you're not awesome. You're the captain of this team. It's your job to raise her to another level.

Your wife is everything you've made her to be. When you don't see your wife as serious anymore, you have to ask yourself if you've been serious in your love toward her. If she's not loving you, maybe it's because you haven't been loving her. If she's not turned on, if she's not on fire, maybe it's because you haven't been turned on fire. If she's not filled with joy, maybe it's because you haven't been filled with joy.

Your wife is the garden that has grown up from the seeds that you've sown into her. Your wife brings forth your fruit. Her life exposes your life. As Jesus said, "You will know them by their fruits."[1] Maybe it's time to sow some different seeds. Maybe it's time to start being cheerleaders for each other again.

When a star player has an off night, faithful fans keep cheering. They remember all the times she came through for them, and don't dog her out for one bad day. They know that if they keep cheering, she'll eventually come out of her slump.

GOD'S GAME PLAN

God Is the Team Owner and the Coach

With the home-court advantage, there's constant cheering, because you and your wife know that *God* put your team together. That's a real crowd pleaser, if you think about it. God made your marriage. Like the old saying, "Marriages are made in heaven." That means your marriage was great from the beginning! "God saw all that he had made, and it was very good."[2]

Your wife loves to hear the heartfelt, sincere reassurance that God made no mistake in bringing the two of you together. Don't hesitate to remind her that she's the perfect wife for you. Be extravagant in saying "I love you" from a sincere heart. Don't let her beat you in expressing more love for you than you express to her. No one is going to beat Jesus in loving us. Remember these words every day, and do them: "Husbands, love your wives, even as Christ also loved the church, and gave himself for it; that he might sanctify and cleanse it with the washing of water by the word."[3]

You sanctify and cleanse your wife with your words as well as with God's Word. If you bless her with your words, she feels clean. If you curse her or speak ill of her, she feels dirty.

> **Watch your wife when you speak to her. Which of your words bring a glow to her face? Which words bring a cloud of darkness?**

When you compliment your wife whether she's all dressed up or she's not, you are seeing her through the eyes of Jesus. When she first wakes up in the morning, does she need to have her hair combed, her teeth brushed, and her makeup on to look beautiful to you? Does she have to do that for God?

Watch your wife when you speak to her. Which of your words bring a glow to her face? Which words bring a cloud of darkness?

Regardless of what she says or does to hurt you or hinder your success, should you ever want to bring darkness to your wife's face?

You want to bring her light, just as God brings light to you. "The Lord is my light and my salvation; whom shall I fear? the Lord is the strength of my life; of whom shall I be afraid?"[4] That's something worth cheering about.

Marriage is teamwork. Yeah, team!

Do you still love to go home to your wife? Marriage isn't a one-night stand. It's bigger than a sports franchise. It's something God sets up, a team for life—a great life! *This is it!*

In the Garden of Eden, Adam knew that he had the home-court advantage as soon as he saw his wife. The Living Bible has a great way of describing how he got her and what he said after she showed up: "Then the Lord God caused the man to fall into a deep sleep, and took one of his ribs and closed up the place from which he had removed it, and made the rib into a woman, and brought her to the man. '*This is it!*' Adam exclaimed. 'She is part of my own bone and flesh! Her name is "woman" because she was taken out of a man.' This explains why a man leaves his father and mother and is joined to his wife in such a way that the two become one person. Now although the man and his wife were both naked, neither of them was embarrassed or ashamed."[5]

When you have the home-court advantage in your marriage, you're not embarrassed when you're together. You always want to go home to your wife. What would it look like if a team didn't want to enter its own gym for a game? In your home court there's a comfort zone you enter whenever you're alone. When your "nakedness is exposed"[6] (things you do that make you look stupid), nobody's booing you. Nobody's calling you names. The cheers never stop, because cheers are a much better incentive for scoring than boos.

Be a Faithful Fan to Your Wife

Make your life a love letter to your wife. In the old days the wedding ceremony described the home-court advantage of marriage with words about mutual joy, comfort in all circumstances, nurturing children in the love of the Lord.[7] When you have the home-court advantage, your life is a love letter to your wife. She gets joy and comfort just from hanging around you, and so do your kids.

You should write love letters to your wife. You should say "I love you" a lot. But your best love letter is *you*. Whenever she sees you looking at her, she gets goose bumps. When you do thoughtful things for her, she gets warm fuzzies inside. Even if she doesn't respond this way initially, you're bound to break through if you remain faithful to flooding her with love and attention. Come on! How can you let those crazy sports fans show more persistence in loving their heroes than you do for your wife?

When fickle fans boo them, a home team loses its advantage. Even when they're not playing their best, they still need the cheers. Be a faithful fan. Stay in there with your wife. Don't boo her. If she blows it, keep cheering. Stand beside her. Stand up for her even if everyone else turns against her. Stick it out. That's what husbands are for. That's what God does for you, right? He said He would never leave you or forsake you,[8] like a fickle fan would. Jesus is your model of a faithful fan.

Love her even when she's on the disabled list. What if your wife suffers from morning sickness during one of her pregnancies and doesn't have the stomach to cook you bacon and sausage in the morning? Are you going to stop complimenting her as you did when she could throw down a great breakfast every morning? Or are you going to love her when she's on the disabled list and pick up some slack yourself?

Jesus is a faithful fan. "Even when we are too weak to have any faith left, he remains faithful to us and will help us, for he cannot disown us who are part of himself, and he will always carry out his promises to us."[9]

So never heckle her. Never nag. Never bring up her faults from the past. Just cheer and keep on cheering! Give her the home-court advantage all the time.

> You and your wife are on the same team. When you turn on her, it's like scoring a basket for the other team, on purpose.

Don't Boo Like the Devil, Cheer Like the Lord

You know who is good at booing? The devil. He's always accusing, always committing fouls against us that cause injuries. Do you want to do the devil's work just so you can even a score? Then you must have forgotten that you and your wife are on the same team. When you turn on her, it's like scoring a basket for the other team, on purpose, just because you got mad at one of your teammates. She's not your enemy. Stop the real enemy in his tracks. The Bible says the devil is defeated, and the way the saints overcome him is with the blood of the Lamb—which cleanses all of us from sin, including you and your wife—and the favorable words we speak about God's work in our lives.[10]

Christ defeated him. The devil scores only when we slack off on defense. We have more intensity to beat him when we are willing to die to our selfish desires. Dying to self is tough. Sometimes it's easier to imagine sacrificing your life to rescue your wife than it is to imagine laying down your pride, but that's the way to get the home-court advantage. That's the way to drive the accuser out of your life. He feeds off your pride, so when you kill your pride, the devil has nothing to eat. You know he's not into fasting, so he's outta there.

HOME-COURT ADVANTAGE IS UP TO YOU

Play the Game of Life the Way Jesus Did

Jesus is the greatest player of all time. After He completed His game on earth, He left us a complete Playbook, and a Coach so we could become as great as He is.

A few years ago my wife and I went on a tour of Israel at the invitation of Ben Kinchlow, former cohost of "The 700 Club" on CBN. I had certain preaching assignments as we rode the bus to the various sites where it was said Jesus had walked. As we went to the tomb, the Garden of Gethsemane, and the remnants of Herod's Temple, a contrast struck me. It was the difference betweeen what most people expect to get out of a trip like that—to walk *where* Jesus walked—and the actual assignment Jesus left for us to do—to walk *as* He walked.

You have to go to Israel to walk *where* Jesus walked, but you can walk *as* He walked every day in your home. That's how you maintain the home-court advantage. That's how you demonstrate the anointing. You walk *as* Jesus walked. You play the game of life the way Jesus did.

How would Jesus walk through married life? We know that He never married at the human level, but we know without a doubt that if He had He never would have been divorced. He never would have committed adultery. He never would have hit His wife or hurt her with His words. He would have been faithful. At all times His heart would have been pure and filled with unconditional love. Anyone would get excited about marrying a Husband like that.

You Can Be a Team Player Like Jesus

You know, you can be that kind of husband. That's His call on your life now that you're saved. "If you've gotten anything at all out of following Christ, if his love has made any difference in your life, if being in a community of the Spirit means anything to you, if you have a heart, if you *care*—then do me a favor: Agree with each other, love each other, be deep-spririted friends. Don't push your way to the front; don't sweet-talk your way to the top. Put yourself aside, and help others get ahead. Don't be obsessed with getting your own advantage. Forget yourselves long enough to lend a helping hand.

"Think of yourselves the way Christ Jesus thought of himself."[11] That's the winning attitude you need for every game.

Carry Your Family to Victory, Even on "Off Nights"

Champions pull off the tough ones. During game five in the 1997 NBA finals between the Chicago Bulls and the Utah Jazz, Michael Jordan was sick as a dog. He looked as if he could pass out at any time. Meanwhile, his team was really having an off night. Nobody could seem to get the hot hand. But before the game was over, somehow the champion inside Jordan rose up. He scored a game-high thirty-eight points, and carried his team to the win, sickness and all.

> When we turn on our wives in tough times, the devil doesn't even
> have to show up. We give him the victory by forfeit. . . .
> When she gets down, don't step on her. Help her up!

Champions don't turn against their teammates. When Jesus went to the cross, He demonstrated one of the most powerful principles of human relationships—being a helper for the helpless. When you are hurting and you start to get down on your wife because she has an attitude, you need to get your thinking converted to that of Christ. Instead of going on the attack, see her with anointed eyes. See her as helpless before the onslaught of evil. When she gets down, don't step on her. Help her up! That's what Jesus would do. That's what He did for you.

"When we were utterly helpless, with no way of escape, Christ came at just the right time and died for us sinners who had no use for him. Even if we were good, we really wouldn't expect anyone to die for us, though, of course, that might be barely possible. But God showed his great love for us by sending Christ to die for us while we were still sinners."[12] That's the kind of love Christ has for the Church, and that's the kind of love He expects you to have for your wife—if you're a real man.

What would it have looked like if Michael Jordan had driven the guys on his team out of the place because they couldn't step up the pace when he was hurting? For one thing, they would have had to forfeit the game.

That's exactly what we do when we turn on our wives in tough times of personal challenge. The devil doesn't even have to show up. We give him the victory by forfeit.

When God created a woman for Adam, He took her from his side, the place closest to his heart. He didn't create her from his feet to be stepped on, but from his side so they could be one. So don't you step on your wife. She's not your opposition. Step on the devil. Love and embrace your wife. Keep her by your side. That's where she belongs. You still need her with you on your team, even when she's not playing her best.

Show Your Wife How Much You Value Her

The eight-cow woman. There once was a town where men paid the dowries for their future wives in cows. The highest dowry that a man had ever paid a father for his daughter's hand in marriage was four cows.

One father in the town had a daughter who was very plain and unattractive, and most of the townspeople doubted if she would ever find a husband. However, one day a rich, successful rancher who owned many cattle saw the woman and fell in love with her. He went to the girl's father and began negotiations for the dowry. Everyone expected him to ask for a bargain, because no one had ever made an offer on her before, but he said, "I will pay you eight cows." They were shocked! But even more shocking was what happened next.

That homely girl became the most beautiful woman in town. Because her husband valued her, she began to carry herself differently. She stood straight and tall. She dressed well. Her whole countenance changed because of the value placed on her by someone who loved and cherished her.

As a man, your goal should be to make your wife feel cherished like this "eight-cow woman." Go after your wife as if she were the best catch in town, because she is, to you. Bless her in any way you can, and watch her flourish under the nurture of your love. If she likes gifts, give her gifts, and give her the kind she likes. Does she like flowers? A dinner out in a nice restaurant? A hike in the woods? A new ring? Or does she just want uninterrupted time every night to be alone with you?

God, your team owner, paid the highest price for every player at the cross. Show your wife how much you acknowledge her value. Treat her as if she's worth the blood of Jesus.

When You Cherish Your Wife, She Dazzles You

Visiting teams can tell when a wife feels cherished. There's something special about a couple who have been married to each other for many years. They've weathered storms, survived tragedies, and served each other for most of their lives. They eventually even start to look alike. They go together like a seasoned pair of players on a team. One person's action sets in motion the other person's reaction, often without a word. You can always recognize it as a marriage where a man has cherished his wife.

Christ cherishes His bride, the Church. "The husband provides leadership to his wife the Christ does to his church, not by domineering but by cherishing. . . . Christ's love makes the church whole. His words evoke her beauty. Everything he does and says is designed to bring the best out of her, dressing her in dazzling white silk, radiant with holiness."[13]

Christ loves the Church. The Greek word for church is *ekklesia*.[14] It means those who are called *by* and *to* Christ. Just as the Church is called *by* and *to* Christ, the wife is called *by* and *to* her husband. She is called into a cherishing! He calls her to be the most significant person in his life for as long as he lives. As far as the husband is concerned, his wife is set apart from the rest of the world. He only has eyes for her.

When you cherish your wife, you do things that give her a sense of value. That's what makes her dazzling. Nothing is too much for her. If you have a little money, you buy her something. If you have a little time, you give her first priority. If she wants a house, you find her a house. If she wants a new car, you find her a car. If she likes an intimate breakfast in bed, you take care of the details.

When you continue to show your wife that you cherish her the way you did when you said "I do" on your wedding day, her performance on the home court will continue to dazzle you.

> Some wives just can't take all that negative input.
> After a while, she stops trying and goes into hiding,
> or she starts fighting back.

No Intentional Fouls with Your Mouth

Cherishing your wife is just the opposite from crushing her, yet husbands crush their wives all the time with their words, just the way soldiers crush their enemies in battle with their guns.

When I was in Vietnam, I remember how I felt lying on a hill in Pleiku under the roar of support mortars. There was no escape from the danger. My fear never left me.

Some men have a way of committing intentional fouls against their wives with words of disapproval that really hurt. No matter how hard she tries, he always finds something wrong. Maybe his motives aren't that bad. He may think he's helping by giving her correction, but some wives just can't take all that negative input. After a while, she stops trying and goes into hiding, or she starts fighting back.

Some women have a mouth like the M-50 machine gun I carried in the army. It mows you down like a hurricane-force wind. Getting the brunt of an angry wife's words is worse for a man than being punched in the mouth. It can destroy him for days.

It's not so much what couples say to each other that destroys the home-court advantage. It's the spirit of revenge behind it. They aren't telling the truth in love. They aren't just correcting each other. They're getting the other person back for hurting them. They're giving out "truth" with a sting to it. They've both forgotten whose team they're on, and keep adding to the devil's score.

The "Plus-Minus-Plus" Formula for Correction

There is a right way and a wrong way to give correction to your number-one teammate. If you want to correct something about your wife, use the "plus-minus-plus" formula: Say at least *twice* as many positive things as you say negative things, and use the positives to suround the negatives so you leave her with something good.

Negative words wrongly said are like curses. They make you feel as if you're in hell, not heaven. Positive words will build you up. Your words can destroy your wife or build her up, so be careful what you say and how you say it. If your wife is showing she is in a weakened condition, by criticizing you, speak to her with kindness. Even if you have to be honest about her faults, love her to pieces in the midst of it and say something nice as well.

When you watch your words, you're remembering what a huge role your mouth plays in making your home heaven or hell. "A bit in the mouth of a horse controls the whole horse. A small rudder on a huge ship in the hands of a skilled captain sets a course in the face of the strongest winds. A word out of your mouth may seem of no account, but it can accomplish nearly anything—or destroy it!"[15]

"You can tame a tiger, but you can't tame a tongue—it's never been done. The tongue runs wild, a wanton killer. With our tongues we bless God our Father; with the same tongues we curse the very men and women he made in his image. Curses and blessings out of the same mouth!"[16]

Good home crowds don't curse their players. They bless them. They don't dog them out. They give the team courage to take the next step.

Let's face it: We're all sinners. We all fall short. If you get on someone because she doesn't change fast enough to suit you, you destroy her will to keep trying. Any rebuke or correction should be motivated by obvious, unconditional love.

You Are Called to Speak Blessings

Good words are not just a good strategy; they carry heavenly re-wards to those who speak them. "Summing up: Be agreeable, be sympathetic, be loving, be compassionate, be humble. That goes for all of you, no exceptions. No retaliation. No sharp-tongued sarcasm. Instead, bless—that's your job, to bless. You'll be a blessing and also get a blessing."[17]

> Whoever wants to embrace life
>   and see the day fill up with good,
> Here's what you do:
>   Say nothing evil or hurtful;
> Snub evil and cultivate good;
>   run after peace for all you're worth.
> God looks on all this with approval,
>   listening and responding well to what he's asked;
> But he turns his back
>   on those who do evil things.[18]

Jesus can help you to bring life back to your marriage through your words. "Death and life are in the power of the tongue, and those who love it will eat its fruit."[19]

Handling Problems with Maturity

Step to the sidelines to see what's really happening. If you'll do what the Bible says, you can get past problems without losing your mate, because you'll learn to handle disagreements in a constructive way. When you don't see eye to eye, you'll step to the sidelines for a min-ute so you can see what's really hapening on the court and what's at stake in the development of godly character in both of you. If your wife gets you so mad you are ready to go up side her head, that shows God how immature you are. You'll have to calm down, grow up, and look for ways to help her develop her character. She's a weak part of yourself that you have to take time and exercise to strengthen.

Don't shift the weight. When you watch basketball on TV, you can usually tell which players aren't giving it everything they've got. You may see some pretty stupid mistakes from lack of concentration. In spite of that, you almost never see a post-game interview where the losing coach or losing player admits, "Yeah, man, it was all my fault we lost. I blew it and it cost us the game." You know they almost always find somebody else to blame.

It was the same thing when Adam and Mrs. Adam sinned: She blamed the serpent and he blamed her, and both of them turned away from God. Husbands and wives have been shifting the weight just like that ever since. Until Jesus.

What could you change about *yourself* to make some "home improvements" in her attitudes on the home court? Repent when you're wrong—or when you could possibly be wrong. And then, always believe in her, always expect the best of her, and always stand your ground in defending her.[20]

Die to your pride. Jesus is called the Last Adam. He succeeded where Adam failed. He died to His pride. He can give you the power to die to your pride. He can help you say, "I'm sorry. I was wrong." He can help you love your wife when you want to be mad at her. He can restore your home-court advantage.

A WINNING MARRIAGE

Preparing to Win

We're ugly, but Jesus makes us beautiful. Jesus loves us, so He has taken on the responsibility of making us—His Church, whom everybody knows can get pretty ugly—into a beautiful Bride "without spot or wrinkle."[21] When we get to heaven, we'll have the home-court advantage all the time. That's the model that He's set up for human marriages. That's the way your love life is supposed to affect your bride—make her beautiful. Prepare her to be the Bride of Christ, even as you are preparing yourself.

Keep working on the details. In preparing for the game of life, you pay attention to the details, the same way you prepare yourself for a game. In basketball, you work out with weights and run and practice your shooting until you become the best you can be. In God, you keep working on every detail that He says is important for perfecting your game, because He's the coach and you're only a player He can choose to disqualify.

"Don't put it off: don't frustrate God's work by showing up late, throwing a question mark over everything we're doing. Our work as God's servants gets validated—or not—in the details. People are watching us as we stay at our post."[22]

> **When the scouts from the devil's team see humility, they recognize it as something that can't be beat.**

Humility gives you power. Pride distracts you from the game plan. It makes you miss the mark. Humility gives you power to concentrate on the goal. "We give no offense in anything, that our ministry may not be blamed. But in all things we commend ourselves as ministers of God: in much patience, in tribulations, in needs, in distresses, in stripes, in imprisonments, in tumults, in labors, in sleeplessness, in fastings; by purity, by knowledge, by longsuffering, by kindness, by the Holy Spirit, by sincere love, by the word of truth, by the power of God, *by the armor of righteousness on the right hand and on the left.*"[23]

What is the armor of righteousness on the right and left? It relates to your whole walk as a Christian. Your right standing. Your righteousness. Your ability to develop weak areas of yourself and the weaker side, your wife. Then you will be approved of God. Notice it says "by the power of God." You get the power of God through your lowliness. If you follow His principles you'll have power. If you will humble yourself you'll be exalted. "Humble yourselves in the sight of the Lord, and He shall lift you up."[24] Humility is power. It's giving God something He can reproduce in society.

Yieldedness builds team spirit. When the scouts from the devil's team see humility, they recognize it as something that can't be beat. If you want to revive your home team's spirit, don't just pray for revival. Pray for contriteness in yourself. "For thus says the High and Lofty One who inhabits eternity, whose name is Holy: 'I dwell in the high and holy place, with him who has a contrite and humble spirit, to revive the spirit of the humble, and to revive the heart of the contrite ones.' "[25]

When you realize that something has happened to your heart to bring a yieldedness, that's the beginning of revival. Your conditioning has made your heart ready for the Holy Spirit to work. He only works in line with what is true to the nature of God, and it is His nature to flow into you when you're yielded.

> If you praise her when she demonstrates a meek and quiet spirit—especially if you're being a pain in the neck at the time—that's a whole different ball game.

Inward Qualities of Winners

Show her it's what's inside that counts. You could get any group of good-looking, muscular guys to put on basketball uniforms and look like a team, but inside they wouldn't know diddly about how to play. No manager in his right mind would want them.

Most wives want to be physically attractive to their husbands. That's what they usually focus on every morning. But the Bible tells the woman to spend her energy in another area, also—developing her inner strength, "the hidden man of the heart, in that which is not corruptible, even the ornament of a meek and a quiet spirit, which is in the sight of God of great price."[26]

That's where you come in. She's going to respond to what you tell her is attractive to you. If her physical appearance is what turns you on and provokes the most favorable comments out of you, then guess where she'll place her focus? But if you praise her when she demonstrates a meek and quiet spirit—especially if you're being a pain in the neck at the time—that's a whole different ball game.

The Bible is not talking about a meek and quiet spirit as something that's put on to fool people. Meekness and quietness are inward qualities. In other words, even if her husband is wrong, she doesn't let it corrupt her. If anyone treats her mean on the outside, she keeps looking good on the inside—building character.

Strength of character comes from within. The Greek word *prautes*, translated "meek," is the attitude of spirit in which "we accept God's dealings with us as good and do not dispute or resist." It is "a condition of mind and heart which demonstrates gentleness not in weakness but power. It is a balance born in strength of character."[27] It's hard to believe, but the meekest one is the strongest one, because that person is most fully yielded to God.

The Bible says a woman is most effective in changing her husband when she stays quiet and puts her confidence in the Lord. "Be good wives to your husbands, responsive to their needs. There are husbands who, indifferent as they are to any words about God, will be captivated by your life of holy beauty. What matters is not your outer appearance—the styling of your hair, the jewelry you wear, the cut of your clothes—but your inner disposition.

"Cultivate inner beauty, the gentle gracious kind that God delights in."[28]

Build up your wife as if you wanted her to be a team player with depth, not just a player who looks good on the picture side of a trading card but has no credible game stats on the back. Sow into her what she needs to be recognized in the next world, not this one.

You should be your wife's model of meekness. If her husband is a flake, where does the wife get the model for meekness? She gets it from Jesus, but she should be able to get it from you. When a husband is nose to nose with his wife all the time, or else ignoring her and not giving her what she wants, his will is fighting against her will. Does that please God? Of course not. But He has other ways of accomplishing His will if you're not cooperating with His game plan.

Here's what the apostle Paul said to a bunch of flaky Christians: "I'm completely frustrated by your unspiritual dealings with each other and with God. You're acting like infants in relation to Christ, capable of nothing much more than nursing at the breast. Well, then, I'll nurse you since you don't seem capable of anything more. As long as you grab for what makes you feel good or makes you look important, are you really much different than a babe at the breast, content only when everything's going your way?"[29]

Grown-up husbands and wives increase in meekness over the years. This is of great value to God, because it means the husband or wife will have the patience and godly character to build a proper foundation for the home—a solid foundation of Christ-likeness that will last when the storms of adversity come. Then they will be able to demonstrate godly virtue for the witnesses in heaven, and will be able to face the probing of Jesus at the Judgment Bar.

Meekness gets rewards in eternity. "Let each carpenter who comes on the job take care to build the foundation! Remember, there is only one foundation, the one already laid: Jesus Christ. Take particular care in picking out your building materials. Eventually there is going to be an inspection."[30]

If her man treats her wrong, she can still act right. That represents the kingdom of God. If she represents the kingdom of God on earth, then she represents the kingdom of God in eternity, and there will be rewards for that. We don't get rewards by gender. We get rewards by obedience. You may not see your wife doing anything that brings visible rewards on the earth, but God may be teaching her how to be a leader in the next world by being subjected to an unrighteous husband like you right now. In heaven, her rewards will be just as great as a world leader's, because it takes just as much of the right stuff under harsh conditions at home as it would have taken her to win a world war.

Remember, you don't get rewarded for position; you get rewarded for possession of Christ-like behavior. The same principle applies to men and women alike. When you're treated badly, stay quiet and let God set things straight. When you're quiet, God opens your eyes so you can see that your enemy's attacks come out of his weakness, not his strength. Then you can help. But when you defend yourself, you refuse to help your wife in her weakness because you're giving in to your own.

Jesus' Model of Authority Through Meekness

Jesus treats His team with respect. You know what Jesus is doing right now in prayer? He's preparing His team for eternity. How does He treat us? With love and respect. He knows we're puny in His eyes, and He has all authority in heaven and earth, but He treats us as if we've already arrived where He wants us to be in the New Jerusalem. God wants us to be like Jesus, so He tells us to submit.

Your domineering attitudes expose your level of submission to Christ. You show how much you are submitted to Christ by your treatment of those under your authority, like your wife. If she's not submitted, maybe you're not submitted, and Christ can't endorse your authority in heaven.

Anyone can be the daddy if he's just the guy with the money. Is it like Jesus to lord it over your wife by using your money as a weapon to enforce your authority? Some husbands say to their wives and children, "As long as I make payments on this house, you'll do what I say!" Is that a good team spirit? Would Jesus treat them that way? No way! If His wife had the wrong attitude about submission, He'd say, "I need to have the right attitude for her."

Bro', if the foundation for your authority is economics, you're out of there when your cash runs out. Anyone can be the daddy if he's just the guy who pays. The foundation for your authority should be your Christ-likeness, not your money. You have only as much true authority as the degree to which you are submitted to Jesus, because He is the source of your authority. All power was delegated to Jesus, so he can delegate authority to believers.

Authority isn't granted by gender but by relationship. It isn't just men who get authority from Jesus. He delegates it to those with whom He has a relationship, and they use it according to their relationships with others. Your wife isn't submitted to you because she's a woman, but because she's your wife.

Misuse of authority means you're out of bounds and can't score. If you got the ball and then let your foot get out of bounds, you could make the most flashy slam dunk anyone ever saw and still not score a point. That's what it's like when you misuse your authority—you think you're scoring, but you're disqualified for not doing it God's way.

Leaders Develop Their Weak Side

You can't hit the ball right with one weak side. I like to play golf. I'm naturally right-handed, but to have a good golf swing, I have to develop my left hand, too. One brother said all his habits had changed since he started seriously playing golf. He said, "I do everything with my left hand now. I eat with my left hand and I drive with my left hand." He knows that in order to have the control he needs in his swing, he has to work on his left hand to make it equal to his right. If he doesn't work on his left hand, then his right side will dominate his left and he won't be able to hit anything straight.

The Bible says that David's soldiers could throw stones with both the left hand and the right hand.[31] You know that most of them were probably not born with that ability. There was just something about being a soldier for David's army that made people get serious about getting strong. They learned how to overcome their weaknesses.

God gave you a wife to develop your weak points. Everybody has weak points that need to be developed in the same way as you develop weak muscles into strong ones. The wife is sometimes called "the weaker vessel," not in a derogatory sense but in the sense of her needing a man to protect and help her. In Genesis 2, when it says that God took the rib out of the man to make the woman, in the literal Hebrew it says God took the other half of the man. The woman is the other half, the weaker half, just as the Church is weaker than Jesus. You have to work on your weaknesses.

If your woman gets under your skin and you fight back at her, she has just been used to expose *your* weakness. Your weakness is your inability to deal with her in *her* weakness. You need to develop that weak side of you until you have enough strength of character to carry her and yourself both out of the ditch, if necessary. If she seems out of bounds, follow the plus-minus-plus method of giving her correction, and pray for her. Say two nice things for everything you say that is critical. The evidence of your strength will be in her change.

Growing Older and Wiser Together

Marriage is a team for life. Your rookie years may be filled with making mistakes and learning from them. But eventually, you'll be veteran players with a wealth of wisdom and experience for the next generation. At the time they get married, most couples don't think about the wisdom they will gain in future years as they grow old together, but wisdom increases with age for all who are seekers of God, and even more so for those who seek God together.

Wisdom is the greatest inheritance you can attain in this life to pass on to your children. If it was your goal to pass on to your heirs money in the bank, you would spend time advancing yourself at your job, working the stock market, or creating your own company. You also have to spend time to develop a portfolio of wisdom. God's wisdom comes from spending time with God, God's Word, and godly people like your spouse, and with your pastor and Christian brothers, who help disciple you so you can better disciple your wife.

Paul instructed Timothy, "Guide older men into lives of temperance, dignity, and wisdom, into healthy faith, love, and endurance. Guide older women into lives of reverence."[32]

Wisdom is part of the furniture when you have heaven in your home. Your home court is a holy temple, a sanctuary where people come to be fed from His table. "Now devote your heart and soul to seeking the Lord your God. Begin to build the sanctuary of the Lord God, so that you may bring the ark of the covenant of the Lord and the sacred articles belonging to God into the temple that will be built for the Name of the Lord."[33]

Embrace Life with Your Wife

Embrace life with your wife. Fill up her days with good things. Cultivate the good life for her, and God will approve *your* life. Your wife doesn't have anyone else to encourage her at that level. You don't have anyone either. You need to be the greatest encouragers for each other. Value each other exceedingly and speak to each other in love, even when there are times when you have to keep each other straight. Speak respectfully to your woman. Cut her some slack. Stay humble. Don't get rough. "The poor man uses entreaties, but the rich answers roughly."[34]

In the Church, every married couple is supposed to be awesome, because God is our Father and He builds only wholesome families. In God, the divorce rate disappears off the charts because of the home-court advantage. No manager in his right mind is going to split up the players on a winning team.

HOW TO KEEP THE HOME-COURT ADVANTAGE ALL THE TIME

Respond when God calls you to have fellowship with Him, for the sake of yourself and your family. When you have been in that secret place with God, where He has called you to rise up and become more like Him, the winter of your discontent with your marriage changes into a springtime of agreement.

Let the Word of Christ have the run of the house. "Let the peace of Christ keep you in tune with each other, in step with each other. None of this going off and doing your own thing. And cultivate thankfulness. Let the Word of Christ—the Message—have the run of the house. Give it plenty of room in your lives."[35]

Put on love and godly character like a team uniform. "So, chosen by God for this new life of love, dress in the wardrobe God picked out for you: compassion, kindness, humility, quiet strength, discipline. Be even-tempered, content with second place, quick to forgive an offense. Forgive as quickly and completely as the Master forgave you. And regardless of what else you put on, wear love. It's your basic, all-purpose garment. Never be without it."[36] Love is your uniform. If the captain doesn't wear the uniform, neither will the team.

Stay calm. When the storms of life come upon you, that's when you have an opportunity to prove your relationship with God and with each other. Any team does a lot better when the captain keeps his cool.

Recognize that the storms of life are temporary, but God and His love in you are eternal. As the old mothers used to say, "I've never seen a storm that didn't pass."

Fly above the storm. Just as an airplane rises above a storm to get to its destination, you need to rise above your circumstances to the calm air, where you can get moving again in the direction of Christ-likeness.

Rise up inside, in that secret place where God dwells. Ask Him for prophetic insight to see where He is taking you so you can set yourself on the proper course.

Follow the Golden Rule as a lifestyle. "Do unto others as you would have others do unto you." Jesus said, "Here is a simple, rule-of-thumb guide for behavior: Ask yourself what you want people to do for you, then grab the initiative and do it for *them*. Add up God's Law and Prophets and this is what you get."[37]

Out-serve each other. "But it shall not be so among you: but whoso-ever will be great among you, let him be your minister; And whoso-ever will be chief among you, let him be your servant: Even as the Son of man came not to be ministered unto, but to minister, and to give his life a ransom for many."[38]

Take your wife out to dinner or away on a trip with you, even as God tenderly takes you with him. In the Song of Solomon, you can see God calling us to times of intimate fellowship when He can bring us up to another level—for our own sake and for the sake of our families: "My beloved spoke, and said to me: 'Rise up, my love, my fair one, and come away. For lo, the winter is past, the rain is over and gone. The flowers appear on the earth; the time of singing has come, and the voice of the turtledove is heard in our land. The fig tree puts forth her green figs, and the vines with the tender grapes give a good smell. Rise up, my love, my fair one, and come away!' "[39] You can bless your wife and encourage her to come up to another level with you when you take her away with you for special times of personal and spiritual intimacy, which are so vital to the health of a marriage.

Develop in oneness. Oneness is greater than unity. In unity you can get together on something. In oneness you are lost in each other. Two become one, with one purpose, one destiny, one focus. You don't lose your personality in oneness, but you lose your self-centeredness. You become one as husband and wife.

Be a peacemaker. Being a peacemaker means dying to your own will and living to God's will. "Be cheerful. Keep things in good repair. Keep your spirits up. Think in harmony. Be agreeable. Do all that, and the God of love and peace will be with you for sure."[40]

Focus on the future you have together in God. Don't get hung up on the petty problems of the present moment. All of those will pass.

Pay attention if your wife doesn't want you to go into the ministry. She may have some good reasons. If your home-court advantage is not yet secure, you don't even need to be thinking about going into the ministry. I hear Christian brothers talk about how they can't do ministry because "My wife doesn't see me being in the ministry. She's not with me." You can get into all that pious pouting and excuse making, but that doesn't fool God. Maybe she can't imagine you being in the ministry because you haven't developed enough yet. She's probably doing you a favor. There are a lot of ministers out there whose wives should have headed them off before they started pastoring a church. If your wife doesn't respect you, maybe you haven't paid enough attention to her, and she knows you wouldn't pay attention to your church, either. Or maybe you would pay so much attention to it that she would be totally ignored. And she definitely isn't seeing that. She wants the home-court advantage in her home.

Show your love by your actions. You've been paying attention to yourself all your life. It's time to pay attention to her. Don't just *say* "I love you." *Show* "I love you" by the way you prioritize your life for her. Love is felt more than told.

Remember that you're getting on-the-job training for eternity. The greatest training school for taking worlds is right in your own home. You learn where real power comes from when you learn selflessness, servanthood, and unconditional love.

PRAYER: A CLASSIC PRAYER FROM THE WEDDING CEREMONY IN THE *BOOK OF COMMON PRAYER*[41]

"Eternal God, creator and preserver of all life, author of salvation, and giver of grace: Look with favor upon the world you have made, and for which your Son gave his life, and especially upon this man and this woman whom you make one flesh in Holy Matrimony.

"Give them wisdom and devotion in the ordering of their common life, that each may be to the other a strength in need, a counselor in perplexity, a comfort in sorrow, and a companion in joy.

"Grant that their wills may be so knit together in Your will, and their spirits in your spirit, that they may grow in love and peace with you and with each other all the days of their life.

"Give them grace, when they hurt each other, to recognize and

acknowledge their fault, and to seek each other's forgiveness and yours.

"Make their life together a sign of Christ's love to this suffering and broken world, that unity may overcome estrangement, forgiveness heal guilt, and joy conquer despair.

". . . Grant that the bonds of our common humanity, by which all your children are united to one another, and the living to the dead, may be so transformed by your grace, that your will may be done on earth as it is in heaven; where, O Father, with your Son and the Holy Spirit, you live and reign in perfect unity, now and for ever. . . .

"O God, you have so consecrated the covenant of marriage that in it is represented the spiritual unity between Christ and his Church: Send therefore your blessing upon these your servants, that they may so love, honor, and cherish each other in faithfulness and patience, in wisdom and true godliness, that their home may be a haven of blessing and peace; through Jesus Christ our Lord, who with you and the Holy Spirit lives and reigns, one God, now and for ever. Amen."

SELAH

Part 1

Here's the key Scripture for the subtitle of this book, "How You Can Have Heaven in Your Home." It's from Deuteronomy 11:18–21 in the King James Version. Apply the commentary notes below the Scripture to your own home situation.

Moses told Israel that the Word should fill your home so much that it would be on your face, on your clothes, in your conversation, and written on your walls. Every time you turn around, there's Word and more Word, because that's the way to get heaven on earth. Moses preached it!

He said, "Therefore shall ye lay up these my words in your heart and in your soul, and bind them for a sign upon your hand, that they may be as frontlets between your eyes. And ye shall teach them [to] your children, speaking of them when thou sittest in thine house, and when thou walkest by the way, when thou liest down, and when thou risest up. And thou shalt write them upon the door posts of thine house, and upon thy gates: That your days may be multiplied, and the days of your children, in the land which the Lord sware unto your fathers to give them, as the days of heaven upon the earth."[42]

Lay up these words in your heart (your inner man, your spirit).

Lay up these words in your soul (your mind, will, emotions).

Bind them for a sign upon your hand. You are reaching out to your wife and children, using your hands to teach, help, and heal, never hurt. You never, ever hit your wife. You bless her with your touch.

That they may be as frontlets between your eyes. As far as your eyes can see, the Word is going forth from you as the husband in your house. Your eyes see the potential in every member of your family, because you know God made them, and you know God's ability to bring change.

Teach your children:
While sitting in your house (speaking and teaching the Word of the Lord).
While walking by the way (in your public lifestyle).
When you lie down (before the family goes to bed at night).
When you rise up (before sending them off to work or school for the day).

Write them on your doorposts. Live out the Word among yourself, your wife, and your children so that in-laws, neighbors, and other visitors can see something different as soon as they walk in your door.

Write them on your gates. As you leave your house for the day, you take the Word out with you—whether husband, wife, or children—because the Word is written on your heart before you go out to face the world.

Part 2

So much happened on your wedding day that the questions the minister asked you may be long since forgotten. Maybe these weren't the exact questions he asked, but it might be refreshing to answer them, to renew your convenant with your wife, and increase the home-court advantage.

Will you have this woman to be your wife?
Will you live together in the convenant of marriage?
Will you love her?
Will you comfort her?
Will you honor her?
Will you keep her, in sickness and in health?
Will you forsake all others?
Will you be faithful to her as long as you both shall live?

"And this I pray, that your love may abound still more and more in knowledge and all discernment, that you may approve the things that are excellent, that you may be sincere and without offense till the day of Christ, being filled with the fruits of righteousness which are by Jesus Christ, to the glory and praise of God."[43]

6

$\mathcal{H}$OW LOW WILL YOU GO FOR YOUR WIFE?

"The accuser of our brethren, who accused them before our
God day and night, has been cast down. And they overcame him by the
blood of the Lamb and by the word of their
testimony, and they did not love their lives to the death."

—Revelation 12:10–12 NKJV

A few years ago, Ministries Today *did an interview with me called "Is Racial Reconciliation Possible?" In that interview, I talked about the fictional slave character Uncle Tom as a role model for blacks.*

One black professor at a Christian university got so mad about my "Uncle Tom" comment in the interview that he wrote me a letter saying, "You're suffering from pathological self hatred and co-dependency!"

That was so funny, because that's nothing but the truth! I absolutely hate the self life, and I'm totally dependent upon God! *However, he totally missed my point.*

Maybe he had never read the book Uncle Tom's Cabin *by Harriet Beecher Stowe. Most people haven't. Most blacks hate to be called "Uncle Tom" but many of them haven't the slightest idea what that fictional character was like.*

Later in this chapter, I'm going to quote some of the story of Uncle Tom for you so you can learn something about Jesus. I will especially be focusing on Uncle Tom's Christ-like relationship with his wife and his lowly lifestyle, because it was full of the substance and power of God. The level of humility and sacrifice his character demonstrated is virtually unknown today. Most of us haven't begun to be like Christ in His sacrificial love and humility.

A CHRIST-LIKE EXAMPLE OF LOWLINESS

The fact that being an "Uncle Tom" is considered a negative stereotype in our society is evidence not only of how little people read, but also of how much we hate to be humble. The subtitle of *Uncle Tom's Cabin* is "Life Among the Lowly" because the author took her readers to the lowliest part of nineteenth-century American society to teach them—rich and poor, black and white—an important lesson about life. She wrote the book in 1852 to crusade against slavery, but the book also has application to the Christian life. God hates pride and the high look,[1] and loves humility and the low look. But, you know, most men are just the opposite. They hate to "go low" and hate to keep quiet when someone else is getting his way instead of them. They do just the opposite of the Bible. They hate the low look and love the high look.

If you walk in on some dudes at a corner store in the inner city, those brothers will *all* give you a high look. They will sure enough stare you down until you want to crawl back out the door, totally intimidated.

Maybe you aren't that obvious about it, but I bet you love to stay in control. You like to look down on the other person from a place of "I'm right and you're wrong." Even though God tells us to be humble, most of us fight giving up our pride. Most of the time we don't even realize it when we're being prideful, and we don't see that we're listening to the voice of Satan more clearly than the voice of God. If you want to be like someone who never went low for anyone, Satan is your model. Satan said to himself, "I will ascend to heaven and rule the angels. I will take the highest throne. I will preside on the Mount of Assembly far away in the north. I will climb to the highest heavens and be like the Most High."[2] "I" and "I" and "I"— Satan always put himself first, on center stage. He loved himself and he thought he was bigger and better than God. So God had to kick him out of heaven. There was no place for him there because he was so full of pride.

You can't have heaven in your home when people are prideful. The Bible says God told Satan that He would personally humiliate him and "you will be brought down to the pit of hell, down to its lowest depths. Everyone there will stare at you and ask, 'Can this be the one who shook the earth and the kingdoms of the world?' "[3]

Jesus hated pride in His disciples. One time they wanted to kill some Samaritans who were cursing Him, so He rebuked them, saying, "You don't know what spirit you are of."[4] If you're the kind of husband who always wants to get even and won't humble himself for his wife's sake, you're showing her just what it would be like to be married to the devil.

God Won't Promote Pride

God wants you to have a humble spirit, not for the purpose of self-hatred and codependency, in a negative sense, but so that He can promote you and trust you with real authority in your family and in the world. When you're in pride He has to oppose you, because you misrepresent His ways. We have to forgive everyone in our past who has hurt us personally or hurt our people, and have compassion on them. We've got to stay humble. God can't promote a prideful spirit.

As a husband, you must constantly be on guard to examine your own spirit in your relationship with your wife. If your wife provokes you and you think she's wrong, it's so easy to snap back in self-righteous pride and put her in her place. What you're really doing, in the eyes of God, is putting forth the wrong spirit. When you try to correct her—or anyone else, for that matter—with the wrong spirit, you misuse the authority God gave you, and He can't legitimately promote you in His kingdom. You're unfit for leadership in heaven, and so you're not bringing heaven to your home.

Unselfish Love for Your Wife Means a Death

Do you love doing what is right more than preserving your own life? Jesus said, "Greater love hath no man than this, that a man lay down his life for his friends."[5] The Greek word for "love" in this quote is *agape,* the unselfish love that's so awesome that only Almighty God can give you the ability to do it. It's the kind of love God wants you to have for your wife. The only way you can demonstrate agape is to go low, so low that you lay down your life for her. Agape is not some surfacy emotion to make you feel good or make your wife feel good. It's a sacrifice. It takes sensitivity. It takes death to self.

Most of the world doesn't understand agape. Otherwise we wouldn't have so many men divorcing their wives. It's a word that gets its meaning from Christ. The lowest you can go is to die to yourself and lay down your life for others, and that's also a great way to silence the voice of Satan. He's called "the accuser of our brethren,"[6] so guess what kind of thoughts he puts in your mind?

"My wife's not like my momma."

"My wife doesn't treat me right."

"My wife has an easy life and all I do is work."

The blood of Jesus defeated Satan on your behalf, but you have to personally overcome Satan every day with your testimony that you follow Jesus. You take up your cross daily and follow Christ. You love your wife as Christ loved the Church. You lay down your life for your wife.

The right spirit is a crucial character quality for God's people, because people judge God by what spirit they see in us. Jesus represented the Father's Spirit with His life, and if we have received Him, we represent Him, too. At the Judgment Bar, just like now, God will judge our spirits and decide if we have something He wants to promote in eternity. Would you want Him to seal you with the kind of spirit and thought-life you have right now?

The best place for God to check you out to see what spirit you are of is in your home. That's why a candidate for church leadership is not approved until the committee looks into his relationships with his wife and children. Those relationships in the home expose his true character. If he has any of the lust of the flesh, the lust of the eyes, or the pride of life,[7] somebody at home is going to see it.

If your relationships at home are not in order, it just means that you love your self-life more than you love doing what is right. You would rather sacrifice relationships with your family to preserve your own self-life, rather than sacrificing your self-life for those you love.

A Faithful and Sacrificial Husband

The title *Uncle Tom's Cabin* refers to the place where Uncle Tom and his wife hosted their simple prayer meetings for the plantation. Slaves would gather there to hear the Word and sing songs about freedom and the Lord.

At the beginning of the book, Uncle Tom is secretly sold by his slave master, Mr. Shelby, to satisfy the master's outstanding debts. Uncle Tom's life was so valuable that the price paid by the slave trader in that private sale almost entirely wiped out the master's debts and saved all the other slaves on the plantation from being sold. One man's life laid down bought all the others.

Uncle Tom was a valuable slave because after he became a Christian, he became a man of absolute integrity. He kept his word. He was trustworthy. He was a faithful servant, husband, and father. There is an economic value to holiness. That applies as much today as it did then. Do you have as much character as Uncle Tom? You can decide after you read the excerpt later on in this chapter.

In the story, a young slave named Eliza found out that Uncle Tom was about to be sold and rushed to warn him. He could have escaped, but he didn't. He found out that if he gave up his life, the others on the plantation—including his wife and children—would be kept safely together. That is agape.

Throughout the book, time after time, Tom's Christ-like character makes the difference in countless lives, and in the end he dies a martyr for not revealing the hiding place of two female slaves who were being used for sex by their master. He never saw his wife again, but he stayed faithful to her until his death, and she to him.

If being an Uncle Tom means having the substance of God in my life, then I'll be an Uncle Tom.

If being an Uncle Tom means having Christ-like integrity, trustworthiness, and faithfulness, then I'll be an Uncle Tom.

If being an Uncle Tom means laying down my life for my family, then I'll be an Uncle Tom.

If being an Uncle Tom means having an opposite spirit from the people who oppress me, then I'll be an Uncle Tom.

If being an Uncle Tom means forgiving those who hurt me, then I'll be an Uncle Tom.

UNCLE TOM, MODELED AFTER CHRIST, CHANGED HISTORY

Uncle Tom's Cabin was created from true-life accounts of slave incidents by Harriet Beecher Stowe, a Christian abolitionist in the North who felt that God had driven her to write. Her father, Lyman Beecher, and brother, Henry Ward Beecher, were two of the most effective pastors and evangelists of their day. At the time she wrote, Mrs. Stowe was a housewife living in Maine, far away from the Southern plantations. However, she was deeply troubled because the supposedly anti-slavery North was enforcing the Fugitive Slave Law against slaves escaping from the South. She was also appalled that, by and large, the Church—both North and South—was not speaking out against slavery. She said, "I will write! I will write if I live!"

She was driven to write something that would confront the nation with slavery as a sin. *Uncle Tom's Cabin* called Christians to account on the basis of their own proclaimed faith in the One who came to seek and save the lowly—Jesus Christ.

In the process of awakening "sympathy and feeling for the black race," the author created a beautiful love story. A wife and mother herself, she presented slaves as real people with real families, people created in the image of God, many of whom had become sincere Christians. She showed agape love in action as she portrayed Tom, sold into the hands of a slave master who took him away forever, laying down his life for his wife and family.

First in weekly installments and then in the completed book, *Uncle Tom's Cabin* had such an international impact that almost overnight it turned public opinion against slavery. Readers in America, France, England, and around the world came to love Uncle Tom. As they saw in Uncle Tom's life the application of Christ-like love, many Christians become horrified at their complicity in slavery. By not speaking out against it, they saw that they had committed a sin against God. From then on, many said, the course of history was changed.

> The book *Uncle Tom's Cabin* caused a worldwide turnaround
> in people's attitudes toward slavery. Abraham Lincoln
> would say later that it was the single greatest
> cause of the Civil War.

Christ Left You an Example

The title character and his wife, Tom and Chloe, demonstrated that sincere family ties were a reality, even in slavery.

The Scripture says Christ suffered for us, leaving us an example that we should follow. "When the time came, he set aside the privileges of deity and took on the status of a slave, became *human*! Having become human, he stayed human. It was an incredibly humbling process. He didn't claim special privileges. Instead, he lived a selfless, obedient life and then died a selfless, obedient death—and the worst kind of death at that: a crucifixion.

"Because of that obedience, God lifted him high and honored him far beyond anyone or anything, ever, so that all created beings in heaven and on earth—even those long ago dead and buried—will bow in worship before this Jesus Christ, and call out in praise that he is the Master of all, to the glorious honor of God the Father."[8]

Do You Love Your Wife as Christ Loves the Church?

As you read the excerpt from *Uncle Tom's Cabin* in this chapter, watch for this:

- A man of character who was willing to live a lowly lifestyle and lay down his life because he knew it would save the lives of his wife and children
- The love of a married couple for each other, committed until their deaths
- A couple's trust in Jesus Christ, even in the most adverse, inhumane conditions

After you read this, I want to challenge you to love your wife as Uncle Tom loved his wife, because that is how Christ loved the Church. He "gave himself for it."[9]

Satan was thrown out of heaven, but Jesus voluntarily went down out of heaven. He humbled Himself, and therefore God exalted Him.[10]

Satan exalted himself, so God had to humble him.

Which one do you want to be like? Only one way will give you a real sense of power and dignity in your home.

The apostle John wrote of Satan's defeat and our victory if we stay in Christ-likeness and voluntary death to our self-life: "Then I heard a loud voice saying in heaven, 'Now salvation, and strength, and the kingdom of our God, and the power of His Christ have come, for the accuser of our brethren, who accused them before our God day and night, has been cast down. And they overcame him by the blood of the Lamb and by the word of their testimony, and they did not love their lives to the death.' "[11]

An Excerpt from Uncle Tom's Cabin[12]

According to the story, the cabin of Uncle Tom and his wife was a crude building that served as a home for his family and a prayer house for the slaves. Every week for several years, ever since he had given his life to the Lord, Uncle Tom had served as a minister to his people. He was also the spiritual mentor of a white boy, George Shelby, the son of the slave master. Young George always read aloud from the Bible to the mostly illiterate slaves. The famous Uncle Tom was described this way by Harriet Beecher Stowe:

> Mr. Shelby's best hand . . . was a large, broad-chested, powerfully made man, of full glossy black, and a face whose truly African features were characterized by an expression of grave and steady good sense, united with much kindliness and benevolence. There was something about his whole air self-respecting and dignified, yet united with a confiding and humble simplicity. . . .

> Uncle Tom was a sort of patriarch in religious matters, in the neighborhood. . . . he was looked up to with great respect, as a sort of minister among them. . . . But it was in prayer that he especially excelled. Nothing could exceed the touching simplicity, the childlike earnestness of his prayer, enriched with the language of Scripture, which seemed so entirely to have wrought itself into his being.

Mrs. Stowe paints a wonderful picture as she writes of Tom's wife, Chloe, in this description from the book:

> A round, black, shining face is hers, so glossy as to suggest the idea that she might have been washed over with white of eggs,

like one of her own tea rusks. Her whole plump countenance beams with satisfaction and contentment from under her well-starched checked turban, bearing on it, however, if we must confess it, a little of that tinge of self-consciousness which becomes the first cook of the neighborhood.

Why Uncle Tom Was Sold

Near the beginning of the story, Tom and Chloe are awakened after one of their prayer meetings by the knock of the agitated Eliza, a slave who was the personal servant to Mrs. Shelby, the slave master's wife. Eliza had been terrified to overhear her master and mistress arguing after he had sold Uncle Tom to a slave trader to satisfy his debts. Mr. Shelby was also throwing in Eliza's little son as an addition to the sale.

Here is a scene from the married life of Tom and Chloe at the time of their greatest personal crisis:

> "Good Lord! what's that?" said Aunt Chloe, starting up and hastily drawing the curtain. "My sakes alive, if it ain't Lizy! Get on your clothes, old man, quick!—there's old Bruno [the dog], too, pawin' round; what on airth! I'm gwine to open the door."
>
> And, suiting the action to the word, the door flew open, and the light of the tallow candle, which Tom had hastily lighted, fell on the haggard face and dark wild eyes of the fugitive.
>
> "Lord bless you!—I'm skeered to look at ye, Lizy! Are ye tuck sick, or what's come over ye?"
>
> "I'm running away,—Uncle Tom and Aunt Chloe,—carrying off my child,—Master sold him!"
>
> "Sold him?" echoed both, lifting up their hands in dismay.
>
> "Yes, sold him!" said Eliza, firmly; "I crept into the closet by Mistress's door to-night, and I heard Master tell Missis that he had sold my Harry, and you, Uncle Tom, both to a trader; and that he was going off this morning on his horse, and the man was to take possession to-day."
>
> Tom had stood, during this speech, with his hands raised, and his eyes dilated, like a man in a dream. Slowly and gradually, as its meaning came over him, he collapsed, rather than seated himself, on his old chair, and sunk his head down upon his knees.

"The good Lord have pity on us!" said Aunt Chloe. "Oh, it don't seem as if it was true! What has he done, that Mas'r should sell *him?*"

"He has n't done anything—it is n't for that. Master don't want to sell; and Missis,—she's always good. I heard her plead and beg for us; but he told her 't was no use; that he was in this man's debt, and that this man had got the power over him; and that if he did n't pay him off clear, it would end in his having to sell the place and all the people, and move off. Yes, I heard him say there was no choice between selling these two and selling all, but the man was driving him so hard. Master said he was sorry, but oh, Missis,—you ought to have heard her talk! If she an't a Christian and an angel, there never was one. I'm a wicked girl to leave her so; but, then, I can't help it. She said, herself, one soul was worth more than the world; and this boy has a soul, and if I let him be carried off, who knows what'll become of it? It must be right; but, if it ain't right, the Lord forgive me, for I can't help doing it!"

Run Away, Tom!

"Well, old man!" said Aunt Chloe, "why don't you go, too? Will you wait to be toted down river, where they kill niggers with hard work and starving? I'd a heap rather die than go there, any day! There's a time for ye,—be off with Lizy,—you've got a pass to come and go any time. Come, bustle up, and I'll get your things together."

Tom slowly raised his head, and looked sorrowfully but quietly around, and said,—

"No, no—I an't going. Let Eliza go,—it's her right! I would n't be the one to say no,—'t an't in *natur* for her to stay; but you heard what she said! If I must be sold, or all the people on the place, and everything go to rack, why, let me be sold. I s'pose I can b'ar it as well as any on 'em," he added, while something like a sob and a sigh shook his broad, rough chest convulsively. "Mas'r always found me on the spot,—he always will. I never have broke trust, nor used my pass no ways contrary to my word, and I never will. It 's better for me alone to go, than to break up the place and sell all. Mas'r an't to blame, Chloe, and he'll take care of you and the poor"—

Here he turned to the rough trundle-bed full of little woolly heads, and broke fairly down. He leaned over the back of the chair, and covered his face with his large hands. Sobs, heavy, hoarse, and loud, shook the chair, and great tears fell through his fingers on the floor: just such tears, sir, as you dropped into the coffin where lay your first-born son; such tears, woman, as you shed when you heard the cries of your dying babe. For, sir, he was a man—and you are but another man. And, woman, though dressed in silk and jewels, you are but a woman, and, in life's great straits and mighty griefs, ye feel but one sorrow!

Only Uncle Tom's Consecration Could Keep Him

Eliza makes a dramatic escape, but true to his word Uncle Tom stays behind to face the awful separation for the sake of his wife and children's safety. Like a sentence of death, being sold "down the river" meant it would be a miracle if he ever saw any of his loved ones again.

He also knew he faced an uncertain future of humiliation, pain, and suffering, helpless in the hands of a slave master from whom no law would protect him. *Only his consecration could keep him.*

The next morning, as Chloe tried to iron her husband's shirt one last time, she broke down and wept. Tom responded, in his uncommon wisdom,

"There'll be the same God there, Chloe, that there is here."

"Well," said Aunt Chloe, "s'pose dere will; but de Lord lets dreful things happen, sometimes. I don't seem to get no comfort dat way."

"I'm in the Lord's hands," said Tom, "nothin' can go no furder than he lets it;—and thar's *one* thing I can thank him for. It's *me* that's sold and going down, and not you nur the chil'en. Here you're safe;—what comes will come only on me; and the Lord, he'll help me—I know he will." . . .

Here one of the boys called out, "Thar's Missis a-comin' in!"

"She can't do no good; what's she coming for?" said Aunt Chloe.

Mrs. Shelby entered. Aunt Chloe set a chair for her in a manner decidedly gruff and crusty. She did not seem to notice either the action or the manner. She looked pale and anxious.

"Tom," she said, "I come to"—and stopping suddenly, and regarding the silent group, she sat down in the chair, and, covering her face with her handkerchief, began to sob.

Tom Meekly Followed His Master

"Lor, now, Missis, don't—don't!" said Aunt Chloe, bursting out in her turn; and for a few moments they all wept in company. And in those tears they all shed together, the high and the lowly, melted away all the heart-burnings and anger of the oppressed. Oh, ye who visit the distressed, do ye know that everything your money can buy, given with a cold, averted face, is not worth one honest tear shed in real sympathy?

"My good fellow," said Mrs. Shelby, "I can't give you anything to do you any good. If I give you money, it will only be taken from you. But I tell you solemnly, and before God, that I will keep trace of you, and bring you back as soon as I can command the money; and till then, trust in God!"

Here the boys called out that Mas'r Haley was coming [the new slave master, who had been trying to catch the fleeing Eliza,] and then an unceremonious kick pushed open the door. Haley stood there in very ill humor, having ridden hard the night before, and being not at all pacified by his ill success in recapturing his prey.

"Come," said he, "ye nigger, ye 're ready? Servant, ma'am!" said he, taking off his hat, as he saw Mrs. Shelby.

Aunt Chloe shut and corded the box, and getting up, looked gruffly on the trader, her tears seeming suddenly turned to sparks of fire.

Tom rose up meekly to follow his new master, and raised up his heavy box on his shoulder. His wife took the baby in her arms to go with him to the wagon, and the children, still crying, trailed on behind.

Tom Was Meek—Not Weak—and a Holy Man of God

As Stowe puts it, "Tom rose up meekly to follow his new master." Uncle Tom had come to a time in his life when he accepted a new Master into his life, the Lord Jesus Christ, so he could be meek as a slave when he had to lay down his life for his family.

When God sees meekness, He says, "Now you're ready to serve me, because you no longer live for yourself."

When you have the character quality of meekness, God can teach you secret things and give you authority, because He knows you'd never take advantage of anyone. But the only way He can train you is by presenting you with challenging situations until you get it right. If you argue, if you raise up, if you have to be right in everyone's eyes, God says, you can't be a leader.

You might be articulate; you might be educated; you might have a good mind; you might even be in a position of leadership, but you're not God's leader, you're man's leader. God says you've got to become a slave before you can be a master in the kingdom. That's how He did it with Jesus.

Black folks call people an "Uncle Tom" when we think they are selling out, but the real Uncle Tom was absolutely the opposite. He refused to sell out to bitterness and resentment. He held on to his holiness.

The truth is we hate to be holy. We associate meekness with weakness, but Uncle Tom was meek and incredibly strong.

Jesus said it was a blessing to be meek—to refuse to turn into a snake when you are stepped on—to lay down your life for others. He said, "Blessed are the meek: for they shall inherit the earth."[13]

Jesus said that "unless a grain of wheat falls into the ground and dies, it remains alone; but if it dies, it produces much grain."[14] Uncle Tom's death to his self-life produced a great crop of change in the lives of others.

Throughout the course of the book, Tom is sold and resold and finally ends up in the hands of one of the great villains of American literature, Simon Legree. Cassy and Emmeline, two slave women on the plantation where he lived whom Legree uses for sex, go into hiding. Because Tom will not reveal their whereabouts and because he tells Legree he needs to repent and be saved, Legree has him beaten until he is near death. In Tom's dying moments, far from his family but true to his Lord, he produces much grain for the kingdom.

Despairing Slaves Found Christ as Tom Lay Dying

Here's another dramatic scene from the story:

Tom had been lying two days since the fatal night; not suffering, for every nerve of suffering was blunted and destroyed. He lay, for the most part, in a quiet stupor; for the laws of a powerful and well-knit frame would not at once release the imprisoned spirit. By stealth, there had been there, in the darkness of the night, poor desolated creatures, who stole from their scanty hours' rest, that they might repay to him some of those ministrations of love in which he had always been so abundant. Truly, those poor disciples had little to give,—only the cup of cold water; but it was given with full hearts.

Tears had fallen on that honest, insensible face,—tears of late repentance in the poor, ignorant heathen, whom his dying love and patience had awakened to repentance, and bitter prayers, breathed over him to a late-found Saviour, of whom they scarce knew more than the name, but whom the yearning ignorant heart of man never implores in vain.

Cassy, who had glided out of her place of concealment, and, by overhearing, learned the sacrifice that had been made for her and Emmeline, had been there, the night before, defying the danger of detection; and, moved by the few last words which the affectionate soul had yet strength to breathe, the long winter of despair, the ice of years, had given way, and the dark, despairing woman had wept and prayed.

The Lord Was with Him, and Took Him Home

Tom had been gone from the plantation in Kentucky for many years, but his sacrifice for his family had not been in vain. His wife and family had stayed together because of it. Chloe had never given up hope that she might see her beloved husband again. She had even been earning the money to buy his freedom. Mrs. Shelby followed Tom's whereabouts so that as soon as she had the finances, Chloe could have him back.

Finally, Mr. Shelby died and his widow sent her son, George, now a man, to find the man who had loved him and mentored him in his slave cabin as a spiritual father, and to bring him home. And so, at Tom's death, there was young George, this son of the former slave master, a white man who as a boy used to read the Bible for the slaves in their Bible studies. There was one more life for Uncle Tom's meekness to reach for Christ.

"Bless the Lord! it is,—it is,—it's all I wanted! They have n't forgot me. It warms my soul; it does my old heart good! Now I shall die content! Bless the Lord oh my soul!"

"You shan't die! you must n't die!, nor think of it! I've come to buy you, and take you home," said George with impetuous vehemence.

"O, Mas'r George, ye're too late. The Lord's bought me, and is going to take me home,—and I long to go. Heaven is better than Kintuck."

"O, don't die! It'll kill me!—it'll break my heart to think what you've suffered,—and lying in this old shed here! Poor, poor fellow!"

"Don't call me poor fellow!" said Tom, solemnly. "I *have* been poor fellow; but that's all past and gone, now. I'm right in the door, going into glory! O, Mas'r George! Heaven has come! I've got the victory!—the Lord Jesus has given it to me! Glory be to His name!"

George was awestruck at the force, the vehemence, the power, with which these broken sentences were uttered. He sat gazing in silence.

Tom grasped his hand, and continued,—"Ye mus n't now, tell Chloe, poor soul! how ye found me;—'t would be so dreful to her. Only tell her ye found me going into glory; and that I could n't stay for no one. And tell her the Lord's stood by me everywhere and al'ays, and made everything light and easy. And oh, the poor chil'en, and the baby!—my old heart's been most broke for 'em, time and agin! Tell 'em all to follow me—follow me! Give my love to Mas'r, and dear good Missis, and everybody in the place! Ya don't know! 'Pears like I loves 'em all! I loves every creatur' everywhar!—it 's nothing *but* love! Oh, Mas'r George, what a thing 't is to be a Christian!"

At that moment, Legree sauntered up to the door of the shed, looked in, with a dogged air of affected carelessness, and turned away.

"The old satan!" said George, in his indignation. "It's a comfort to think the devil will pay him for this, some of these days!"

"O, don't—oh, ye must n't!" said Tom, grasping his hand; "he's a poor mis'able critter! It's awful to think on't! O, if he only could repent, the Lord would forgive him now but I'm feared he never will!"

"I hope he won't!" said George; "I never want to see *him* in heaven!"

"Hush, Mas'r George!—it worries me! Don't feel so! He an't done me no real harm,—only opened the gates of the kingdom for me; that's all!"

Death Had No Hold on Uncle Tom

When George Shelby came to him he said, "Uncle Tom, I found you and I've come to take you home." That would have made a great ending, right?

But Tom said, "You can't take me home; I'm about to go home to be with my Lord." Look at this! The kingdom was real to him! His wife's love was still real to him, but the kingdom of God was pulling him even more strongly.

George said, "Oh, look at what he did to you! This is terrible!"

But Tom said, "He didn't do anything to me but open up the doors of heaven so that I can go to be with my Father." Death had no hold on him. As the Scripture says, "We are confident, yes, well pleased rather to be absent from the body and to be present with the Lord. Therefore we make it our aim, whether present or absent, to be well pleasing to Him. For we must all appear before the judgment seat of Christ, that each one may receive the things done in the body, according to what he has done, whether good or bad. Knowing, therefore, the terror of the Lord, we persuade men."[15]

WALKING OUT THE CHRIST-LIKENESS
OF AN UNCLE TOM

Uncle Tom was abounding in the riches of Christ, so he knew that his life was pleasing to God. He was a slave, but he was able to love without a slave mentality, because he did not see himself as a slave of man but a slave of righteousness, the Bride of Christ. Even in his final hours he sought to persuade those around him that they must believe in the Lord Jesus Christ that they might be saved.

I am an Uncle Tom.

I am a slave of righteousness.

I want to walk in the faith of Uncle Tom, who saw the glory of God throughout his sufferings and lived in Christ's light eternally.

PRAYER FOR HUMBLING OURSELVES IN OUR RELATIONSHIPS

Father, in Jesus' name, I thank You now for the revelation of what You're speaking to me and what You're doing in me to make me humble. I want the full power of the measure of God worked in my life and in my home. Jesus, I realize that if I don't go down in my relationships and serve others, especially my wife, I won't be qualified to serve and lead in any other area of life. You said whoever is greatest among us must be a servant. Help me to serve today. Help me to take the lowest place. Help me to go down so You alone can raise me up.

God, I've been a prisoner to my own selfish desires. I'm so sorry. My hope has been diminished because I am so unlike You. So I'm asking You now, Lord, give me the vision for being loosed from my strongholds of pride, jealousy, and talking too much and too fast, and being ruled by my emotions and unforgiveness. Loose me from them, Father. Thank You for Your Word today. It's keeping me. I love You for it. I'm being changed from glory to glory. Purify my heart. Keep me in Your presence.

In Jesus' name I pray. Amen.

SELAH

1. Make a conscious effort to lay the same kind of spiritual foundation as Uncle Tom had, something that will withstand opposition to what you know is right. I recommend that you buy the book and read it.

2. Have you ever laid down your life for someone, either literally or figuratively? How did you feel about it afterward?

3. Have you ever sacrificed for someone, only to find out later that they were unworthy? That hurts. Imagine what depth of character it took for Jesus to do that for the whole human race. Write out some Scriptures related to His death, burial, and resurrection from the final chapters of the four Gospels. Meditate on their meaning for your life.

4. Considering what you have read from *Uncle Tom's Cabin,* meditate on the depth of character in the following prayer. Apply it to those in your own life who sometimes cause you to have "bad wishes in your heart."

A Slave Woman Prays for Her Master's Soul [16]

"O Lord, bless my master. When he calls upon thee to damn his soul, do not hear him, but hear me—save him—make him know he is wicked, and he will pray to thee.

"I am afraid, O Lord, I have wished him bad wishes in my heart—keep me from wishing him bad—though he whips me and beats me sore, tell me of my sins, and make me pray more to thee—make me more glad for what thou hast done for me, a poor [N]egro."

7

$\mathcal{I}$N-LAWS ARE NOT OUTLAWS

"Honor thy father and thy mother:
that thy days may be long upon the land
which the Lord thy God giveth thee."
—Exodus 20:12 KJV

At most wedding ceremonies, the father of the bride says only two words: "I do." He doesn't even create this little speech himself. At the wedding rehearsal, he's instructed to say those two words when prompted by the minister's question, "Who gives this woman to be married to this man?" That's all the input he gets to have in the service.

The fact is, the girl's daddy probably isn't giving the girl away at all. Probably the groom never asked his girl's daddy if he could marry her. He just asked the girl and she told her father.

Nobody consulted Daddy about the marriage. The speech by the father of the bride is just a formality. The wedding was all set up between his daughter and some guy she met.

RECAPTURING THE RIGHTFUL PLACE OF IN-LAWS

The father of the bride these days is like a farmer who works a field all his life until it becomes productive, only to have it snatched from him without his consent. This guy got to "harvest a field [he] never worked. Without lifting a finger, [he] . . . walked in on a field worked long and hard by others."[1]

It's time to recapture the rightful place of in-laws in the marriage of their children. We need to look again at how the destinies of two families are being changed forever when two people are married. Two children who have grown up under the covering of their parents are being merged into a whole new family line.

It hasn't been too long since a young man was expected to go to his girl's father and ask for her hand in marriage. In the Bible, not only did the man have to get permission from his girl's daddy for the hand of his daughter, he also had to pay a dowry. Here are two examples from Scripture.

In the book of Genesis is the story of how Laban told Jacob he could have his daughter Rachel in marriage if Jacob worked for him for seven years.[2] The Bible says, "Jacob served seven years to get Rachel, but they seemed like only a few days to him because of his love for her."[3] Because of Laban's trickery, however, when the wedding night came, Jacob actually consummated that marriage with Rachel's sister, Leah. He had to make a commitment to work for Laban another seven years to get Rachel, too.

In the book of 1 Samuel is the story of how King Saul set the price of one hundred dead Philistines for David to marry his daughter Michal. That was after David had already killed Goliath to get her.[4] David didn't care. He went out and killed two hundred Philistines. Saul was not the most righteous father-in-law. He was a lousy king. But David still respected him until the day he died, and when someone came and told David that he had killed Saul, expecting David to be happy that he could now take over as king, David had that person executed.[5]

How things have changed since those days. Now the father not only doesn't receive a dowry, he usually has to bear the full cost of the wedding—and still not get to say anything but "I do."

Commandment to Honor Father-in-Law and Mother-in-Law

The fifth of the Ten Commandments says "Honor thy father and thy mother."[6] When it speaks of the father and mother, it includes the father-in-law and mother-in-law, because of course they are one partner's parents.

In a practical sense, the in-laws (referring here to the bride's parents) were vitally involved in a wedding in Bible times because of the way the relationship was sealed. (You will find more details in Chapter 10.) First came a period of approximately one year of espousal. Then, when it was time for the wedding, instead of everybody going out to the synagogue for a brief service the way we do, the bride put on her gorgeous white robe and jewels and waited at her father's house for the groom. The groom, along with a noisy crowd of friends and music makers, came to the home of his bride's parents and received his bride with their blessings.

Then the groom took everybody to his own house or his father's house, accompanied by more music makers and merry-making friends, for the wedding feast. Often the whole community would get involved and join in.

In the evening, the bride's parents escorted her to a private room and the groom was taken there also, either by his friends or the bride's parents. The marriage was consummated while the guests continued the festivities. The bedsheet was saved by the bride's father. It was stained with blood if she was a virgin and therefore having intercourse for the first time, so he kept it for proof, in case her virginity was ever questioned.

No one ever questioned if the bride's parents and the groom's parents should be given a prominent place. It was obvious to everyone. God affirmed that with the commandment to honor them.

The word translated "honor" or "respect" is the Hebrew word *kabad,*[7] which means "weight." When you give weight to your in-laws' input, you honor their years of experience—including their raising your wife to be the person you wanted to marry. You give weight to the words that they speak. You especially honor them because God has commanded you to do it.

JETHRO: THE FATHER-IN-LAW OF MOSES

One of the most powerful examples in Scripture of a man honoring his in-laws is the story of Moses and Jethro. Moses was the man who met with God to receive the Ten Commandments, and who carried them to the people. I don't know if this scene made it into the movie version of *The Ten Commandments,* but after God met Moses at the burning bush and told him to go and rescue the Israelites in Egypt, Moses immediately took off to talk to his father-in-law, Jethro, before he went anywhere. Even though he had heard directly from God, Moses honored his father-in-law enough to ask his permission to leave town.

"Moses returned home and talked it over with Jethro, his father-in-law. 'With your permission,' Moses said, 'I will go back to Egypt and visit my relatives. I don't even know whether they are still alive.'

" 'Go with my blessing,' Jethro replied."[8] Moses was eighty years old at the time. That's a pretty serious in-law relationship, and Jethro wasn't even a believer. He was just a gracious father-in-law who was open enough for God to use.

We know from the Bible that Jethro later allowed his daughter and grandsons to return to his house for safety sometime during the siege in Egypt or the wandering in the wilderness, because there is a grand reunion scene when Jethro traveled to Moses' camp to bring the wife and children back.

While Moses was on the front lines for God, his father-in-law had been there for him. He had given Moses' wife and children a place of refuge. There is no record that he resented it. He just did it. And when Jethro returned them to his son-in-law, the two men who had spent forty years together tending Jethro's flocks had a joyful reunion. The Bible says, "And Moses went out to meet his father-in-law, and did obeisance, and kissed him; and they asked each other of their welfare; and they came into the tent."[9]

The words "did obeisance"[10] mean that Moses went all the way down on the ground and prostrated himself, the way that people did in those days to honor royalty or God. Moses, that great man of God, is a biblical example of a man who knew he was the product of all that his father-in-law had sowed into him, and Jethro is a biblical example of all that a father-in-law should be. Moses met God during the forty years he served in Jethro's house, working for his in-laws on the backside of the mountain. He did not meet Him during his forty years in the palace of Pharaoh.

Elders of Israel Honored Jethro

After the reunion scene, "Moses told his father-in-law about everything the LORD had done to Pharaoh and the Egyptians for Israel's sake and about all the hardships they had met along the way and how the LORD had saved them. Jethro was delighted to hear about all the good things the LORD had done for Israel in rescuing them from the hand of the Egyptians. He said, 'Praise be to the LORD, who rescued you from the hand of the Egyptians and of Pharaoh, and who rescued the people from the hand of the Egyptians. Now I know that the LORD is greater than all other gods, for he did this to those who had treated Israel arrogantly.' Then Jethro, Moses' father-in-law, brought a burnt offering and other sacrifices to God, and Aaron came with all the elders of Israel to eat bread with Moses' father-in-law in the presence of God."[11]

Because of Moses' attitude of respect, he opened the way for his father-in-law to come to know the true and living God. The elders of Israel also came to respect Jethro, and God came down in their midst as they all sat at the table together.

Jethro Had Seen the Potential in Moses

Jethro had substance. He also had a shepherd's heart. When Moses first met Jethro in Midian, he was an escaped murderer—a criminal on the Most Wanted List of the Egyptian Pharaoh. He had murdered someone because he had the desire to deliver his people from Egypt, but he did not have the heart to do it right.

Jethro saw enough potential in Moses to let him marry his daughter Zipporah and tend his flocks for the next forty years. During the early years of Moses' marriage, Jethro stuck with him. He gave him the support he needed. During that time he gave Moses the right heart for the calling that God was about to place on his life. Even after Moses had assumed leadership of the multitudes, he still honored his father-in-law, and still allowed Jethro to have valuable input into his life. This time, when he came to Moses in the wilderness, Jethro taught Moses how to shepherd the people of Israel.

Moses Received His Father-in-Law's Wise Advice

Listen to the great advice that Moses' father-in-law gave him about how to rule:

"The next day Moses took his seat to serve as judge for the people, and they stood around him from morning till evening. When his father-in-law saw all that Moses was doing for the people, he said, 'What is this you are doing for the people? Why do you alone sit as judge, while all these people stand around you from morning till evening?'

"Moses answered him, 'Because the people come to me to seek God's will. Whenever they have a dispute, it is brought to me, and I decide between the parties and inform them of God's decrees and laws.'

"Moses' father-in-law replied, 'What you are doing is not good. You and these people who come to you will only wear yourselves out. The work is too heavy for you; you cannot handle it alone. Listen now to me and I will give you some advice, and may God be with you. You must be the people's representative before God and bring their disputes to him. Teach them the decrees and laws, and show them the way to live and the duties they are to perform. But select capable men from all the people—men who fear God, trustworthy men who hate dishonest gain—and appoint them as officials over thousands, hundreds, fifties and tens. Have them serve as judges for the people at all times, but have them bring every difficult case to you; the simple cases they can decide themselves. That will make your load lighter, because they will share it with you. If you do this and God so commands, you will be able to stand the strain, and all these people will go home satisfied.'

"Moses listened to his father-in-law and did everything he said. He chose capable men from all Israel and made them leaders of the people, officials over thousands, hundreds, fifties and tens. They served as judges for the people at all times. The difficult cases they brought to Moses, but the simple ones they decided themselves."[12]

Jethro didn't see Moses as so highly elevated in leadership that he couldn't still give him input, and Moses wasn't so stuck on himself that he couldn't receive input from his father-in-law. Moses was being used by God to help the people settle their disputes, but Jethro, in the wisdom of his years, saw that the method Moses was using would wear him out. Because of the in-law relationship they had developed, a whole nation was affected.

"Then Moses sent his father-in-law on his way, and Jethro returned to his own country."[13] Jethro had the wisdom to know that

Moses' destiny was not his destiny. He went back to his own land, entrusting the care of his daughter and grandchildren to his son-in-law and God.

IN-LAWS CAN HELP A MARRIAGE

When my daughter Nicole decides she wants to be married, I know my wife and I will enter into the process knowing that we are not about to sever ties with someone who has spent all her life with us as our daughter. If a young man wants to separate a young lady from her parents, he is not the man for her.

At this point in time, we know our daughter better than he could possibly know her, just because of all the time that we have had her. We can help him to understand her and to love her more just on the basis of our experience. We can help him understand how she sees herself, what particular gifts and abilities she has that she might be too shy to tell him. If he respectfully encourages her to maintain close communication with us, even after they are married, their marriage will benefit because we will be just as committed to their marriage covenant as they are.

> Marriage is a merger—not just of a man and woman but also of their two families.

Marriage should be an extension of both family trees, with both sets of parents as full participants. Grandparents and great grandparents back through the generations all contributed something to what they are today.

A Wedding Ceremony Honoring In-Laws

As the mother and father of the bride, my wife and I would expect to be a vital part of the ceremony. One of the new elements I would introduce into the ceremony is an interchange between the father of the bride and the groom.

Charge to the Groom from the Father of the Bride

If I were presenting my daughter to the young man she was about to marry, this is what I would like to say:

Today I am here to present to you my daughter's hand in marriage.

My wife and I have provided for her needs. We have given her practical understanding of life, and supported her dreams. We have stood by her in the challenges that have come her way. At crunch times, when it seemed as if no one else cared, we were there for her. I was available to talk to her when she needed someone.

I have brought her up to be a woman of God suitable to marry a man of God. From the time my daughter was a child, we prayed that she would have a godly husband like you, a man who knew Jesus Christ as Lord and Savior. Her mother and I raised her in the fear and admonition of the Lord. We prayed for her and gave her the Scriptures. From her mother's womb I spoke the will of God into her life. I was an example before her as her father, and at some point, when she was mature enough, I asked her if she would want her husband to be like her daddy. She is a young woman of godly character, and we love her deeply. She may leave our house, but she can never leave our hearts.

I have brought her this far. Will you take her to the next level? If the answer to me is yes, I present her to you as a virgin, as God will present the Church as a virgin to marry Jesus Christ. I give her to you now, so that you may be for her not only what I was as a father, but also what only you can be to her as a husband. I will respect your relationship with her and the home that the two of you will establish. I will pray for you that you will be the kind of husband to her that Christ is to the Church, and that she will be a godly wife and helper to you.

As God blessed the first man and the first woman, who were created in His likeness, I bless my daughter, who has the likeness of her mother and me, and I bless you. And I say to you, "Be fruitful, and multiply, and replenish the earth, and subdue it, and have dominion."

May God bless the union of you and my daughter, and may

He always keep us close to one another in our hearts.

Groom's Response to the Father of the Bride

This is how the groom would respond:

Thank you for the gift of your daughter. I accept her with great humility and gratitude. I acknowledge and respect your position as her father and my father-in-law. I honor your wife as her mother and my mother-in-law. I pray that our relationship will be like Moses who, even when he grew into manhood and had a significant leadership role in history, retained a godly meekness and submission to his wife's father, Jethro.

It is my intention to give your daughter a home that is full of love and respect. She is a wonderful person from wonderful parents. I appreciate all that you and your wife have sown into her to help her become the person I am marrying today. She is the fruit of what you have given her.

This is my commitment to you, to her, and especially to God. As you have covered her with your name, I will cover her with my name. I will be a man of God for her. I will be a faithful husband. I will pray for her. I will take her to the next level. I will seed into her a new potential. I will love her unconditionally. I will provide for her. I will be a godly example to her.

I will believe God for our children to come, who will also be your grandchildren. I will teach them to respect you and I will raise them in the fear and admonition of the Lord. Our family will model out the kingdom with unconditional love. We will carry the godly seed you have sown into her into the next generation.

Occasionally I will present her to you so that your own personal times with her may continue. You will always be welcome in our home. When you come to visit us, you will see that she is becoming even more beautiful, both on the outside and on the inside. She will be growing more beautiful as she grows older, because of the loving care I intend to give her. She will realize the greatest joy and happiness as my wife, because I will be committed to her for the rest of my life.

The Minister's Charge to the Guests

Here is a response from the pastor after the interchange between the father of the bride and the groom, as he looks out at the wedding guests in the congregation:

You are witnesses of this covenant between the bride's father and the groom. You are about to be witnesses to a covenant between this man and this woman. Today you are adding your faith to these people that this marriage will succeed. If this marriage is not what God ordained it to be, you will be held to account. I am charging you that you must pray for them. You must support them. If this marriage becomes something that it ought not to be, if there is any violation, then you as a brother or sister must hold them accountable to do what God has ordained through their covenant.

RELATIONSHIPS OF RESPECT

How Husbands Can Show Respect for Their In-Laws

After the excitement of the wedding is over and the marriage begins, there will be a day-to-day realization of all that these people have promised to one another.

Here are some practical things that you as a husband can do to show respect for your in-laws and your parents.

Pray for them daily. Seek insight from the Bible about how you should relate to them in a godly way.

Find out from your in-laws what they want you to call them. Respect their age and position by not using their first names unless they specifically instruct you to do so.

Develop your own separate identity, but also let them have input in the early stages of your marriage, unless their presence is obviously destructive.

Stay sensitive to their financial needs, and help them whenever necessary, even if it's a sacrifice. Jesus challenged the scribes and Pharisees, "Why do you use your rules to play fast and loose with God's commands? God clearly says, 'Respect your father and mother,' and, 'Anyone denouncing father or mother should be killed.' But you weasel around that by saying, 'Whoever wants to, can say to father and mother, "What I owed to you I've given to God."' That can hardly be called respecting a parent."[14]

Encourage your wife to spend time with her parents, even if you can't always accompany her.

Encourage your wife to call her parents regularly. Call them occasionally yourself. Develop a level of intimacy with them as a member of the family. Don't allow yourself to feel like an outsider, even if some family members treat you that way.

Invite them to your home. Make them feel that they are always welcome. Prepare gracious meals when they come, and take them out to dinner sometimes.

Go easily and often to their home, if their home is open to you, and always find ways to help out when you're there. If they need extra help fixing something, mowing the lawn, etc., go there for that purpose on the weekends.

Discover what are their interests and become informed about them so you can carry on enjoyable, intelligent conversations. Don't always expect them to ask you about your interests. Ask about theirs. You will increase in wisdom and knowledge if you are willing to learn from them. "The father of the righteous will greatly rejoice, and he who begets a wise child will delight in him."[15]

If your father-in-law gives you instruction you don't think you need, don't get offended. Don't get inner conflicts. Listen to him. You might learn something. Keep the right attitude. That will please your Father in heaven. "My son, hear the instruction of your father, and do not forsake the law of your mother; for they will be a graceful ornament on your head, and chains about your neck."[16]

Don't worry if you don't seem able to measure up to their expecta-tions. If you are legitimately wrong or immature, they can help you. If you are right and they are wrong, the Lord can use them to teach you humility—if you stay low.

Try to please them, but don't be overly dependent on their approval of you. Honor them, and seek the approval of God.

Even if your in-laws are unfriendly, maintain the character of Christ toward them. How can you cherish your wife unless you try to win over her parents as if they were your own?

Don't speak against your in-laws to others. Speak well of them. Even if you have to privately seek counsel for a difficult situation, keep your manner as respectful as possible, even when they aren't there to hear you. "There are those who curse their father and mother, and feel themselves faultless despite their many sins. They are proud be-yond description, arrogant, disdainful. They devour the poor with teeth as sharp as knives!"[17]

Never try to turn your wife against her parents, even if they have been abusive to her in the past. Be supportive of her needs, but don't encourage her complaints or old hurts. Help her to forgive and trust God for the past. Help her to look at their positive side. Everybody has one. "[D]iscover beauty in everyone. If you've got it in you, get along with everybody. Don't insist on getting even; that's not for you to do. 'I'll do the judging,' says God. 'I'll take care of it.'"[18]

Thank them for the way they raised your wife. Show an interest in your wife's growing-up years, and look at old photos. If they seem open, ask about grandparents and other relatives in a friendly, posi-tive way.

Help your wife to remember their birthdays and anniversaries, and make sure there is always money budgeted for cards and gifts. Call or visit together on those days, and on Christmas, Easter, and other holidays like Mother's Day and Father's Day. Balance your visits so that both parents and in-laws receive time and attention.

When you make a mistake, admit it. Allow them to see your weaknesses sometimes. Their input may save you from making the same mistake again. "A man who refuses to admit his mistakes can never be successful. But if he confesses and forsakes them, he gets another chance."[19]

Teach your children to respect their grandparents. Encourage each child to develop a relationship with Grandma and Grandpa.

As they grow old and infirmities set in, continue to respect and seek out their wisdom. "Listen to your father's advice and don't despise an old mother's experience. Get the facts at any price, and hold on tightly to all the good sense you can get."[20]

If they are not Christians, love them into the kingdom. Don't drive them into hell with your superior "witnessing" attitude. "Winning souls" is not just about street-corner evangelism. It's also about lifestyle and relationships. It takes wisdom to win souls.[21] Remember how Moses won his unbelieving father-in-law to the true God by honoring him and respecting his counsel.

If someday they need to live with you, if at all possible let them move in with you, and be gracious about it. If they saw fit to take the trouble to raise your wife, you should take the trouble to care for them in their last years. Don't make them feel guilty. They might have just a little time left. The Bible says to "not hide yourself from your own flesh,"[22] or as it says in another version, "don't hide from relatives who need your help."[23]

How In-Laws Can Show Respect for Their Child and Their Child's Mate

If you are reading this book and you have children who are already married, or even if you are not at that stage yet, these next points can help you to be a godly in-law someday to your children's spouses.

Pray for them. God has called you to create a legacy for the kingdom of the Lord. When people follow your trail, it should lead them straight to the face of God, the will of God, the ways of God, the

mind of God. Your heart is crying out, "God, speak to me and somebody else's life will be changed. What you speak to me will be carried
out, because I will yield."

Guard your heart. Your children will be able to receive from you a
lot better if your heart toward them is right. Don't let the annoying
"little foxes"[24] in your relationship build up into something that sep-
arates your families. If they don't call often enough, so what? If they
don't write or send gifts, don't get an attitude about it. Don't even
bring it up. That's all in the flesh. You just focus on blessing them
regardless of what they do. That's what God does to you. "Don't
you realize how patient he is being with you? Or don't you care?
Can't you see that he has been waiting all this time without punishing
you, to give you time to turn from your sin? His kindness is meant
to lead you to repentance."[25]

Keep the right spirit when you speak to them. They will be willing to
take anything from you if they sense you have the right spirit.

*Don't try to control your children's lives. Let them make a few mis-
takes.* If they don't want your input, don't force it on them. Keep
loving them and praying for them. You may not even be right. Let
God give you an opening, and if He doesn't, keep quiet. Remember
that they are adults finding their way just as you did at their age.

Praise them with your words. Grown children need encouragement
even more than advice. Remember the "plus-minus-plus" formula—
give them twice as many compliments as correction. Here is an example of praising a godly woman from the Bible: " 'Many daughters
have done well, but you excel them all.' Charm is deceitful and
beauty is passing, but a woman who fears the Lord, she shall be
praised."[26]

Be an example and role model for them. "And here you yourself
must be an example to them of good deeds of every kind. Let everything you do reflect your love of the truth and the fact that you are
in dead earnest about it."[27]

As the father or father-in-law, be "serious and unruffled . . . sensible, knowing and believing the truth and doing everything with love and patience."[28]

As the mother or mother-in-law, "be quiet and respectful in everything [you] do. [You] must not go around speaking evil of others . . . but [you] should be teachers of goodness."[29] When the occasion arises, teach the wife how to love, honor, and serve her husband. "These older women must train the younger women to live quietly, to love their husbands and their children, and to be sensible and clean minded, spending their time in their own homes, being kind and obedient to their husbands so that the Christian faith can't be spoken against by those who know them."[30]

Talk to them as often as they seem to want to hear from you, but don't be calling them all the time, either.

Listen to them and show an interest in their affairs—without being bossy and interfering. "Your conversation should be so sensible and logical that anyone who wants to argue will be ashamed of himself because there won't be anything to criticize in anything you say!"[31]

Get to know the parents and family of your child's mate.

Be willing to share resources to help your children get started in their married life. Everyone needs more support in the early years than they do after they get rolling. Don't keep them dependent on you, but don't be afraid to rescue them occasionally, either, even with financial help. Don't put them down because they can't make it on their own. They don't know everything you know. Be kind and generous, and in the process, teach them good stewardship and a sense of personal responsibility. It should not be your goal to keep them in a position of begging for money from you for life, but to train them how to exercise stewardship and increase their resource base. In the process, you will be demonstrating your love and commitment in very practical ways.

Show your support in every way possible, especially in times of crisis. Don't look at your child's marriage as an escape from your responsibility. Your support relationship is for life.

If your son or daughter shows poor judgment, be merciful. Remember that you raised them, and some of what they are doing is probably what you taught them.

Don't let your child think he or she can move home with Momma if things get a little tough in their marriage. Help them to grow up by telling them, "I'm always available to talk to you, but this house is no longer available as a place for you to live. You're married now. You have to work things out. Marriage is a point of no return. God placed you together. There will be no divorce and no separation. I'm not someone you can run back to, unless it's to hear my counsel. The Bible says to leave your father and mother. I have to enforce that. The Bible says to cleave to your mate. I'm going to back God on that. You will be trying to make me sin if you come against this."

Show appreciation for your child's mate. Praise them for their accomplishments in education and career. Compliment their clothes, cooking, landscaping, artistic ability, etc.

Don't spoil the grandchildren (well, not too much), but do be attentive to them. Go to their games and recitals. Give them gifts that they like and are also approved by their parents.

Don't undermine your grandchildren's relationship with their parents. Reinforce to the grandchildren that their parents have wisdom and authority in their lives and that they are accountable to obey God's commandment to honor them.

If your child or their spouse is not a serious Christian yet, speak to them about your faith out of the compassion of Christ. Let them see your heart for them. I heard about one of the old-time preachers who had a great ministry, but when he told people about hell, someone said, it felt as if he were sending you there. When Billy Graham talks about hell, however, he has so much compassion you can tell he wants to keep you out of hell. You need to have that spirit.

Don't criticize their character. Help them grow up. People don't do what they are required to do for various reasons: irresponsibility, lack of knowledge, selfishness, rebellion. There can be too much emphasis on blaming them. Sometimes they just don't know how to do it right and need a father willing to teach them. "And now a word to you parents. Don't keep on scolding and nagging your children, making them angry and resentful. Rather, bring them up with the loving discipline the Lord himself approves, with suggestions and godly advice."[32]

Don't take sides when they have a dispute unless the matter is of grave importance. Don't favor your daughter or son over his or her mate. Don't say anything that could cause division between them. They are one flesh now, and so both of them are your children. They need wisdom, and so do you. Someone may not be telling you the whole story, anyway.

IN-LAW INTERVENTION

According to the biblical model, there are times when in-laws are justified in coming on with strong intervention in a marriage. An example from the book of Deuteronomy involves the issue of the bride's purity.

From the Bible: If the Wife's Virginity Is Questioned

In the Old Testament, as mentioned in Chapter 2, when a husband falsely accused his wife of not being a virgin when he married her, it was the father's responsibility to clear her name in court. He was the one who had retained the proof of her virginity from the marriage bed (the bloodstained sheets) for just such an unwelcome eventuality.

The accusation against the wife was considered a wrong against the father, and the father received compensation. Because of her father's protection, which lasted even into the time of her marriage, and his diligence to clear her name, after the trial was over the daughter received the assurance that her husband could never divorce her. "The judges shall sentence the man to be whipped, and fine him one hundred dollars to be given to the girl's father, for he has falsely accused a virgin of Israel. She shall remain his wife and he may never divorce her."[33]

Today: A Son-in-Law's Adultery

The father of the bride has the right to confront his son-in-law when he has committed adultery. He can go to him and say, "You had a covenant with me. You broke your covenant with me and with my daughter."

As I described it earlier in Chapter 3, the basis on which the father-in-law goes to his daughter's husband is this:

- *As her father*
- *As a witness at the wedding*
- *As a brother responsible for bringing sin to the attention of another man,* lest that man's blood be upon his hands [34]

A FATHER'S WORDS TO A SON-IN-LAW COMMITTING ADULTERY

If the son-in-law commits adultery, the father-in-law could confront him with words like these: "What are you doing by committing this terrible sin of adultery against my daughter? You have sinned against her and against me and against all the other witnesses who were with you at your wedding. I'm more than your father-in-law. I am a man of God. You are more than a son to me. You are a brother in the Lord. I heard you make a covenant with my daughter, and I am holding you to account for that vow. I have to hold you to account, because if you die in your sins and I don't tell you right now, your blood will be on me. You get yourself right before God and before my daughter. You come back to my daughter and repent at her feet."

How many fathers today are righteously intervening to save their daughter's name and protect her from divorce? (See Chapter 3 for additional details on addressing this problem.)

IN-LAWS ARE A BLESSING

God is blessed when He sees in-laws who love their children and their mates, and children who love and respect their in-laws. People once used the expression, "I'm not losing a daughter, I'm gaining a son." That's a good way for in-laws to look at it—gaining a full son.

My In-Laws Helped Me Grow

I'm glad now that I always allowed my mother-in-law and father-in-law to give input into our marriage. In my early stages of ministry, I had a heart for God and a vision for where God was leading us, but not much godly wisdom. My father-in-law gave me wisdom. He had always been a responsible person. He was a colonel in the army when not too many black men were being elevated to that rank. I didn't have too many positive experiences with a father, and he did some of the things a natural father would do.

One time he put himself on the line for me. My credit was so bad that I couldn't even rent a house, so he rented it for us on his credit and I paid him back. On our next house he paid the rent for a whole year. He was very much involved in helping me reestablish credit.

At the same time he was giving us that kind of financial help on his credit, he was advising me how to get my own financial house in order. I was a slow learner. He had a lot of patience with me, but one time he gave me a stern word I will never forget. He said, "You are a grown man now with your own wife and children. You can handle things a lot better than this. If you don't handle it this time, don't come back for any more money."

That sure speeded up the process of my development! Subconsciously, in the back of my mind, I still thought I could always go back, so I wasn't careful enough. He took that thought away and forced me to become a man.

My mother-in-law would say things to me about how I should run the house. Even though I didn't always agree with her, I gave her the freedom to speak her mind and didn't get defensive. She meant it for my good. Instead of avoiding her, I invited her input. Instead of insisting that my wife leave them and cleave to her husband, I initiated visits and communication so my wife didn't feel she had to have a secret relationship. I knew ultimately I would have to make the decisions in the house, but it was God-honoring to honor them. When my mother-in-law passed a few years ago, I was so glad I had encouraged my wife to spend so much time with her.

People Investing in People—That's Love

The best investment anyone can make is investing in people. It's the only investment we'll take with us to heaven. The Bible says, "All the special gifts and powers from God will someday come to an end, but love goes on forever."[35] Love is expressed in commitment—the willingness to give your best to someone, to give your all, to do things for people even when you think they don't deserve it, helping them up one more time when you know they might fall down again. That's what my in-laws did for me.

PRAYER OF GRATITUDE FOR PARENTS

Father, thank You for the revelation of Who You are, for an understanding through the washing and cleansing of the blood, found only by the reality of the Holy Spirit.

Thank You for the preparation of our fathers and mothers for us. Thank You for parents who had the substance of gold, some of silver, some of brass, some of wood, but with all of them a preparation was made for our future. We need their substance and Yours for what You are preparing us to be in the world to come.

Thank You for what You are building in Your house, which we are. Thank You for what You are building in the homes of our families. You have translated us out of this world into the power and kingdom of Your dear Son, walking not according to the dictates of this realm but of Your realm.

Father, we ask You for help because we need it so badly. Focus our hearts on Your Word. We need Your Word moment by moment. Strengthen us in our weaknesses, in the tender years. Launch us when it is time for us to reach the age of accountability.

Open our eyes. Open our ears. Open our hearts so that we might become even more tender as You speak to us.

In Jesus' name we come against all works of evil. We stand strong in His finished work on the cross. With His stripes we are healed—in our body, soul, and spirit.

In Jesus' name we pray. Amen.

SELAH

1. Read in the Bible the stories of Jacob and David mentioned at the beginning of the chapter. (See Notes for references.)
2. Create your own charge for the father of the bride and response from the groom that could be used in a wedding ceremony. If you have a daughter, personalize it for her.
3. Look again at the section on how to have a better relationship with your in-laws, or how to be a better in-law. List personal applications that you can carry out in your own family.
4. Read the Scriptures below for information and revelation on family relationships.

Exodus 20:12 (KJV)
Exodus 21:15 (NIV)
Exodus 21:15 (TLB)
Exodus 21:17 (TLB)
Leviticus 19:1–3 (NKJV)
Leviticus 19:32 (NIV)
1 Kings 2:19 (TLB)
Proverbs 1:7 (TLB)
Proverbs 15:5 (TLB)
Proverbs 20:20 (NIV)
Proverbs 23:22 (TLB)
Proverbs 28:24 (TLB)
Proverbs 30:11 (NKJV)
Proverbs 30:17 (TLB)
Malachi 1:6 (NIV)
Malachi 4:4–6 (NKJV)
Matthew 10:21 (KJV)
Romans 1 (*The Message*)
1 Timothy 5 (*The Message*)

8

CHILDREN ARE A BLESSING FROM THE LORD

Three of the most important sentences
you can say to your children are these:
I love you.
I believe in you.
You can do it.

Jesus said, "There was once a man who had two sons. The younger said to his father, 'Father, I want right now what's coming to me.'

"So the father divided the property between them. It wasn't long before the younger son packed his bags and left for a distant country. There, undisciplined and dissipated, he wasted everything he had. After he had gone through all his money, there was a bad famine all through that country and he began to hurt. He signed on with a citizen there who assigned him to his fields to slop the pigs. He was so hungry he would have eaten the corncobs in the pig slop, but no one would give him any.

"That brought him to his senses. He said, 'All those farmhands working for my father sit down to three meals a day, and here I am starving to death. I'm going back to my father. I'll say to him, "Father, I've sinned against God, I've sinned before you; I don't deserve to be called your son. Take me on as a hired hand."' He got right up and went home to his father.

"When he was still a long way off, his father saw him. His heart pounding, he ran out, embraced him, and kissed him. The son started

*his speech: 'Father, I've sinned against God, I've sinned before you;
I don't deserve to be called your son ever again.'*

"But the father wasn't listening. He was calling to the servants,
'Quick. Bring a clean set of clothes and dress him. Put the family
ring on his finger and sandals on his feet. Then get a grain-fed heifer
and roast it. We're going to feast! We're going to have a wonderful
time! My son is here—given up for dead and now alive! Given up for
lost and now found!' And they began to have a wonderful time.*"[1]

That is Jesus' parable of the prodigal son.

PRODIGAL CHILDREN

A Modern-Day Prodigal Son

A few years ago, the wife of evangelist Billy Graham, Ruth Graham,
wrote a book about her journey through the youthful spiritual tur-
moil of her son Franklin. She called it *Prodigals and Those Who
Love Them*.[2]

You would never know it today, but at one point in his life, Franklin was a prodigal—an absolute rebel who acted more like one of his
father's opponents than his son. As a young man in his twenties, he
smoked and drank, rode a motorcycle, and shot machine guns for
fun, while still trying to keep a foothold in the door of the Church.

As he tells it, on his twenty-second birthday in 1974, his father
once again confronted him with the same truth with which the elder
Graham has confronted millions of people during his fifty-plus years
in ministry: the love of God and the claims of Jesus Christ on his
life. The elder Graham said, "You can't continue to play the middle
ground. Either you're going to choose to follow and obey Him or
reject Him."

Without committing himself, Franklin went off on a trip to the
Holy Land, but in a hotel room near Jerusalem, God got hold of him
and wouldn't let him go. As Jesus said in the parable of the prodigal
son, he "came to himself."

Franklin said later, "I put my cigarette out and got down on my
knees beside my bed. I was His. . . . The rebel had found the cause."

The verse from the Bible that meant the most to him at that time
was this one from Romans 8:1: "There is therefore now no condem-

nation to them which are in Christ Jesus."[3] I know Franklin didn't have perfect parents, even though they're famous Christian leaders, but he did have parents who loved him and believed in him. They didn't condemn him. They always tried to show him the way out. Maybe that gave him the hope and perseverance to find out how much God loved him and believed in him, too.

Parents, Like God, Don't Give Up

Parents who refuse to give up on their wayward children are just like God. They don't stop valuing them when they become an embarrassment and a source of frustration, because that is not like the Father. Our Father is like the prodigal's father. We can come to Him with a wasted life, having ruined ourselves financially and every other way, and He's just glad to see that we've come home.

In Franklin Graham's case, this once prodigal son is poised to someday take over the leadership of one of the greatest evangelistic ministries of all time. Potentially millions of souls could be affected.

God the Father sent His Son to die for Franklin Graham before he ever did anything to deserve it. That unconditional love of the Father is a quality God longs to see in parents everywhere, because it is absolutely awesome when parents act like God!

Parents Love the Real Person Inside

At the end of Jesus' parable of the prodigal son, the elder brother had his say. He was mad! He didn't see why his brother should be given a party after the terrible things he had done. His standard of value was based on accomplishment, and he didn't see anything worth valuing in his wastrel brother. He challenged his father's judgment and called attention to his own superior value, *in his eyes,* because he had followed the letter of the law.

The elder brother didn't understand that his father wasn't endorsing the prodigal's sin. The father was choosing to value *who he was* more than *what he had done.* We have to learn to value who our children are more than what they do—both good and bad.

The father loved both his sons and he believed in them. When he saw his son coming home, he knew that his character had conquered. He had come to a place of brokenness that was promotable and to be praised, while the elder son demonstrated only pride. The prodigal had come back with the right heart, ready to submit to his father, while the elder son was ready to be superior to his father. Only the first quality was worthy of celebration.

Jesus told the rest of the story: "The older brother stalked off in an angry sulk and refused to join in. His father came out and tried to talk to him, but he wouldn't listen. The son said, 'Look how many years I've stayed here serving you, never giving you one moment of grief, but have you ever thrown a party for me and my friends? Then this son of yours who has thrown away your money on whores shows up and you go all out with a feast!'

"His father said, 'Son, you don't understand. You're with me all the time, and everything that is mine is yours—but this is a wonderful time, and we had to celebrate. This brother of yours was dead, and he's alive! He was lost, and he's found!' "[4]

The prodigal's father paid attention to his son when he came home because he saw something genuine that had changed in his character. When Jesus said he "came to himself," he also could have said that he died to himself. He died to the desire to sin, and that is a major accomplishment in any son's life. The son was dead, but he came to life again when he thought of going to his father. That's the way we are to be with God: "dead indeed unto sin, but alive unto God through Jesus Christ our Lord."[5]

RELATING TO YOUR CHILDREN IN CHRIST-LIKENESS

Are Your Children Bothering You?

It's interesting to watch what happens on Sunday mornings when children burst out of their classrooms and children's church and rush in to be with their parents. Sometimes it's not only interesting, it's overwhelming! If nobody stops them, those crumb-snatchers end up running around the sanctuary after one another, beating on the drums, and picking up thousand-dollar microphones as if they were toys. They usually start by pulling on their parents to interrupt their conversations, but the parents are so involved in talking to their friends whom they haven't seen since last Sunday that the kids don't get much attention. That's what opens the floodgates for the kids to start their demolition derby.

The things you reinforce by your attention are the things you'll get from that child on a consistent basis. And most of the time what you reinforce is what meets *your* needs, not necessarily his or hers. You don't want him bothering you. You don't want to be disturbed. You have something else you would rather do. You get impatient with her childish ways. All of those feelings make you want to put a lid on your child, but not necessarily to teach her what is right.

How Your Pride Hurts Your Child

Let's face it. Another motivation that is very strong in child-raising is pride. For example, your excitement over the child's first step may be motivated by a desire to tell people about it—to boast. That's one of the hard things about having a handicapped child. You can't feed your pride because you can't compete on the same fleshly level as everybody else.

One of the reasons that parents disown their wayward children is that the prodigal's erratic behavior cuts into their bragging rights. Most parents, if they're honest, will admit they are in competition with other parents over the accomplishments of their children. Because of their insecurities, they want to find things to boast about to other parents from the time that the child is born. They boast about when he sits up, when she has started teething, how early he walks, when she says her first words. We need to look at what kind of psychological impact that train of thinking has on our children.

There's nothing wrong with encouraging our children to be the best they can be. Kids learn fast that they need to perform to get your attention, and that the requirements keep getting higher. That can have a positive effect on their advancement, but not when their achievement becomes tied to their value, especially in the eyes of their parents.

Your boasting could be a bad seed that will eventually take your child into the wrong kind of competition. He tries to excel in school so you will approve of him and can boast about him. His whole sense of your love comes from his performance. If you promote that kind of thing, you totally miss his true value inside. You are instilling in your children that they have to be at the top of the class, because that makes you feel the most proud, instead of rewarding them for doing the best they can.

There's nothing wrong with striving to excel, and we should, because God is an excellent God. If it turns out that your child ends up at the top of the class through hard work and faithfulness, that's great, but don't make yourself in some subconscious way seem better than other parents because your child makes better grades or stands alone on top of his peers. That's not a true analysis of value.

It could be that your child has the personal gifts to lead the class, but maybe she doesn't. Maybe she accomplishes more among people in private, when nobody's watching, which has just as much long-term value. If your children work hard and do the best they can and still don't make first place, don't let them get discouraged. Tell them, "Do your best again the next time! That's all that's required. That's a seed. God is watching. He knows if you're doing your best and still not seeming to win."

Parents should reinforce to their children as they grow up a balanced desire to be the best they can be but with the understanding that they may need more knowledge or more character development to increase their level. That's why children need love and acceptance and somebody to say "I believe in you," whether they get a good grade or a promotion or not. Those things don't determine intrinsic value. You're valuable, period, because you're made in the image of God. Everybody learns differently and at different speeds. Lots of people who did poorly in school ended up as a success in life when they entered into their destiny from God. And most successful people had at least one person who loved them and believed in them, not necessarily their own parents. Somebody else's child may need your love and encouragement, too.

Giving Extravagant, Unexpected Love

If you want to create a divine wonder in your children, show them extravagant love when nothing special is happening. They aren't doing anything to get your attention. They haven't done anything remarkable lately. They're just sitting there minding their own business and you start loving up on them. That will help them understand in a small way the wonder of God's awesome love for us.

Give them a hug and say to them something like this:

"I just love you because you're my child!"

"I'm so glad God gave you to me!"

"You're so wonderful!" (They did nothing special to cause you to say that, they just *are* special.)

"Come here and hug me. Give me a hug."

They'll probably start laughing and say, "What did I do?" Or if they're cynical they may ask, "What do you want?" But you let it all roll off and you say, "You don't have to do anything. I just love you because you're my kid and you're wonderful. You're God's gift to me. There's nothing you could do to make me love you more. I love you!"

Wow! There was no performance attached to it. No having to earn a hug or earn words of commendation. You're reaffirming to them that they're special just because of who they are. "You're my kid. Your Dad just loves you." That will be so tremendously helpful to your family if you can keep doing it.

Telling Your Children That You Believe in Them

I'm moved by this phrase "I believe in you," because I think that's what God sent His Son for—not only to be a sacrifice but also to prove with His sacrifice that He believed in you, before you could ever accomplish anything to please him.

God says "I believe in you" while you're still a rebel, or unproved, and then sows into you what's necessary to bring your change. The prodigal's father gave him the family money and then he gave him a ring and a party, because he sensed that each time that gift was what the young man needed to bring his change. God's love and acceptance make it possible for you to accomplish the things that please Him. Condemnation and judgment could never accomplish that. That's something to remember when you are trying to figure out how to raise your children.

I continually have to ask God to help me to love my children more, the way He loves me. I don't ever want them to think I don't believe in them. I have a lot of spiritual children as well as natural ones. Probably the thing that hurts me about myself the most is when I fall below God's standard, and let a person's faults take out of me the faith that he can rise up and be changed.

It bothers me when I realize the times that I have not seen the potential in someone and have been moved only by their outward character, especially when their bad attitudes have been directed toward me. That's when I need to be the most like God, because my unconditional love in crunch time can direct them to my Father. If I'm not an example of His unconditional love in that way, that drives me into His face. And as the prodigal's father shows us, God's unconditional love is demonstrated through us not only by words but also by deeds.

> **Your child will change through your change.**

Admitting Weaknesses Helps Your Child Change

One of the keys in successful parenting is taking the focus off the child's faults and on your own. If you make a commitment to strive for Christ-likeness in your parenting, your child will change through your change. If all you ever see is the child's weaknesses and none of yours, they will lose the motivation to do what is right. You may think you are always winning because none of your faults are being exposed and all of theirs are, but nobody is really winning. Total integrity is the answer. Admitting your faults, saying to your child "I'm sorry" when you're wrong, disciplining them but then having a reunion after it's over—all of that helps heal the hurts of growing up into Christ-likeness.

It may go against your nature to make yourself vulnerable to your children by admitting your faults, but it will bring a breakthrough in your relationship with them. You don't have to detract from your position as their parents and become their buddy to do it, either. They are still to honor you as the head of the family team.

Your Commitment to Your Children as They Change

Robert Schuller tells the story of one public-school teacher who influenced a whole generation of ghetto children by loving them and believing in them. A study had been done of these particular elementary-school children to determine their potential for success. The prediction was dismal: The study concluded that most of them would end up dead or in jail within a few years. Many years later, another study was done, and the researchers were astounded; Almost all of them had led successful lives. Only a handful had even minor trouble with the law. When the researchers tracked down the reason why these kids beat the odds, almost all of them pointed out one particular teacher they had along the way. She made the difference because she loved them and believed in them and taught them what they needed to know—not only in the classroom but also in life.

If one teacher who had those children for a few hours a day for a single year could make that much difference, what effect could you expect from parents who love and believe in their children for life? If you are a parent, what are you doing with your time that is more important than sowing your love and capabilities into your children? God has equipped you with what you need not only to be a successful husband but also to be a successful father.

YOUR ATTITUDES DETERMINE YOUR ALTITUDE

If you want God to move you into a more influential position in your children's lives, don't just look at *their* attitudes, look at *your own*. In God, your attitudes determine your altitude. He can raise you up only to the extent that you are willing to go down and yield to Him, letting Him make you more like Jesus.

Gaining Confidence for Raising Children

I think past generations had a lot more confidence in the way they raised their children. They believed that what they were doing would make a difference in the way the kids turned out. They followed this old adage from Proverbs: "Train up a child in the way he should go: and when he is old, he will not depart from it."[6] Maybe that's because he had parents who helped him find his way.

Finding the way a child should go is the responsibility of the parent, not the child. It involves years of prayer to find that out, and a lifestyle of building on the abundance of positives you see in your child instead of harping on the few negatives. It takes faith in God that He called you to raise these particular crumb-snatchers for His glory.

Lifting Them Up, Not Putting Them Down

Children demand attention by doing "bad" things, make no mistake about it. But if you're always looking at something that's wrong rather than looking for something that's right, your focus is all wrong. You get stopped in the process of finding the way your child *should* go because you're so busy telling them the way they *shouldn't* go. You put them down when you should be raising them up. Instead of being a supply to help them get off the ground, you become a weight to keep them grounded.

What if Jesus were like that? If He wanted to micromanage us, He would find so many things wrong He wouldn't be able to do a thing for us. But He knows our need and He gets more pleasure meeting those needs than pointing out our faults. Jesus knew both the Spirit and the letter and He still died for us.

Conviction of Sin Includes Comforting

The Holy Spirit convicts us of sin, but in a spirit of comfort. When the Holy Spirit fills our homes, we have heaven there. Home is not a place of discomfort. It's a place of comfort. It's a place where the whole world can be against you, but you can come home and find help. Somebody said, "Home is the place where when you go there they have to take you in." The Lord wants heaven in your home because that's a natural example of what you're going to have when you get before the Father. He'll say, "C'mon in! I've been expecting you!" and you'll walk right in as if you'd been there all your life, because of course you have. Heaven is just an extension of the way you've been living on earth.

Giving Children the Home-Court Advantage

When you have heaven in your home, you have peace. At home there's joy. At home there is someone on your side. At home you have unity. At home you have love unconditionally. At home you're not vying for position.

The home-court advantage for children means that the only time a child gets booed is when they sin, but even then they know they're not being rejected. Only their sin is getting rejected. They can change and get rid of the sin. Anybody can. That's our destiny, to continually clean away the sin areas and be pure.

The home-court advantage means that you have fans who keep cheering you on just because you suit up. Even if you sit on the bench, you get cheered, because the issue isn't performance. It isn't even winning in natural terms. The issue is winning in Christ. Your actions become more like Jesus than like the world.

Your children are not your enemies. Your enemies are their sins. Your enemies are the worldliness in your children. Your enemies are the works of the flesh and the devil's influence over your children. That's the issue. If you defeat the right enemies, you can keep the home-court advantage because your actions show you appreciate your children and want them to have every advantage in their home.

Children may rebel but won't permanently turn against their fans—their parents. They'll try to do things to please you, and seek your applause, knowing inside when your praise is motivated by genuine love and confidence in them and their future greatness.

A child's home-court advantage means that regardless of what they do—right or wrong—they still have favor. They know that their parents will never turn against them. You may disapprove of their actions and discipline them accordingly, but you never disapprove of *them*.

On the home court, a child receives attention all the time. He is always on display, always getting cheers. Children don't always know the boundaries and do a lot of things to gain attention, even when you have company or are on the phone. As parents, you have to learn to discern the difference between a kid acting up and acting out a need. You have to learn the difference between whining and crying out of a legitimate hurt.

When he has the home-court advantage, a child gets corrected into Christ-likeness. As their parents, you are noncompromising on shaping the character qualities they need to see their sins and their absolute need for God. You teach them how to be honest when they have sinned, to repent, to receive if necessary whatever penalty has been set out beforehand, and then to receive God's forgiveness through your forgiveness.

On the home court, children don't become spoiled-brat superstars. They become trained for the challenging encounters that come with life.

Changing Your Children Inwardly Takes Love, Not Just Law

"[W]e can't round up enough containers to hold everything God generously pours into our lives through the Holy Spirit!

"Christ arrives right on time to make this happen. He didn't, and doesn't, wait for us to get ready. He presented himself for this sacrificial death when we were far too weak and rebellious to do anything to get outselves ready. And even if we hadn't been so weak, we wouldn't have known what to do anyway. We can understand someone dying for a person worth dying for, and we can understand how someone good and noble could inspire us to selfless sacrifice. But God put his love on the line for us by offering his Son in sacrifical death while we were of no use whatever to him.

"Now that we are set right with God by means of this sacrificial death, the consummate blood sacrifice, there is no longer a question of being at odds with God in any way. If, when we were at our worst, we were put on friendly terms with God by the sacrificial death of his Son, now that we're at our best, just think of how our lives will expand and deepen by means of his resurrection life! Now that we have actually received this amazing friendship with God, we are no longer content to simply say it in plodding prose. We sing and shout our praises to God through Jesus, the Messiah!"[7]

We have a loving God who believed in us before we ever did anything to make Him believe in us. He just loved you and said, "I believe in you."

The Lord changes us by love—not by Law. The Law was already there but we remained unchanged. Our Father changes us by His grace, His unmerited favor, His unconditional love that reaches out to us without condemnation in spite of His knowing everything bad about us that we've ever done.

Parents who try to control their children only from the outside—by laying down the law—won't reach the child's inner man, where godly character and zeal for God are developed. They have to do that through love.

When you're dealing with discipline, you keep your children's flesh from causing anarchy in your house by law and punishment, but that's not the sole basis on which you build your relationship. You have to lay aside your wrath, then reach their hearts with unconditional love, just as God did for us "while we were still sinners."[8]

You control the flesh of a child from the outside, but you change him from the inside. That's how God works in us. God changes us from the inside out. As we yield our hearts and minds to Him, He brings everything under His control. He made us, so He knows what we need to get the kind of order in our lives that will make us blessed.

Loving Children Before They Change

Singing and shouting praises to God comes naturally when we love Him with all we've got. If we don't love God extravagantly, as Jesus taught, how can we love our children and our neighbors?

"Jesus said, 'The first in importance is, "Listen, Israel: The Lord your God is one; so love the Lord God with all your passion and prayer and intelligence and energy." And here is the second: "Love others as well as you love yourself." There is no other commandment that ranks with these.' "[9]

The same verses from Mark 12 in the familiar words of the King James Version sound like this: "The first of all the commandments is, Hear, O Israel: The Lord our God is one Lord: And thou shalt love the Lord thy God with all thy heart, and with all thy soul, and with all thy mind, and with all thy strength: this is the first commandment. And the second is like, namely this, Thou shalt love thy neighbor as thyself. There is none other commandment greater than these."[10]

Children need to be loved before they can change their behavior. Law can control behavior, but love is needed to permanently change it. Law is temporary, but love is eternal. You can have someone checking up on your behavior all day long and you will follow the letter to stay on their good side, but as soon as they're gone you're a wild man, following your inward desires.

When we're raising children, we first write the Law on their minds by the letter, but then God writes it on their hearts by the Spirit. First the natural, then the spiritual. First the temporal, then the eternal. That's part of the great mystery of life. That's why we can keep believing in our children regardless of all the outward "yuk." God created them, so God placed in them the potential for right behavior.

God changes behavior by the Spirit. The fruit of the Spirit is love, joy, peace, patience, kindness, goodness, gentleness, faithfulness, and self-control.[11] Fruit produces after its own kind, so the fruit of the Spirit you exhibit toward your children will be reproduced in their lives, too. These inner attributes will keep working even if nobody is around to enforce them, because they come from a force within that makes you want to be good, and kind, and faithful, and loving, just as a matter of course.

The Law is good, as Jesus said, but when you rely exclusively on the Law, you're only into sin management by authority figures, not permanent change. When you get to know God, His love and confidence in you change your life forever. That's one reason we must make sure our children come to know God—not just so they can escape from hell and go to heaven but also so they can get that impartation of Christ-likeness inside.

One of the goals God has for parents is to develop the inner man of their child. They do it by instruction, "line upon line, here a little, and there a little,"[12] and they also do it by example. Just as parents study the Bible in order to be more like God, our children are studying us. "Be ye therefore followers of God as dear children."[13] "Watch what God does, and then you do it, like children who learn proper behavior from their parents. Mostly what God does is love you. Keep company with him and learn a life of love."[14]

Rewarding Your Child's Growth in Maturity

God grants increased authority based on increased character development, just as a father gives children increasing privileges as he sees that they have mastered increasing levels of responsibility. If children consistently come home on time at one certain hour, they may be allowed to stay out later to see if they are also able to keep that deadline. If children faithfully do their homework without being told, they don't have to be accountable to you every day to report that they have done it.

Present stewardship determines future responsibility. What you steward well now gives you the experience and credibility to steward something else later.

Children develop character and stewardship ability from their parents most effectively when the children submit to them. Those principles are worked out in simple ways at first, such as being responsible for picking up their little clothes and toys and helping out around the house. If they are faithful with those things, maybe they will be allowed to take care of a pet and eventually the family car. What children learn at home about being responsible is their introduction to authority and submission. These principles and practice will help them become a success in life.

SUBMISSION IS THE MODEL

God Set Up the Submission System

All authority is delegated authority. God delegated authority to parents over their children by saying to all children everywhere, "Honor your father and mother."[15] He delegated authority to the husband as head of the family, and delegated authority to his wife as his helpmate and confidante and covenant partner in their responsibilities.

As parents you have to deal with a lot of subtle and not-so-subtle attacks on the biblical structure of authority and submission you are trying to teach your children. You expect it from their peers, but you also get challenges from schoolteachers, television, movies, magazines, and newspapers. Public figures are often rebels, from sports stars to recording artists and from movie stars to public officials, and their words and attitudes are contagious to your children.

Jesus Loved Seeing Submitted People

Jesus loved to see proper authority structures in action, because He knew it represented the stability of the kingdom. When a Roman centurion came to Jesus,[16] to plead with him to heal his servant, Jesus offered to go to his house. The centurion was a humble man, in spite of his position, and he also understood the powerful concept of authority. His acceptance of the importance of authority and submission in human relationships actually showed him something about God that increased his faith. He saw what God could accomplish with His absolute authority over the universe, because he knew what he could accomplish with his limited authority over his small world of influence. The temporal was a model of the eternal.

Parents who let their children get away with rebellious attitudes toward them are not only setting them up for failure in the "real world" of social structures in church, school, and business, they are also depriving them of future faith in the power of God. If their parents are powerless against them, how can they believe in an all-powerful God?

HOW TO TEACH YOUR CHILDREN TO RESPECT YOU

- *Jesus as the head of the family.* Make Jesus the head of your family, and follow Him. Seek to meet *His* needs with your marriage and family, not your own needs.
- *Prayer.* Pray for your family, asking God to help all of you with your attitudes.
- *Bible teaching.* Teach your children what the Bible says about honoring parents and people in authority, including Bible stories that demonstrate those principles.
- *Godliness.* Interact with one another with the same level of respect that the Father, Jesus, and the Holy Spirit use in their interaction with one another. They don't fight with one another out of pride. The devil is the one who does that.
- *Husbands modeling respect.* Love your wife as Christ loves the Church. Always show respect for your wife in front of your children. Love her as Christ loves the Church. Penalize your children's disrespect for your wife, including times when you're not around and she reports on secret acts of rebellion.
- *Wives modeling respect.* Submit to your husband as you submit to the Lord. Always show respect for your husband in front of your children. Acknowledge him as head of your family. Don't let your children speak to you in ways disrespectful of their father. Correct them. Build him up in their eyes.
- *Corporate agreement.* Work out a plan for your family as a husband-wife team. God put you together because you both need each other's input.
- *Disagreeing but maintaining respectful attitudes.* If you disagree on something as husband and wife, speak about it to each other in a Christ-like way, as a model for the children, or work it out privately.
- *Bottom-line decisions left to the husband.* In the rare instances where a husband and wife cannot agree, she must submit to the husband's final word, remembering that meekness is not weakness, but strength, and that God is the ultimate Judge of right and wrong. If the husband is in sin, as a wife pray for God's mercy on him, because no one can escape His wrath.
- *Faithfulness in your position.* Don't strive for more rights. Be

faithful in whatever roles and responsibilities you have now, and let God be the one to promote you.

· *Acting like an adult.* Children fight to gain a high position. Mature adults fight to stay low.

· *Continually seeking to build Christ-like character.* Study the ways of Jesus, and prayerfully model your life after Him.

· *Remembering God's role for you in eternity.* This life is just on-the-job training for the future. God can't use you as a ruler in His eternal realm if you always fight back like a child now.

Submission in Family Relationships

Respect never gets outdated. In previous generations, respect for parents was not optional. It was required. Disrespect was punished severely with the rod of correction! However, these days there is so much rejection of biblical standards of submission and authority, especially by misguided women's groups, that children are growing up as rebels. The blame must also fall heavily on the men, who are un-Christ-like—either in a heavy-handed approach toward their authority over their wives, or in a refusal to take unpopular actions at all.

My kids don't mess with my woman. People learn about authority and submission from watching other people. I teach my children to respect their mother by respecting her myself and submitting to her in all the appropriate ways. I tell my children, "If you mess with my woman, you've earned my wrath." They know I mean it. I may not be there in person all the time, because of my ministry travel schedule, but if they are messing with her, I'll probably find out, and then they're in trouble (*troublllle!!!*).

In the same way, my wife knows how important it is for her to affirm my authority to them. Kids are great at trying to play one parent against the other, or to see if they can find ways that one parent resents the other so they can use it to get their own way. My wife doesn't put me down to the children. She builds me up.

My wife's acknowledgment of my position as head of the family is a source of strength in our home, and is one of the ways we teach our children about the realm of the eternal. When you don't love your wife as Christ loves the Church, it causes stress—not only for her, but also for the children, because it doesn't represent God. In the same way, when your wife is not submitted to you as the Church is submitted to Christ, it hurts not only your relationship with her but also the relationships both of you have with your children. It also sets in motion anti-social attitudes for their future on earth, when they get out into the world, and their future life in heaven, beyond this earthly dimension.

Gaining the strength to submit. Certain cults make a lot of Jesus' words "my Father is greater than I,"[17] saying it proves He was not *God* but was only *a* god. But within the eternal nature of God, just like within the nature of a godly marriage, there is an interplay of authority and submission that is awesome. There is a give-and-take, a dividing of responsibilities. At the time Jesus spoke, He was fulfilling His divine role as a man, fully submitted to His Father's will for the purposes of the kingdom. He had taken on a body of flesh, but He was never ruled by the flesh. He was ruled by the Spirit. *That's why He had the strength of character to submit!*

When men and women deal with authority and submission from the position of their flesh, according to their earthly nature, they totally miss what God wants them to see spiritually. With God it's not *position* that's important. It's your *faithfulness* in that position. Women's groups who get in the news by complaining loudly about this or that Christian group teaching about submission of women are missing the point and therefore missing a blessing by their complaining. Many men don't like to submit, either—in the church, on their jobs, and even the submission that is required in laying aside certain career plans to serve the needs of their families. Men and women who get hung up on their position don't realize that godly submission, like meekness, is not weakness but strength. Anything that matches God's model for mankind is strength!

It takes a lot more strength of character for a child to submit to his parents than it does for a child to rebel. Kids are rebels from day one. It's only as they grow that they develop the character to be obedient. As children of God, we may be adults in terms of our age, but childish in terms of our character. If God says, "Wives, submit to your own husbands,"[18] then wives need to submit to their own husbands, because God says to submit! The full text of that verse is "Wives, submit to your own husbands, *as to the Lord.*"

> I could ask wives, To what degree are you submitted to the Lord? That's the same degree to which you are able to submit to your husband.

Our attitudes in the natural realm expose our commitments in the spiritual realm. If wives have truly made Jesus the Lord of their lives, they won't have any problem *obeying Jesus* by making their husbands the head of their homes. Submission has nothing to do with value or influence. It has to do with maturity in the kingdom of God. It's a strategy God uses to accomplish His will on the earth, and to build character into people to prepare them to rule in eternity.

If you fight God's standards of submission now—whether you're a man or a woman—you're a rebel, and He can't use rebels in the next world. If you obey Him now, and keep the right attitudes in your relationships, you may even be qualified to rule galaxies when you reign with Him in eternity. You don't know what great things are coming through your obedience. "But it is written, eye hath not seen, nor ear heard, neither have entered into the heart of man, the things which God hath prepared for them that love him. But God hath revealed them unto us by his Spirit: for the Spirit searcheth all things, yea, the deep things of God."[19]

> God's purpose in marriage isn't meeting *your* needs. It's meeting *His* needs. He's the Owner and Coach! That's why you need to be a team.

God made marriage to meet His *needs, not necessarily yours.* The biggest problems in husband/wife relationships arise when men and women forget the real purpose of marriage. It isn't to meet *their* needs. The purpose of marriage is to meet *God's* needs. God created marriage so that the woman could help the man and together they could fulfill their destiny, including the bearing of children and taking dominion over this world and the next.

If people are more into self-fulfillment than fulfilling the purposes of God, they will never be truly happy, and neither will their children. Life has to be lived in the context of God's higher purposes. That's why there is no conflict in the kingdom of God.

When you have heaven in your home, the husband, wife, and children are all in places that God designed for them in His creative order: The man was created first, then the woman, then the children, who came forth from their unified relationship.

Fulfillment in the home comes when the wife is a covenant partner to her husband, and under his leadership they corporately and in agreement rule over their children. The husband doesn't unilaterally decide what is best for the home and then issue decrees to make everyone do what he wants. He consults with God on the best way to serve his family so that the family will fulfill its God-given destiny. He consults with his wife, because God gave her to him to help him do what is right.

Most of the tension and striving for position between men and women is totally temporal and fleshly. It is the fruit of envy and selfish ambition. It doesn't serve the purposes of God. It doesn't help the children.

Striving for rights doesn't represent Jesus. Jesus doesn't strive with the Father to get His rights. The devil was the one who did that, so God had to kick him out of heaven, because striving doesn't represent His ways. Jesus and the Father are one in love. They stay together for the sake of the children—us! They live all the time in a heavenly atmosphere of peace. And it's not a temporary peace, where they "agree to disagree." They are living in permanent, blissful unity for eternity. What do they have that we need to obtain for ourselves? They have love. They have wisdom. They have corporate purpose and the order necessary to fulfill that purpose, each one understanding His part in the overall plan.

A family is like a body, just as the Church is like a body. A body can have only one head, or else it's a monster! At crunch time, some important decisions may have to be made where you and your wife absolutely cannot agree. That's the time when because of her calling as a wife, God says for her to give in. That's the bottom line. She doesn't have to give in to sin. She doesn't have to give in to breaking the Law of God. But outside of that she has to yield to her husband's will. That's how the family stays in a place of peace. And remember, if you are wrong and you blow it, forcing your wife to miss God's will, He will absolutely deal with you later for your sin, but He will reward your wife for staying low.

EVERYONE SUBMITS IN PURE AND PEACEFUL FAMILIES

"Who is wise and understanding among you? Let him show it by his good life, by deeds done in the humility that comes from wisdom. But if you harbor bitter envy and selfish ambition in your hearts, do not boast about it or deny the truth. Such 'wisdom' does not come down from heaven but is earthly, unspiritual, of the devil. For where you have envy and selfish ambition, there you find disorder and every evil practice. But the wisdom that comes from heaven is first of all pure; then peace-loving, considerate, submissive, full of mercy and good fruit, impartial and sincere. Peacemakers who sow in peace raise a harvest of righteousness."[20]

God isn't waiting for you to get yourself together. He came to get you together. Stop striving and ask Him for His help.

TAKING TIME FOR CHILDREN

Quantities of Time Help Your Children Become Like You

When you first get married and you have no children, your attitudes pretty much just affect the two of you, but when the children come, you are spreading what's inside of you—either good or evil—to a lot more people. You have even more reason to demonstrate Christ-like love when you're influencing your children's minds and hearts.

You become like the people you hang out with. Your children are becoming like you to the extent they spend time with you. If they spend more of the day with other people—from day care to public school—they will become more like them.

Your children need to get from their time with you the inner qualities that will help them qualify not only for this life but also for the life to come. When you really get hold of the Lord, His life works in you both in time and in eternity.

There's no getting around it. Children require *quantities* of time, not just *quality* times. Everyone has the same twenty-four-hour day to work with. Where do you place your priorities? Where *should* you place them? Which of your activities will be most pleasing to your Father in heaven?

Some men who have a heavy work schedule and long commuting times need to look at some other options in order to spend more time at home. Children don't raise themselves. They need constant love and attention from their father and mother. Maybe you can bargain for time on your job by time sharing, flexible hours, or doing more work at home. Maybe you can use your computer for telecommuting. Stay flexible. Be consistent with times you spend with your family. Eat together with the TV turned off so you can talk to one another. Look for God every day and report it at the dinner table.

Time to Teach Children to Handle Money

Children will eventually need to learn how to handle a checkbook, but since there will be no checkbooks in heaven, there must be some other eternal principles they should learn first. Teach them accountability, discipline of soul and mind, and stewardship and faithfulness over the little things that they own. Those qualities are inward qualities. Then they track what they do with their money. They may not know the best accounting procedures, but they can track what comes in, what goes out, where it goes, and what it's used for. They can ask themselves: Does it glorify Jesus? Does it just please me? What is the percentage I spend on myself as opposed to the percent I spend on God? Do I tithe? All of that comes under the matter of stewardship. You can teach a person how to handle a checkbook, but he still may not have the character to handle it. However, if you teach a person how to have character and to live with a sense of accountability to the Lord at any moment, then that checkbook will get in order.

Time to Train Children to Be Loving

In all the training we do with our children, we also need to train them to be loving. That takes time! All of the problems we face in raising a family become smaller when we have love. Love is of God.

"My dear, dear friends, if God loved us like this, we certainly ought to love each other. No one has seen God, ever. But if we love one another, God dwells deeply within us, and his love becomes complete in us—perfect love!"[21]

"God is love. When we take up permanent residence in a life of love, we live in God and God lives in us. This way, love has the run of the house, becomes at home and mature in us."[22]

There is a lot we can learn from children who are born imperfect. God sends them to us for a purpose. Some of the most loving, affectionate children are those who are considered mentally disabled. Their minds don't get in the way and overrule their hearts. We have to consciously choose to love, but they love naturally. Their appearance might tend to repel us, but we are won over by their abandonment to love.

Sometimes we become so conscious of our own outward appearance and our own inner conflicts that we lost the ability to love that we had as innocent children. Life robs us of our abandonment to love, especially if we are too impatient to hang around children. We need children around us just to refresh us in our ability to love and be loved.

Jesus "called a little child and had him stand among them. And he said, 'I tell you the truth, unless you change and become like little children, you will never enter the kingdom of heaven. Therefore, whoever humbles himself like this child is the greatest in the kingdom of heaven.' "[23]

Jesus said that "out of the abundance of the heart the mouth speaketh."[24] If you are full of pride, it overflows into impatience, but if you are full of love, everything you do and say speaks of love.

Teaching Children to Be Happy

How do children learn to be happy? By being around happy people. Are you a happy person? Do your wife and children and their friends love to be around you because you're so happy all the time? Eugene Peterson wrote in his introduction to Philippians something about apprenticeship that is relevant to fathering, both natural and spiritual.

Philippians "is Paul's happiest letter. And the happiness is infectious. Before we've read a dozen lines, we begin to feel the joy ourselves—the dance of words and the exclamations of delight have a way of getting inside us.

"But happiness is not a word we can understand by looking it up in the dictionary. In fact, none of the qualities of the Christian life can be learned out of a book. Something more like apprenticeship is required, being around someone who out of years of devoted discipline shows us, by his or her entire behavior, what it is. Moments of verbal instruction will certainly occur, but mostly an apprentice acquires skill by daily and intimate association with a 'master,' picking up subtle but absolutely essential things, such as timing and rhythm and 'touch.' "[25]

You're an apprentice to God, and your children are apprentices to you. What you are learning from God, you can pass on to your children. It also works in reverse. As you see in the natural realm what your children need from you and how much they bless you with their lives, you can learn more about God. You gain understanding of the Father God as you walk out being a father yourself.

AN EXAMPLE FROM THE LIFE OF FREDERICK DOUGLASS

The following excerpts from a letter[26] by Frederick Douglass (1817?–1895) to his former slave master are an expression of how slavery attempted to destroy the family unit, and one man's gratitude for his children's freedom. The letter describes the traumatic life of a slave child, and a father's gratitude that God had spared his children from such a fate. A slave father and mother knew that at any time their child could be snatched from their arms or simply disappear because "Massa" had coldly sold the child to another owner. Douglass loved his freedom from those fears.

Historical Sketch of Frederick Douglass's Life

Douglass wrote this letter ten years after escaping from the plantation and establishing himself as a free man in the North. He had become an eloquent spokesman against the evils of slavery, and was in the process of becoming a standard of reconciliation for both black and white, Christian and non-Christian. People can look at his life, follow his model, and in effect "get some of that."

Frederick Douglass was born a slave on the Eastern Shore of Maryland in about 1817. The actual year of his birth can only be approximated, since few accurate records were kept of slave births and deaths. From the time he was a child of six, Douglass had been determined to run away. His mother died when he was seven. When he was a teen, he brazenly took on his slave master in a physical fight that could have cost him his life. He defied the stereotype of an ignorant slave by first learning to read by bribing white boys with food, and then studying in secret for years.

As a child he tried to answer the heart-rending question, "Why am I a slave?" He wrote, "When I saw the slave-driver whip a slave-woman, cut the blood out of her neck, and heard her piteous cries, I went away into the corner of the fence, wept and pondered over the mystery. I had, through some medium, I know not what, got some idea of God, the Creator of all mankind, the black and white, and that he had made the blacks to serve the whites as slaves. How he could do this and be good, I could not tell."

On September 4, 1838, with the help of his fiancée, Anna Murray (whom he later married), Douglass used the documents of a free black seaman to escape from the man who was his slave master at that time, Thomas Auld, and settle with his wife in the North. He would later write to Auld, "[T]hanks be to the Most High, who is ever the God of the oppressed."

Years later, Douglass legitimately paid his former master for his freedom with $700 he had received from friends. A brilliant, self-educated man, Douglass became a powerful public speaker for the abolition of slavery, initially with William Lloyd Garrison and the Massachusetts Anti-Slavery Society, and later independently. In 1845, Douglass increased his abolitionist influence by traveling to England, Ireland, and Scotland to speak out against slavery.

The first of his three autobiographies was published in 1845. In 1848 in Rochester, New York, he became the founder and editor of the anti-slavery newspaper *The North Star.* Honored with public service appointments rarely given to blacks, Douglass became the marshal of the District of Columbia under the administration of President Rutherford B. Hayes. Under President James Garfield's administration, he received the federal appointment of recorder of deeds of the District of Columbia.

In January 1884, two years after his wife's death, Douglass married a white woman. He used his relationship to exemplify racial reconciliation.

Douglass received his third federal appointment as minister-resident and consul general to the Republic of Haiti under President William Henry Harrison. In June 1891, due to illness, Douglass resigned from this appointment, but he continued to write, correspond, and speak until his death in 1895.

Excerpt from a Letter by Frederick Douglass

Asking his former slave master how he would feel if his children were stolen in the same way slave children were stolen:

Your mind must have become darkened, your heart hardened, your conscience seared and petrified, or you would have long since thrown off the accursed load and sought relief at the hands of a sin-forgiving God. How, let me ask, would you look upon me, were I some dark night in company with a band of hardened villains, to enter the precincts of your elegant dwelling and seize the person of your own lovely daughter Amanda, and carry her off from your family, friends and all the loved ones of her youth—make her my slave—compel her to work, and I take her wages—place her name on my leger [sic] as property—disregard her personal rights—fetter the powers of her immortal soul by denying her the right and privilege of learning to read and write—feed her coarsely—clothe her scantily, and whip her on the naked back occasionally; more and still more horrible, leave her unprotected—a degraded victim to the brutal lust of fiendish overseers, who would pollute, blight, and blast her fair soul— rob her of all dignity—destroy her virtue, and annihilate all in her person the graces that adorn the character of virtuous womanhood? I ask how would you regard me, if such were my conduct? Oh! the vocabulary of the damned would not afford a word sufficiently infernal, to express your idea of my God-provoking wickedness. Yet sir, your treatment of my beloved sisters is in all essential points precisely like the case I have now supposed. Damning as would be such a deed on my part, it would be no more so than that which you have committed against me and my sisters.

On the blessed safety of his children in freedom:

So far as my domestic affairs are concerned, I can boast of as comfortable a dwelling as your own. I have an industrious and neat companion, and four dear children—the oldest a girl of nine years, and three fine boys, the oldest eight, the next six, and the youngest four years old. The three oldest are now going regularly to school—two can read and write, and the other can spell with tolerable correctness words of two syllables: Dear fellows! They are all in comfortable beds, and are sound asleep, perfectly secure under my own roof. There are no slave-holders here to rend my heart by snatching them from my arms, or blast a mother's dearest hopes by tearing them from her bosom. These dear children are ours—not to work up into rice, sugar and tobacco, but to watch over, regard, and protect, and to rear them up in the nurture and admonition of the gospel—to train them up in the paths of wisdom and virtue, and, as far as we can to make them useful to the world and to themselves. Oh! sir, a slave holder never appears to me so completely an agent of hell, as when I think of and look upon my dear children. It is then that my feelings rise above my control.

Closing the letter, free from personal malice—"I am your fellow-man, but not your slave."

I shall make use of you as a means of exposing the character of the American church and clergy—and as a means of bringing this guilty nation with yourself to repentance. In doing this I entertain no malice towards you personally. There is no roof under which you would be more safe than mine, and there is nothing in my house which you might need for your comfort, which I would not readily grant. Indeed, I should esteem it a privilege to set you an example as to how mankind ought to treat each other.

I am your fellow-man, but not your slave.

Frederick Douglass

PRAYER FOR THE RESTORATION OF FAMILIES

Father, in Jesus' name, in the anointing of the Holy Spirit, I thank You that these families who read Your Word are blessed beyond mea-

sure. I declare a blessing upon them. No matter when they read it, because the Word of the Lord is truth, I thank You that throughout the years people are always changed.

I thank You that families are being restored. There will be people whose faith will come alive. There will be people who will repent, give their hearts to You, live holy lives, and then be bold to take steps to bring change.

They'll take steps, Lord Jesus, and as You correct them, they'll perfect their ways and take more steps so that You can use them more and more.

Thank You so much, Lord, for what You're doing among the people of God in this hour. You've reserved Yourself a people, Lord, and I thank You that they will not be defeated, because You are almighty God.

We love You now. You're an awesome Father.

Bless our eyes, Lord, that we'd be even more in focus than we've ever been. Bless our ears that we would have a keenness to hear. Bless our hearts, Lord. Let us be so tender that we might have understanding.

In Jesus' name I pray. Amen.

SELAH

How Much Time Do You Spend in Spiritual Training of Your Children Each Week?

Do you remember how the Three Little Pigs built their houses? Do you remember that children's story "The Three Little Pigs"? A couple of the pigs thought they could get by with quick construction. They threw their houses together with straw and twigs. That was no problem for the Big Bad Wolf. He just blew those houses down and ate the pigs. The third pig made his house of bricks. It took more time and money, but when he was finished it had the substance to protect him when the wolf came.

How much time do you spend building your spiritual house? If you're like most men, and I'm talking about most *Christian* men, you spend a whole lot of time building a career and very little time building your spiritual house. Everybody has to earn a living, but what is happening to your calling to minister to your family? Unless you get serious, your family won't have much more protection from the world, the flesh, and the devil than those first two pigs had.

God is calling you to take time out to build your house out of the substance of a consecrated life. If you've built your house on anything but the rock-solid model of Jesus Christ, your house will be washed away.[27] If you've built with wood, hay, and stubble, it's going to burn.[28] Since Jesus is the head of your house, ask Him, "What are *Your* priorities?" and then do those things that He requires.

CHILDREN'S SPIRITUAL TRAINING CHART

Here is a chart where you can shade in the number of minutes you spend with your children in spiritual training each day for one week. Fill out one chart with your baseline goals, then keep track of how you meet those goals for the following week. If you need to make some adjustments, go ahead and do it. Your children will be blessed by your faithfulness.

Children's Spiritual Training Chart
Number of Minutes Spent Daily with Your Children in the Word and Prayer

Sample

Dates:

Minutes	SUN	MON	TUES	WED	THURS	FRI	SAT
120							
110							
100							
90							
75							
60	▓			▓			
45	▓			▓	▓		
30	▓	▓		▓	▓		
25	▓	▓	▓	▓	▓		
20	▓	▓	▓	▓	▓	▓	▓
10	▓	▓	▓	▓	▓	▓	▓

Note: Don't count the church social hour as spiritual training time, unless it is.

Children's Spiritual Training Chart
Number of Minutes Spent Daily with Your Children in the Word and Prayer
Baseline

Dates:

Minutes	SUN	MON	TUES	WED	THURS	FRI	SAT
120							
110							
100							
90							
75							
60							
45							
30							
25							
20							
10							

Children's Spiritual Training Chart
Number of Minutes Spent Daily with Your Children in the Word and Prayer
Goal

Dates:

Minutes	SUN	MON	TUES	WED	THURS	FRI	SAT
120							
110							
100							
90							
75							
60							
45							
30							
25							
20							
10							

9

⸻

ℬE THE MAN OF GOD
YOUR FAMILY NEEDS

> Trust and obey—
> For there's no other way
> To be happy in Jesus
> But to trust and obey.[1]
> —John H. Sammis
> (1846–1919)

Any pastor knows that it's sometimes harder to get his wife's respect for the prophetic Word he says he is receiving from God than it is to get the respect of the Church.

Several years ago, I began to wonder if my wife could respect my words as coming from God on the basis of what she saw of my prayer life. Then I began awaking at 2 or 3 A.M. to use the rest room, and the thought struck me: Why am I waking up? I was conscious of God at those times, and I began to think, How can I be with my wife during the most intimate times of the night but never share intimate moments with God?

So when I awakened in the early hours, as the priest for my family, I began to get down by the side of the bed and pray.

Then after a while I began to physically leave the room and go downstairs to pray. My wife would awaken and call my name. When I didn't answer, she would come looking for me. When she would hear me crying out for her and the children, that increased her respect and love for me more than any of my preaching had ever done.

What had happened was that through my yielding to the call of God to pray and be the priest interceding for my family, I had found a place of rest. My rest in God produced the respect of my family, so they would listen to the prophetic words God gave me for them the rest of the day.

YOUR SPIRITUAL ROLES AND RESPONSIBILITIES IN THE HOME

Your Role as Priest and Prophet in Your Home

Every man of God—as the earthly representative of Jesus for his house—should be both priest and prophet in his home. He should pray in secret as a priest, and He should speak as a prophet what he hears from God in secret prayer.

As priest, you carry your family in prayer. Jesus is the Great High Priest.[2] He fulfilled all the qualifications of the Old Testament priest, whose main responsibility was to pray for the people of Israel. Jesus is still praying for us now. The Bible says that Jesus "has an unchangeable priesthood. . . . He always lives to make intercession."[3]

God wants you to be a priest—a man of prayer—in your home. Jesus said, "My house shall be called the house of prayer."[4] That means *you. You* are God's house. You are someone who prays, especially for your family. When you as a man of God are a house of prayer, your home also will be a house of prayer.

The secret of prayer is prayer in secret. As priest, you pull away daily to be with the Lord alone. You pray that your wife and children will come into God's presence more and more, and you keep on praying that they will stay in His presence. You carry to God the needs of your house, because God is inviting you to bring your needs to Him. "Let him have all your worries and cares, for he is always thinking about you and watching everything that concerns you."[5]

Maybe you can think of carrying your wife and kids to God in prayer like this: You know how you sometimes pack the whole family in the car and go get some ice cream, even when you've got some half-eaten cartons in the freezer? Everybody's hanging out together having a good time (until the crumb-snatchers spill chocolate ice cream on the car upholstery, of course).

That's the way you should carry your wife and kids in prayer before the Lord. Just like you're the one driving the car to get the ice cream, you're the one carrying them in prayer. And you're having such a good time because you're in there with God for people He loves even more than you do.

Priests respond to God's call to pray. Aaron, Moses' brother, was the first high priest. When Aaron went in to God, he carried the names of the tribes of Israel as jewels on his robe,[6] just as I'm telling you to carry your wife and children in to God. Aaron prayed because God told him to do it. Read about God's instructions to him in the Old Testament.

Prayer, where you as the priest in your home hand over your family's cares, is not something that *you* initiate. It's something that *God* initiates, and you become yielded enough to go in there with Him. Then, when you enter into intimacy with Him, you produce the spiritual yield of a prophetic word to give to your wife.

Every wife needs from her husband a "God said," but before you can get a "God said" for your wife, you have to be spending time with God in the intimacy of intercession. As a prophet, you carry back to your wife and children the fruit of what God has imparted to you concerning the needs of your house.

As prophet, share what you receive in prayer. Does your family burst into applause when you speak the Word of the Lord to them? That's what the people did when they heard Jesus. If your family isn't applauding your insights from God, maybe it's because you're not as serious as Jesus was about His prayer life, so they can't respect you as a prophet.

The main role of the prophet in the Bible and in the home is to speak forth the word of the Lord. There may be some "foretelling," in the sense of dealing with future events, but most of what a prophet does is "forth-telling," to help people understand what God wants them to do *now*. The only way a man of God can understand the things of God and speak the word of God is to spend intimate time in prayer with God as a priest.

What It Means to Be Priest and Prophet in the Home

PRIEST	PROPHET
Speaking to God on behalf of your family	Speaking to your family on behalf of God
Praying	Proclaiming
Attitudes	Actions
Being	Doing
Inward work	Outward work
Preparation	Proclamation
Private life	Public life
Seeking the source of God's power	Working with the force of God's power
Impartation	Revelation
Personal confession and repentance	Calling others to confession and repentance
Isolation in the closets of intimacy with God	Manifestation of spiritual fruit gained in prayer
Consecration and sanctification as an inward work	Consecrated and sanctified lifestyle evident to all
Sacrificing secretly for the sake of your family	Speaking openly to keep your family in touch with God
Closets of prayer alone	Concerts of prayer with others
Living in the Most Holy Place of God's presence, symbolized by going behind the veil to the Ark of the Covenant	Carrying God's presence to others, symbolized by moving the Ark of the Covenant on its poles
Anointing yourself with oil	Anointing people with oil for church office and their roles in public affairs (as the prophets did for kings in the Bible)
Development of holiness in your inner man	Exposure of the state of your holiness through your words and deeds

Jesus was the Great Prophet whom Moses predicted would come.[7] Jesus proclaimed the Word of the Lord to His generation and the generations to come, and He wants you to proclaim that Word to your generation, beginning in your own home.

> The greatest vacuum in Christendom is the prayer closet. If your prayer closet is empty, your Christian walk will not bear fruit, but if you make prayer a priority, you and your family will be blessed.

Taking Spiritual Responsibility in Your Home

Prayer cures spiritual barrenness. When you love your wife, you model your life after the example of Christ and the Church. That means that you take spiritual responsibility for your wife and for the home and family you have created together.

It is my prayer that you will develop the sensitivity to see how awesome it is to take spiritual responsibility for your home as a priest and prophet. In this chapter, I want you to see the practical application of the biblical examples of Zachariah and Noah, and to understand that you must *be* a priest and *stay* a priest before you have influence as a prophet.

Much of what is wrong in the home, the Church, and society can be traced to men falling short of their priestly responsibilities in prayer, and then lacking the substance to speak forth the Word of God. When we should be speaking *prophetically* out of our relationship with God and the fullness of *His* Word, we are speaking *pathetically* out of our relationship with man and the barrenness of *his* words.

The greatest vacuum in Christendom is the prayer closet. If your prayer closet is empty, your Christian walk will not bear fruit, but if you make prayer a priority, you and your family will be blessed.

Prayer sets your home on a strong foundation. A wise father builds the life of his family not just occasionally but day by day upon the Word of God and prayer. Jesus said you will be wise in the same way as the man who builds a house upon a rock instead of upon sand.

Jesus said, " 'These words I speak to you are not incidental additions to your life, homeowner improvements to your standard of living. They are foundational words, words to build a life on. If you work these words into your life, you are like a smart carpenter who built his house on solid rock. Rain poured down, the river flooded, a tornado hit—but nothing moved that house. It was fixed to the rock.

" 'But if you just use my words in Bible studies and don't work them into your life, you are like a stupid carpenter who built his house on the sandy beach. When a storm rolled in and the waves came up, it collapsed like a house of cards.'

"When Jesus concluded his address, the crowd burst into applause. They had never heard teaching like this. It was apparent that he was living everything he was saying—quite a contrast to their religion teachers! This was the best teaching they had ever heard."[8]

Win-Win Situations with God

Take a rest from self-effort. When you realize that your responsibilities as priest and prophet are too great for you to handle, it's time for you to enter into God's rest. The Bible speaks of rest in the sense of resting from self-effort. When you enter God's rest, you stop trying to do things in the power of your own strength and instead seek to get things done out of your relationship with God. Instead of trying to work out solutions from what you know, you trust God completely to do what you don't know.

Your level of rest is determined by your level of intimacy in prayer, because the rest of God comes from the presence of God. As a man of God for your family, you seek to enter His rest through prayer, personal consecration, and faith.

In the past, the people of God couldn't enter His rest because they wouldn't trust Him.[9] Their disobedience disqualified them. However, God has never given up hope for a new generation who will trust and obey Him, and therefore qualify to enter into His rest. That's what I'm seeing for this generation. That's what I am seeing for *you*—rest as a result of trust and obedience.

"The promise of 'arrival' and 'rest' is still there for God's people. God himself is at rest. And at the end of the journey we'll surely rest with God. So let's keep at it and eventually arrive at the place of rest, not drop out through some sort of disobedience."[10]

In the Old Testament, God instituted the Sabbath as man's day of rest, just as He Himself had rested on the seventh day of creation. In the Ten Commandments, He said, "Remember the Sabbath day, to keep it holy."[11]

When you are born again, you don't just live your Christian life on Sunday, and you don't just rest on Sunday. Every day is Sunday and every day is rest day because of your dedication to Him. We are living in the"eighth day," where we are always at rest. The Day Star is shining in our hearts.[12] As Israel rested on the seventh day under the Old Covenant, we now "rest" in our hearts by trusting and obeying God in our hearts—twenty-four hours a day, seven days a week.

Happiness comes through obedience. Two key words for entering into God's rest are "trust and obey." Here are some words about how blessed it is to trust and obey God. They are taken from the famous song by John H. Sammis (1846–1919). You've probably sung it before:

> *"But we never can prove*
> *The delights of His love*
> *Until all on the altar we lay,*
> *For the favor He shows*
> *And the joy He bestows*
> *Are for them who will trust and obey.*
> *Trust and obey—*
> *For there's no other way*
> *To be happy in Jesus*
> *But to trust and obey."*[13]

As a true priest, trusting and obeying God, you follow not only the spirit of the Law, as you understand it, but also the letter of the Law—the unchanging standards of righteousness. As you "trust and obey," your obedience to these standards affects your level of holiness—and ultimately your level of success in life—through access to the living God.

Trust and obedience are the keys to every kind of success. When God spoke to Joshua after Moses' death, after Joshua had taken over the responsibility for ruling Israel, He said of His laws, "[I]f you are careful to obey every one of them you will be successful in everything you do."[14] We are not saved from hell by obeying the Law. That comes through trusting in Jesus. But we are saved form a lot of the hell on earth when we follow all the standards of righteousness that God put in the Law for our success.

Martin Luther had a wise wife named Katherine. At one time the great reformer Martin Luther was so discouraged by his own sinfulness, the wretched condition of the world, and the persecution of the Church that he continually walked around the house as if he had a dark cloud over him.

His wife, Katherine (a "Katherine the Great," like my wife Katheryn!), was a godly woman who liked to keep heaven in her home. She knew her husband very well, so she went and dressed herself all in black. As the story goes, Luther noticed and asked the reason for her mourning outfit. "Do you not know," she said, "God in heaven is dead?"

"What nonsense!" Luther said. "How can God die? He is immortal and will live through all eternity."

"And yet," Katherine said quietly, "you go about hopeless and discouraged."

And Luther said, "Then I observed what a wise woman my wife was, and I mastered my silence."

A PRIEST NAMED ZACHARIAH

The Roles of God's Servants

Zachariah's privileges as a priest. One of the stories from the book of Luke that doesn't get told too often at Christmastime is what happened to Zachariah, the father of John the Baptist, as he served as a priest in the temple. Zachariah's wife, Elizabeth, was the cousin of Mary, Jesus' mother.

Zachariah and Elizabeth were good people who followed the Law precisely. To a priest, obedience to the Law was a matter of life and death. It was part of his training to learn that God had the right to kill him in the temple in front of all the people if he disobeyed even a small part of the Law.

At the time of this story, Zachariah and his wife had no children.

If you and your wife have had any trouble having children, you need to read true stories like this one. It's awesome how God supernaturally solves the problem of infertility in the Bible.[15]

When Zachariah's time came to do his priestly duty in the temple, he had the opportunity of a lifetime to pray to God in a place where the whole nation believed that someone could go and God would hear him. As the priest in your home, you have that privilege every day, but priests who lived in the days before Jesus died for the sins of the world might do it only once in a lifetime.

The Old Testament priesthood represented an attitude we've lost—the awe of God, the fear and reverence of God, the amazement that someone so holy and heavenly should take any time to mess with filthy sinners, and the willingness to use their privileged access to pray for the needs of others.

The priest's fear of God. Ask God to give you the same sense of awe that those priests had in the days when the Holy Spirit had not yet come for all the people, and only a few had any real experience with God. They had a much better appreciation of what a miracle it was to talk to God than we do, and especially to get in a place to hear back from Him.

Those men of God had more awe of God because they had a better understanding of God's penalty for sin. It had taken Zachariah a lot of years to reach this high point in his career when he was chosen by lot to go into the Holy Place to burn incense and pray for the people. He couldn't go in if there was any sin in his life. A priest's life was committed to learning how to please God, because as soon as he was chosen to go in there, he had to dot every *i* and cross every *t* or God could kill him right in front of the altar of incense.

God is still dealing with us as priests in our homes, trying to purify every motivation, thought, and word so that we can get into His face without getting killed, because His nature is absolutely holy.

Most people spend their lives trying to please people, not God. You need to come to the place where pleasing God is more important than anything else in your life. You can't work yourself up to being dedicated. Either you're dedicated or you're a sinner. You're either holy or you're defiled. You're either in faith or you're in fear. You're either a hypocrite or you're pure.

To walk in purity as God has ordained is a fight. You have to do battle in prayer and personal consecration, both for yourself and for your home, but the rewards are worth it.

Meeting God's Standards

Walking holy with God's help. It's tough to be pure. Jesus said, "Heaven can be entered only through the narrow gate! The highway to hell is broad, and its gate is wide enough for all the multitudes who choose its easy way. But the Gateway to Life is small, and the road is narrow, and only a few ever find it."[16]

But you don't have to find that way alone. Don't ever be afraid of reaching the goal of God's high standards. Don't drop out of the race before you finish, because the Lord says, "I will not leave you comfortless."[17]

God gives us the goals. He sends the Holy Spirit to comfort us while we strive to accomplish them, and then gives us rewards when we get there! That causes me to go off into praise!

Living as if your life depended on holiness. You need to stop seeing yourself so low. See yourself as a purified priest who is righteous because he knows his very life depends on the level of holiness in his lifestyle.

A priest's whole career success is dependent on his learning how to please God. Success with God is not the same as success with man. To man, success means money or fame, like making it big on the stock market or winning the NBA playoffs. That kind of success is as empty as a leather basketball with air in it. Success with God has substance that lasts. It's sinless. It doesn't have any "morning after" sense of "Is this all there is?"

Remember that even in losing seasons, you're still a winner with God. When you fail God's standard, don't give up. Get up! "For a just man falleth seven times, and riseth up again."[18]

Sins covered by Jesus' blood. Zachariah joins humanity in tracing his ancestry to Adam after the Fall. That means he was born a sinner. When God made Adam and Eve, they were pure. They could talk to God and to each other. They knew that they were naked but they were not ashamed. They felt good about themselves. They had arrived. They had no sense of sin to put a barrier between them and God. Their clothes were invisible but beautiful, because they were made from God's approval. Then they sinned and spoiled everything—for all of us.

As a priest who was born a sinner, Zachariah had to learn all of the laws, statutes, ordinances, and temple procedures by heart so he could avoid God's wrath when his time came to serve in the holy temple. He had to sacrifice animals on the altar of burnt offering to cover his sins, just as God had killed animals to make a covering for sinful Adam and Eve.[19]

After Zachariah went through the purification ceremonies, he could go in alone to the Holy Place and burn incense on the altar of incense. Part of his job was praying for the nation of Israel, and since he was a family man, we can imagine that he took the liberty to put in a word with the Lord for himself and his wife. There was probably something about that moment that brought hope alive in him so this childless husband could say to the Lord that he wanted to have a family. It was the best way he knew how to reach God—follow the letter of the Law, go into the Holy Place of the temple, and then speak what was on his heart.

Zachariah didn't know it yet, but thirty-three years later the whole Jewish temple system of prayers and sacrifices would be blown wide open with the death of Jesus, and a lot more people would be praying and meeting God any place where they desired to seek after Him. The whole world, not just the Jews, would have the potential of being the people of God, whose sins were covered and forgiven because of the blood of Jesus, and who have access to His holy inner court.

A Judgment Day is coming. God is absolutely holy, and anyone varying from God's standard deserves death. Some people who are playing around now will find out when they die and face the Judgment Bar that God still kills sinners, and only those covered by the blood of Jesus, the Lamb of God, will inherit eternal life.

Our sins are covered now, but sometimes we keep sinning in certain areas for a while and have to repent and get ourselves straight so we can go boldly and unashamedly before God again. We don't "get it" totally at first. We have to learn how to continually and consistently drive out the sin that sneaks back in, so we can go before Him naked and unashamed. Then we can reach God for ourselves and our families.

The particular day in the life of Zachariah that we are discussing was not only life-changing for him but also world-changing. The people praying outside, waiting for him to come out, probably thought he was dead because he was in there so long. They thought he had sinned and God had killed him so everybody would find out and be afraid to sin themselves.

These days brothers find out if you're sinning by having fellowship and encounter groups. God knows that you ignore the Holy Spirit, so He has to put you around men who kinda hold you up while you're in your baby stage. They hold you to the consecrated life. "Hey, bro', did you pray yesterday? Did you read the Scriptures?" You know that if you lie about it to their faces, the Holy Spirit convicts you about the fact that you lied to man and you lied to the Holy Ghost. That keeps you straight for now, but you need to grow up past that accountability stuff with man and be like the priests who laid their lives on the line every time they went into the temple. They knew they were holy because they knew they had been in there with God.

Some people come to church and hide out. They aren't under any accountability because they don't want their defiled life to be shown. The Holy Spirit is talking, but they aren't listening. That is the epitome of pride—when you get conviction from God and you reject it. God has given us a better way: "Search me, O God, and know my heart: try me, and know my thoughts: and see if there be any wicked way in me, and lead me in the way everlasting."[20]

Zachariah Blew It, but God Had Mercy

Zachariah was slow coming out of the Holy Place, but it wasn't because he had sinned and died. He had definitely blown it, but God's mercy had let him live to fulfill His will.

Zachariah had seen an angel. This big angel came out of nowhere and stood beside the altar of incense. Zachariah was scared to death! This wasn't one of those Christmas-card angels who looks like a beautiful woman or a little crumb-snatcher with wings on. They don't have any of those in the Bible. Angels in the Bible are great big men! This angel was Gabriel, the same angel who would be speaking later to Mary about the birth of Jesus. Gabriel had also appeared to Daniel centuries earlier, and frightened him, too, so he must have been something serious. Gabriel had told Daniel about the coming Messiah, whom we now know as Jesus, and in Zachariah's day he told Mary and Joseph that the time for the Messiah had come.

Here's the rest of the incident with the angel in the Holy Place of the Tabernacle, as written about by Luke:

"Zachariah was paralyzed in fear.

"But the angel reassured him, 'Don't fear, Zachariah. Your prayer has been heard. Elizabeth, your wife, will bear a son by you. You are to name him John. You're going to leap like a gazelle for joy, and not only you—many will delight in his birth. He'll achieve great stature with God . . . [and] he'll get the people ready for God.' "[21]

Zachariah was like Sarah when the angel said she would get pregnant with Isaac. She didn't believe him, either. Zachariah thought the angel was head-tripping because, after all, he and his wife, Elizabeth, were too old to have kids. Gabriel set him straight, but then he told Zachariah that he would be unable to speak until the day of his son's birth, because of his unbelief. That was his punishment, but at least he was still alive. When the angel finally let him go, Zachariah went back out where the people were waiting, but he could only use sign language. They could tell that he had seen a vision.

Zachariah's Son, John the Baptist

John's God-ordained destiny. When he finished his duties, Zachariah went home, and shortly afterward his wife conceived. Six months into her pregnancy, God sent Gabriel to Mary, and you know the rest of the story of the birth of Jesus. Zachariah's son, John—the future John the Baptist—was born, and Zachariah got his voice back and started praising God. The Bible says that Zachariah didn't blow it this time. He was faithful in naming his child John, as he had been instructed several months earlier by Gabriel, even though he had to write it down because he still was unable to speak. Then, it says in *The Message*, "Zachariah's mouth was now open, his tongue loose, and he was talking, praising God!"[22] He loved having that baby because he knew John had a God-ordained destiny. John eventually fulfilled all the angel's prophecies over his life. John was the one destined to prepare the way for the people to receive Jesus.

Your child's God-ordained destiny. It's great to read the story in Luke and see how happy it made Zachariah to have a child, just in case you haven't been too appreciative of your kids lately, or if you've fallen into the trap that says children are a curse and not a blessing.

God sets the course of a person's life from even before his birth.[23]

That's why unborn children are so precious. They should never be killed. They have a calling even before they are conceived. Not everyone has the calling of John the Baptist, but every unborn child has the same potential for greatness in God's eyes.

The God-Ordained Destiny of Jesus

Jesus had to die for our sins. John the Baptist fulfilled his calling to prepare the way for Jesus. Then he died, and Jesus died, also. The Bible says that Jesus died on a cross, the most cruel method of death in his time. He was stripped naked. Nails were driven through His hands and feet. He hung there on public display until He could no longer push Himself up to get air in His lungs, and then He suffocated. Most of those who were executed by crucifixion died slowly, growing increasingly weak until they faded away. Sometimes it took several days to die. But Jesus was dead within hours, and just before He died, God gave Him the supernatural strength to shout—twice!

Jesus shouted once in despair as God laid the sins of the whole world upon Him.

Then He shouted once in triumph, because His defeat of our sin and death had been completed.

Jesus' death gave us access to God. Luke wrote that while Jesus was dying, even though it was day, darkness came down over the whole earth for three hours, and then the Temple veil was torn. "Then the sun was darkened, and the veil of the temple was torn in two. And when Jesus had cried out with a loud voice, He said, 'Father, into Your hands I commit My spirit.' "[24]

When Jesus died, the thick curtain covering the Most Holy Place— near where Zachariah had met the angel Gabriel many years before—split wide open. It showed all people everywhere that through Jesus' death God had made a way for them to reach heaven.

Through Jesus' death, God had broken through! His eternal plan from the foundation of the world had been fulfilled in the death of His sinless Son. A way of access was made for us to enter into the Most Holy Place of His presence—anytime, anywhere—as long as we come through the way He has made.

While He was on earth, Jesus said, "I am the way, the truth, and the life: no man cometh unto the Father, but by me."[25] He is called the "Lamb of God,"[26] because He replaced all the animal sacrifices. He replaced the altars, the Holy Place, the Most Holy Place, and the veil. They were not needed any longer. He took His own blood to heaven as the Great High Priest of all the ages, and the Father was satisfied that the price had been paid forever for all who might sin. A few years after Jesus' death, the Jewish temple was destroyed. Another way had been made to reach God.

Have you come to the Lamb of God? Have you come to Jesus? Do you really know Him in the secret closets of intercession? You can. The way has been prepared for you to come.

As the old hymn says,

> *Just as I am, without one plea*
> *But that thy blood was shed for me,*
> *And that Thou bidd'st me come to Thee,*
> *O Lamb of God, I come! I come!*[27]

The woman who wrote those words, Charlotte Elliott (1789–1871), was a bedridden invalid for most of her life. She had come to a place of great despair when a famous Swiss evangelist named Dr. Caesar Malan came to her home and told her, "You must come just as you are, a sinner, to the Lamb of God that taketh away the sin of the world."[28] Dr. Malan was quoting the words spoken by Zachariah's son, John the Baptist, when he saw Jesus: "Behold the Lamb of God, which taketh away the sin of the world."[29] Then Miss Elliott gave her life to Jesus.

A PROPHET NAMED NOAH

Noah's Story

The man who "walked with God."[30] If you ask most people who know something about the Bible to name some of the Bible's prophets, not too many would give you the name of Noah. But Noah was definitely a prophet for his time. Noah preached for one hundred years that the people were so corrupt, God was sending a flood to destroy every living thing on the earth. If that isn't a prophecy, I don't know what is. It is not only foretelling, it is also forth-telling. Noah had heard from God as a priest and had come to his family as a prophet. He was a priest/prophet before those orders were established. He could have been an arm of deliverance for the whole earth, if they had listened to him.

Because "Noah found grace in the eyes of the Lord,"[31] God not only preserved his life, He also included Noah's whole family in Noah's deliverance. When you are righteous, you have favor with God, and your favor affects your whole family's blessings from

The Husband as Priest and Prophet in the Home

Priestly Character Qualities

Pained by Sin in Yourself and in the World

Passenger-Carrying in Prayer

Peaceful

People-Loving

Perfected

Perfectly Satisfied with Life

Persevering in Prayer

Personality-Conflict-Free

Personally Committed

Placing Yourself in Isolation for Prayer

Pleasant

Pleasing God

Point of Contact to God

Positionally in Heaven

Potentially Great Because You Practice Holiness

Powerfully Kept by God

Praising and Worshiping to Start the Day

Praying over Meals and Bringing Heaven to Your Home

Precious with the Oil of Anointing

Preferring the Presence of God

Pregnant with Vision

Prejudice-Free

Prepared for Enemies and Offenses

Presenting Yourself Before God to Do His Will

Price Paid and Free

Privately Spending Time with God

Profoundly at Rest

Provided for

Pure in Thought, Word, and Deed

Purged from Sin

heaven. God said to Noah, "I will establish My covenant with you; and you shall go into the ark—you, your sons, your wife, and your son's wives with you."[32]

As a *priest*, Noah had an intimate level of fellowship with God because of his consecration. The Bible says, "Noah was a righteous man, blameless [complete, perfect, having integrity] in his time [generations]; Noah walked with God."[33]

As a *prophet*, he lived a consecrated, obedient life and spoke forth the word of the Lord. He had learned to trust and obey God. "Thus Noah did; according to all that God had commanded him, so he did."[34] "By faith, Noah built a ship in the middle of dry land. He was warned about something he couldn't see, and acted on what he was told. The result? His family was saved. His act of faith drew a sharp line between the evil of the unbelieving world and the righteousness of the believing world. As a result, Noah became intimate with God."[35]

Prophets Respect God's Power

Remember, a prophet is someone who speaks for God by communicating God's message. He may be (1) forth-telling—bringing forth a

The Husband as Priest and Prophet in the Home

Prophetic Character Qualities	
Passing down a Spiritual Heritage	Proclaiming Liberty
Pastoring Your Home and Neighborhood	Producing Spiritual Children
Physically in Shape	Professional
Picturing Jesus for Others When They See Your Life	Pronouncing Blessings
Playing and Having Fun with a Consciousness of God	Prophetic
Preaching	Prospering
	Public Life Equaling Private Life
	Punishing Wrongdoing to Help Children Grow

message as God gives him understanding from the Word; or he may be (2) fore-telling—regarding events in the future.

Death to false-speaking prophets. Anyone who calls himself a prophet—even in his own home—ought to have the fear of God on him, because in the Bible a false prophet could be killed.

There were two main categories of offense for which a false prophet could be executed:

(1) He prophesied a sign or wonder that did take place, but he used his prophecy to turn people away from the true God.
(2) He prophesied something that did not take place, which proved his message was not from God at all.

"If a prophet, or one who foretells by dreams, appears among you and announces to you a miraculous sign or wonder, and if the sign or wonder of which he has spoken takes place, and he says, 'Let us follow other gods' (gods you have not known) 'and let us worship them,' you must not listen to the words of that prophet or dreamer. The LORD your God is testing you to find out whether you love him with all your heart and with all your soul. . . . *Stone him to death,* because he tried to turn you away from the LORD your God, who brought you out of Egypt, out of the land of slavery."[36]

"[A]ny prophet who falsely claims that his message is from me shall die. And any prophet who claims to give a message from other gods must die. If you wonder, 'How shall we know whether the prophecy is from the Lord or not?' this is the way to know: If the thing he prophesies doesn't happen, it is not the Lord who has given him the message; he has made it up himself. You have nothing to fear from him."[37]

Be careful about saying, "God told me." Don't give personal messages from God to people unless you are sure you have heard from God, and it checks out against the Bible and other witnesses, who can confirm that what you have said is true. In other words, don't go around saying, "God told me this or that," or even worse, "God told me this or that *for you,*" and not expect the wrath of God to catch up with you if you're wrong.

All Christians are able to hear from God. The essence of being a Christian is that you'll get revelation. God took the blinders off our eyes. God didn't intend that no one but the preacher would get insight out of the Word. What makes you different from the people in other religions is that you get access before the Father, and in that access you get insight. Ask God for revelation, and ask Him to give revelation to others. That's what the Bible says to do.

The apostle Paul prayed for the church at Ephesus: "I keep asking that the God of our Lord Jesus Christ, the glorious Father, may give you the Spirit of wisdom and revelation, so that you may know him better."[38] You can know the will of God for your family. Your wife and children can know His will, too. Together you can bring your family into the destiny of God.

ANOINTED TO BE A MAN OF GOD

The Oil of God's Anointing

When you become a Christian, God gives you an anointing that breaks every yoke.[39] Some of the yokes you can break because of your anointing are strongholds in your home that keep you and the members of your family bound and unable to walk freely with God. When you're committed to Christ, you're anointed, like the kings and priests of old. The word *Christians,* which first appears in Acts 11:26, is the Greek word *Christianos,*[40] which comes from the word *Christos* [41]—the Greek word for Christ. *Christos* means "anointed," "to anoint," or—in the case of Jesus Christ—"the Anointed One." A Christian is anointed because he has joined himself to Jesus, the Anointed One. The high priest was described as he "upon whose head the anointing oil was poured, and that is consecrated."[42]

Your anointing qualifies you as the man of God for your family.[43] You're someone God wants to work with to bless their lives. Quit making excuses! There's nobody else for God to anoint as the man of God for your home but you.

Give because of your anointing. The anointing is not just for you. The anointing is also to give away. Jesus said, "Give, and it will be given to you: good measure, pressed down, shaken together, and running over."[44] The more you give, the more you receive. Don't let other people's faces fool you when you give them a word of encouragement or prophecy that comes to you because of your anointing. They may act as if they aren't receiving it, but Jesus said, " 'Judge not according to the appearance, but judge righteous judgment.' "[45] To judge righteously, you need to hear from God, and then you need to have faith to speak out what you hear. Have faith that what God has anointed you to do, you will do. Without faith it is impossible to please God.[46] If you've ever been anointed and prayed for, it was probably with "a little dab will do ya." But Aaron had so much anointing oil poured over his head that it ran all the way down to his feet. God is extravagant with His anointing, and He wants you to be extravagant about yours as well.

Bring unity because of your anointing. You are anointed to bring unity to your home. The precious oil of Aaron's anointing was a symbol of the unity of Israel. The anointing for oneness is still flowing over you in your home, through Jesus Christ. Your prayers as priest will bring your family into oneness.

> *"Behold, how good and how pleasant it is for brethren to dwell together in unity! It is like the precious oil upon the head, running down on the beard, the beard of Aaron, running down on the edge of his garments."*[47]

Your Personal Eightfold Anointing

You can personally and privately anoint yourself with olive oil daily. It is a reminder to perform your priestly role in your home in holiness and in unity with your wife. I anoint my body daily with fragrant olive oil as an act of spiritual worship and a reminder that God has set me apart to be holy. My body is the temple of the Holy Ghost. I am not my own. I was bought with a price; therefore, I should glorify God within my body.[48]

The oil reminds me that God has made me one with my wife. We are unified, and our unity brings spiritual growth in our home.

In our ministry, we do an eightfold anointing of ourselves to remind us that we are extravagantly anointed by God. Here are some words of commitment you can use as you anoint these eight parts of your body every day:

Head. Anoint my head, Lord. Make my thinking like Your thinking. Make me walk according to Your Spirit. Give me some sense.

Mouth. Anoint my mouth, Lord. Let my words be uplifting and building. Don't let me say things that misrepresent You. Let me speak the Word and live the Word that I speak. Help me to pray continually, that Your presence will be always with me.

Eyes. Anoint my eyes, God. Let me see what You see from heaven. Don't let me see people where they are. Let me see them for where You ordained them to be.

Ears. Anoint my ears, in Jesus' name. Let me hear so that even though I hear the natural voices, let me hear Your voice, Jesus. As You speak a revelation into my ears—the womb of my spirit—may I become pregnant with vision for myself, my family, and the generation.

Nose. Anoint my nose so that I will have discernment in my relationships with other people, and know what is right before the Lord.

Hands. Anoint my hands, the fruit of my labors. Help me to lay hands on others to bless and heal. Use my hands to anoint kings and the fivefold ministry into office. Let me bear fruit in Jesus' name. (Because I wash my hands all day and therefore wash off the scented oil, I anoint my wrist where I don't typically wash. Then, during the day, if my faith wavers, I can sniff my wrist so that the odor sparks my senses and helps me to stay in the flow of God.)

Feet. Anoint my feet and let my walk be pleasing to You. May I walk with the weight of glory in my life. Let me not walk in any place or destiny that would be not ordained of You. Control me. Cause me to walk in Your will.

Body. Anoint my body. My body is the temple of the Holy Ghost. Don't let my flesh rule over me. Don't let my food take control over me. Keep me in shape physically. Help me to fast and live a fasted lifestyle. Let me be an example of You in every way.

I am anointed, and this is the day that the Lord has made! When You have completed Your personal anointing declare, "This is the day that the Lord has made!"[49]

Anointed to Serve Others

Serving others through prayer. The priests and prophets were anointed to pray. When Zachariah purified himself and went in to burn incense and pray in the secrecy of the Holy Place, he was living out a perpetual reminder that the priests are people who are about the Lord's work.[50] We need to be reminded of that. If you're a Christian, you're a priest. You're an intercessor. You go to God on behalf of others. It's something you inherited along with your salvation. The apostle Peter said that we are "a royal priesthood,"[51] to be exact. We aren't going to be doing what Zachariah did in the natural realm. We may not be earning a salary as a pastor. But we are all priests in full-time service to God. Regardless of our secular occupation, we are working for Him. We are priests. We pray!

Serving others by bringing change. Many Christians I know are not dedicated to God's service. They have forgotten they have a prophetic calling. They are so much in love with the world, they aren't interested in heavenly things. I'm talking about pleasing your own flesh. If you remain as you are—doing your own thing—the world you love so much will stay in the condition it's in. The world isn't like it is because it's evil. The world is like it is because so many people are uncommitted Christians. They go to the church building but they don't take the Church anywhere. They don't speak to others prophetically concerning the things of God. They aren't salt and light. They don't pray for change. We've got to stop blaming the world for being worldly and get transformed into Christ-likeness, so that we can make the world like heaven.

IS YOUR LIFE A PICTURE OF JESUS' LIFE?

As the anointed man of God for your house, stay conscious of your need to act like Jesus, who loves His Bride and is called "a merciful and faithful high priest."[52] Create such a tidal wave of the reality of Jesus in your life that when you're with your family, they feel as if they're with Jesus. You want Jesus to come upon you so strongly that there's hardly any difference between a personal encounter with Jesus and a personal encounter with you. You're changing and impacting their lives as if Jesus were still walking on the earth.

How real is your relationship with Christ, or is it just religion? If it's real, then in your home, they see Jesus in you. When you come into a city, when you go to your job, when you're in a fast food restaurant, when you get in an elevator or walk into an office building, people sense His presence. When you go into the rest room, revival should come into that bathroom when you're in there.

You were created to be like God, so work at it until you get it right. You were made in His image.[53] You have the nature of God. Christians are "partakers of the divine nature."[54] "God . . . decided from the outset to shape the lives of those who love him along the same lines as the life of his Son. The Son stands first in the line of humanity he restored. We see the original and intended shape of our lives there in him."[55]

Consecrate yourself until your life becomes a picture of Christ's life. Clean the sin off and what will shine through is "Christ in you, the hope of glory."[56] He "is able to do exceedingly abundantly above all that we ask or think, *according to the power that works in us.*"[57]

If you have the potential to be like Jesus and you're not, it's because you're not seeing Him very clearly. You haven't been hanging around Him enough to get to know Him. You don't see Him in the Scriptures because you don't feast on His Word. You don't "read the red"—the words of Jesus in the New Testament.

The more clearly you see Jesus, the more you'll become like Him—not only when He appears at His Second Coming, but also when He appears now in your heart. The more you become like Jesus, the more your wife will want to partner with you to bring heaven to your home.

PRAYER TO BE LIKE JESUS

Father, in the name of the Lord Jesus, we thank You that You have given us Your Spirit. You have taken us out of bondage, and Jesus is now ever living to make intercession for us. Insight is coming from Him to us through the Holy Spirit. Power is coming from Him, au-

thority is coming from Him. God, we refuse to go outside of the camp, outside of Your presence and Your anointing. Lord, we stay in the anointing, in the tabernacle, in the fellowship, in the glory, in the honor of God, in the holiness of God.

Take all of the slackness out of us, Lord. Help us to admit where we are in our desires and intention. Don't let us be soft. Let us be just like You in every way.

Lord, hide us from "Egypt," the things of the world. Blind us to Egypt, but help us, Lord, to be wide open to heaven. Help us to see Your ways, to have Your understanding, to reach out and touch others, Lord, not to be so thoughtful of ourselves.

Help us to be a blessing to other people, my Father, through the ministry of the Word, the fresh oil of the anointing. Awaken us constantly out of our sleep and help us to have a pure discernment of our own hearts.

Help us to see the end from the beginning. Help us to look at how You created things in the beginning, and make our relationship with You like Your relationship with Adam and Eve when You originally created them. Help us to do those things that are pure according to how things are going to be ultimately. Thy will be done on earth as it is in heaven.

Lord, when we are tested, help us to see that it is a test, and let us go through it in such a way that it would bring glory to Your name and to Your Son. Thank You, Lord.

Continue in every way to give us increase. Continue in every way to help us to boldly reach out and touch others, to be extravagant in our love, faith, and financial giving in every way.

We are being overtaken by You. You are the tidal wave that has come to us. You brought the earthquake and the water, and the river comes from the throne of heaven. Thank You for letting it travel at a speed unknown to reach us.

In Your precious name we pray. Amen.

SELAH

I try not to close any day before judging myself with the help of the Lord to see if I deserve to go to sleep at night—if I have fulfilled His will for me for that day. Several years ago in our ministry we started using the end-of-the-day checklist on the next page, called "May I Go to Sleep Now, Father?" I challenge you to use it every day for the next season of your consecration.

MAY I GO TO SLEEP NOW, FATHER?

*Before you go to sleep at night, write notes
for each of the areas listed below.
Judge yourself for your level of your
faithfulness in becoming more like Jesus.*

Note: Scripture references are just a few examples. Search for others.

Cultivating your relationship with God

❑ **Personal prayer time and Bible study.** *Luke 18:1, Isaiah 56:7.*
❑ **The secret prayer life.** *Matthew 6:5–6.*
❑ **Awareness of sin** *(evil thoughts; lust of the eyes, lust of the flesh, pride of life). 2 Corinthians 10:3–6; 1 John 2:16.*
❑ **Confession of sin and repentance.** *1 John 1:9, Mark 1:15.*
❑ **Prayer and fasting.** *Isaiah 58.*
❑ **Intercession for others** *(friends; family; the lost; local, national, and international civic leaders; local, national, and international church leaders; social issues; personal ministry; associates). James 5:16, 1 Timothy 2:2.*
❑ **Gratitude.** *Colossians 3:15. Count your blessings, using Philippians 4:8 as a guide (things that are true, honest, just, pure, lovely, of good report, virtuous, worthy of praise). See also the blessings in Deuteronomy 28 and Ephesians 1:3.*

"Finally, brethren, whatsoever things are true, whatsoever things are honest, whatsoever things are just, whatsoever things are pure, whatsoever things are lovely, whatsoever things are of good report; if there be any virtue, and if there be any praise, think on these things" (Philippians 4:8 KJV).

Loving People—1 Corinthians 13.

❏ **Family first.** *Make a daily list of good qualities you see in the people in your family, again using the categories from Philippians 4:8 (above).*
❏ **Personal prayer list.**
❏ **Speaking well of people today** *(blessing people with your words). Proverbs 11:11.*
❏ **Witnessing** *(sowing your life with humility into lost, prideful, or religious people). Acts 1:8.*
❏ **Friendships** *(kind thoughts, words, and deeds toward others, including enemies). Matthew 5:44.*
❏ **Reconciliation** *(everywhere it's needed). 2 Corinthians 5:17–21.*
❏ **Letters** *(personal, witnessing). 2 Peter 3:1–2.*
❏ **Secret acts of kindness** *(secret service, secret giving, giving alms). Matthew 6:1–4.*

Personal Integrity

❏ **Telling the truth.** *Revelation 21:8.*
❏ **Keeping your word** *(by your words you will be justified or condemned). Matthew 12:37.*
❏ **Punctuality.**
❏ **Work ethic** *(reflection on your effectiveness, attitudes, and vision).*

Personal Health

❏ **Exercise.** *1 Timothy 4:8.*
❏ **Eating** *(examining habits, lusts).*
❏ **Fasting.**

Personal Order and Finances

❑ Tithes and offerings
❑ Processing of papers *(mail, bills, etc.—process, decide next step)*.
❑ Evaluation of finances *(paying bills, reconciling bank statements, planning budgets, ending debt)*. *Romans 13:8.*
❑ Money stewarded today. *Matthew 25:14–30.*
❑ Extra-biblical readings *books, newspapers, magazines, etc.)*.
❑ Homework *(office, school, and church)*.
❑ Cleaning *(house, bedroom, office, etc., and describe parts undone)*.
❑ Desk cleared for tomorrow.

Everything released, trusting God.

10

MARRIAGE IS ON-THE-JOB TRAINING FOR THE FUTURE

"That your days may be multiplied, and the days of your
children, in the land which the Lord sware unto your
fathers to give them, as the days of heaven upon the earth."
—Deuteronomy 11:18–21 KJV

*It has been over twenty years since I saw my wife deliver our first
son, Jason, at the hospital, but I'll never forget what an ordeal it was
for her. It wasn't that the labor was long or that she had complica-
tions, it was just that she was in so much pain.*

*Right now the Church of Jesus Christ is in pain. Christ's woman,
the Church, is pregnant with child for the last days. The baby is
coming to term. The membrane is about to burst. His Church is
about to give birth to a great spiritual revival, and God is looking for
the faithful few whom He can trust to be spiritual parents for the
new babies.*

I hope that in learning how to bring heaven to your home you have
also been given a vision of how to bring heaven to your job, your
church, your personal ministry, and society. I hope you want to be
some of those faithful few who have the character qualities of Jesus
and can be entrusted to make an impact in His name—both in this
world and the next.

When Jesus was raised from the dead, He didn't appear to the
crowds. He appeared to five hundred people.[1] Of those, only 120
were willing to wait for Him in the upper room until the Holy Spirit

came. By the time of Pentecost, fifty days after the Resurrection, the Bible says that these disciples had taken care of business details like replacing Judas with another apostle, prayed, and forgotten their past differences to come into one accord. Those present included the apostles, Jesus' mother, Mary, Jesus' brothers, and the women who had followed Him. They all had to wait for God's gestation process to be completed in them before the birthing of the Church.

HEAVEN ON EARTH

Spiritual Parenting

Grow up! The Church of Jesus Christ needs a rebirth. We need to get desperate enough about our immaturity that we seek Him for our change. The shame of Christians is that while they should be spiritual parents, they stay at the level of a babe. They are always acting like little children to God. They pray and say, "God, I want this," "God, I want that." We can't keep coming to prayer meetings and seeking God for ourselves. We need to grow up in God so that we are no longer just asking God to do things for us. We are parents taking the spiritual responsibility for others, and even for the generation. That's what Adam did. That's what those 120 people did in the upper room.

If you know how to bring heaven to your home, you can help bring heaven to all the earth. The concept of parenting goes beyond dealing with being a biological parent. It has to do with having the responsibility of oversight. That's the spirit of a parent. A man can father children and still be totally irresponsible regarding their care. He doesn't have the spirit of a parent. Other people who have no biological children are still parents because they take the responsibility of being a parent in God.

We are called to be spiritual parents who love children (the spiritually immature) and take responsibility for their growth. The word "Adam" means progenitor, the first man. He had the oversight over the entire human race. We are being raised up to be spiritual parents to oversee the creation of God.

Take heaven beyond your home. The subtitle of this book is "How Every Marriage Can Bring Heaven to Your Home." Your marriage and parenting experiences are not just for today and they are not just for yourself and your family. Those experiences are on-the-job training to prepare you to serve the Lord both in time and eternity. Bringing heaven to your home establishes a piece of God's kingdom here on earth.

Take a closer look at the opening Scripture for this chapter and for this book. God is saying in Deuteronomy 11:18–21 that heaven comes to earth when you have the Word of God in your heart and soul, and you teach it and live it out before your family.

The next step for every man of God who brings heaven to his home is to help bring heaven to the rest of the world.

The Bible Begins and Ends with a Marriage

At the beginning of creation, God gave Adam a wife—Eve. The Bible begins with a marriage.

At the end of the Bible, there's another marriage. This one is between the Last Adam, Christ, and His woman, the Church. It's the Marriage Supper of the Lamb.

You know that when the history of the world begins with a marriage and ends with a marriage, there must be something awesome about marriage that we're supposed to see. That's why all the time I've been talking to you about how "your wife is not your momma" I've also been talking about seeing your relationship with your wife as a type of something else that God is doing.

In other words, God isn't only trying to heal marriages, He's also trying to give you Christ's point of view. He's not just trying to help you have a great marriage, He wants you to be great in every area of your life. And He especially wants you to be prepared for eternity. God is in the process of training you to have oversight in this world and the world to come.

Jesus Will Appoint Christians to Rule Over His Kingdoms

Before God made the world, He had a vision of what the world would be like. He also saw what He wanted you and your wife to be like, and He loved you. That's the principle of original intent.

Before the world was started, God knew how it would end. Then He worked backward to make it a reality. That's the principle of last things.

God has made Jesus ruler over all His creation. A time is coming when He will be visibly ruling everywhere. The book of Revelation says, "And there were loud voices in heaven, saying, 'The kingdoms of this world have become the kingdoms of our Lord and of His Christ, and He shall reign forever and ever!' "[2]

Jesus told the apostles that in the world to come they would be assigned responsibilities in His kingdom.[3] He said, "And I appoint unto you a kingdom, as my Father hath appointed unto me; That ye may eat and drink at my table in my kingdom, and sit on thrones judging the twelve tribes of Israel."[4]

That appointment follows creative order. God delegated certain responsibilities over the earth to Adam—animals, birds, creeping things, and fish. Jesus will delegate certain responsibilities over eternity to His Church.

At every moment, we are in on-the-job training for the future. That's why what we are learning about being a servant-leader in the home is so important.

Just before Jesus appointed the apostles to positions of oversight in the kingdom, He had to intervene because they were arguing about who would be the greatest. He told them then what I have been telling you in this book, that "the greatest among you should be like the youngest, and the one who rules like the one who serves."[5]

Humility, service, and a repentant heart not only make you a great husband who brings heaven to his home, they also prepare you to be promoted to positions of greatness, both in this world and the world to come, because God is with you. "For this is what the high and lofty One says—he who lives forever, whose name is holy: 'I live in a high and holy place, but also with him who is contrite and lowly in spirit, to revive the spirit of the lowly and to revive the heart of the contrite.' "[6] When God watches your attitudes as you relate to your family and handle other aspects of your life, He can tell a lot about whether He wants to promote you.

EVERY STAGE OF YOUR LIFE IS A PREPARATION FOR THE NEXT

Jesus told a story about three men who were being tested for promotion by a master who entrusted them with his wealth. Two invested it wisely, and one did not. Those two whom the master considered to be good stewards were rewarded with his highest praise: "Well done, good and faithful servant; you were faithful over a few things, I will make you ruler over many things. Enter into the joy of your lord."[7]

"Well done . . . I will make you ruler . . . enter into the joy." Most of us know that Jesus wasn't just referring to rulership and joy in this world but also in the world to come.

Each stage in life is preparation for future responsibility. When you're a child, your parents prepare you for preschool, then kindergarten and elementary school, then junior high, high school, and maybe college. They also prepare you to be a good employee in the marketplace. It isn't all spelled out like that, but that' what's happening as you grow up under your parents' training.

When you're an adult, instead of parents being the ones to give you the most input for your growth, you have your wife. You also have pastors, managers, overseers, mentors, and spiritual parents. All of them will hopefully help you to be faithful in every area of jurisdiction you encounter. Christ-like character not only makes you a good husband and father but also a good employee, manager, or minister.

> **Your marriage is your most important training program for the next stage of your life.**

In this chapter you will see how God uses your marriage to train you for the next stage of your life.

The first place a man begins to steward the dominion God gave him on the earth is in the area of his relationship with his wife. He represents a seed of what heaven is going to be like. He expresses Christ-likeness to his wife. He is a visible manifestation of Jesus to his whole house.

In marriage, you build character and learn firsthand about life from God. The first reason you seek God's counsel is because you need His help! Then you build character through developing relationships with your wife, your children, and your parents and in-laws. Parents and in-laws are examples for you, to show you what marriage is all about. They have weathered some storms. They know how to overcome challenges, and they can tell you firsthand how to love each other regardless of what happens. All of this is just part of your on-the-job training for the future.

Marriage Lessons Apply to All of Life

As you are trying to be the best husband you can be, you learn not only how to improve your family life but also how to be a better person all around. What you learn in marriage you apply in your workplace, the church, and all your other relationships. Then, as you and your wife grow closer together, you become an example of a good marriage to others. Your marriage becomes a source of hope that it is still possible in this divorce-prone age to find at least one happily married couple.

Each stage of your life is a preparation for the next stage. This life is a preparation for the life to come. There will be a whole new experience waiting for us that God has prepared for those who love Him. That's why you need to get all you can get out of God's training program on earth, especially in your marriage, because that is what He is using to qualify you to rule with Christ in eternity.

If we understood that, we wouldn't keep serving God for His hands instead of serving Him for His feet. We wouldn't keep God in the position of a spiritual Santa Claus. We would see Him as the almighty God of the universe. When preachers tell you how you can get your needs met, instead of how you can meet the needs of God, it's as though God exists for you instead of you existing for God.

God is not your spiritual Santa Claus. Maybe you're wondering why God hasn't removed such-and-such a problem yet. It's because God's main concern isn't trying to remove your problems, He wants to remove your inadequacy to deal with your problems. God can deal with problems. As Christians—Christ-like people—we don't run *from* the problem. We run *to* the problem. We're the salt and light.

Once we start growing up in the realities of the eternal realm and move out of religion into relationship, then we will become the solution solvers in the earth. That is why Adam was originally created—to live forever and rule for God—but when he sinned, God immediately had to disqualify him. From then on He was setting in motion another plan that He would fulfill through His Son. He was always seeing life on earth from the perspective of eternity.

More Joy Ahead If You Refuse to Quit

Everything about God is eternal. If you and your wife can keep your problem solving in the context of eternity, things here on earth won't seem nearly so overwhelming. The Lord has already sown seeds of eternal thinking into our minds. The writer of Ecclesiastes says, "He has also set eternity in their heart, [without which man] will not find out the work which God has done from the beginning even to the end."[8] However, those seeds of eternity are constantly being choked off by "the cares of this world, and the deceitfulness of riches, and the lusts of other things."[9] No matter what problems arise, no matter how hard life seems to get, no matter what tragedies and pains you have to endure, it's not the end. There's always something better up ahead. You never saw a storm that didn't pass!

That's what eternal life is all about. You're on a journey without end, and every place you go, if you know the Lord, is even more awesome than the place you were before.

Think about it. Where does your mind spend most of its time? You probably are dealing mostly with money, your family, your job, your enemies, lots of everyday stuff in the time and space dimension. You are mostly concerned with the situations you're dealing with right now.

That's not where God lives. He lives in the realm of the eternal. The Bible keeps bringing you back to that reality. Even when God helps you out in your everyday situations, He does it because they have implications toward the future. He wants to encourage you by helping you overcome your trials so you will press on into His joy, because "weeping may endure for a night, but joy cometh in the morning."[10]

Since you are being prepared to live with God for both time (now) and eternity (forever), God isn't worried about today's problems, because He already knows how they are going to turn out. He knows the end from the beginning. He's just using them to build character in you and to expose your character flaws, which need your attention so you can correct them now and He can use you in eternity.

A Real-Life Story About Eternity

Here's an example of how a group of Christians in Georgia had to draw on every bit of faith they had in God's eternal realm to survive a sudden, devastating tragedy.

"Get out! Get out! The dam has broken!" It sounded like a pack of freight trains roaring out of the darkness in the early morning hours

of November 6, 1977.[11] Then came the shouts: "Get out! Get out! The dam has broken!" The gentle stream tumbling over forested Toccoa Falls in northern Georgia had become a deadly wall of water. Within seconds, a thirty-foot-high tidal wave had been created as the dam broke and the water bolted over the falls and into the valley below, smashing into the trailers, homes, and campus buildings of Toccoa Falls College. Autumn trees were uprooted like matchsticks. Cars and house trailers became deadly torpedoes. As people struggled to escape the wave, some were swept away. Others watched helplessly as members of their own family drowned before their eyes. The families of this Christian and Missionary Alliance school would never be the same. In a flash, thirty-nine men, women, and children had been sent into eternity.

As the devastating waters receded, incredible stories began to emerge out of Georgia's worst natural disaster in almost forty years. A community of professing Christians had come face-to-face with the reality of their faith in eternal life. And the world was watching to see what they would do.

The Bible says, "Many waters cannot quench love, neither can the floods drown it."[12] These people lost their loved ones, but the love they received from Jesus could not be drowned. Even the members of the press and rescue agencies who came to see what remained of the campus could not believe that the survivors had such peace and joy. They had not lost Jesus, and they knew their loved ones were with Him. They could not just live in the realm of the circumstances they were facing. They had to live in the realm of the eternal. All of their lives had in some way been a preparation for this hour.

Here's one family's experience.

"Come on, kids, get ready. We're going to meet Jesus." In one trailer, Bill and Karen Anderson had been asleep with their five children when a woman ran by shouting, "Get out! Get out! The dam has broken!" Within seconds, the trailer shifted and then a huge force slammed against it, tearing off the roof. They prayed that they wouldn't panic and managed to calm their children by telling them to trust the Lord.

When the next blow came the children cried out, "Jesus! Jesus!" Then the trailer smashed against trees. Bill tossed his oldest daughter, twelve, and oldest son, six, into the branches. Then he heard his wife saying calmly to two of the other children as they stood in the hallway of the sinking trailer, "Come on, kids, get ready. We're going to meet Jesus." And then they were gone. Bill knew they were with the Lord.

Bill and his other daughter managed to survive, along with the two children in the trees. When Bill's unsaved relatives came from Vermont for the funeral service, he discovered that this seeming tragedy had a victorious side. His sister told him, "I've found the Lord." Then his oldest brother said, "I didn't come here for the funeral. . . . I'm here to see you. I want what you've got," and Bill led him to the Savior. Bill knew where his wife and children were, and now he knew that his brother and sister would be with them someday in the future. The deaths had already transcended the realm of time and brought a little of heaven to earth.

Christians Who Die Have a Glorious Future

Most people outside the Church have not experienced the kind of power that comes from God when faith is tested by tragedy. It was obvious that Jesus was real and the eternal realm was real to these survivors. Their Christian walk had been preparing them for the future by faith, and the future had come.

If you are saved, and your marriage is serious, no matter what unexpected events come your way, you can survive, and thrive. It doesn't have to be a death, but that is the ultimate tragedy that proves every time the difference between true Christianity and any other belief system. Christians who die still have a future. It's not the end. It's only the beginning of a new adventure. Marriage is not just a relationship to meet present needs. It is a symbol of heaven, where love goes on forever.[13]

When Jesus is real in your marriage, you don't have to wait until your spouse dies to get people talking about how awesome it is to see your life. If they see you dealing well with your relationship on a daily basis, these days that's news, too! You have died to your self-centered life! It's getting so rare to see a really happily married couple. The adults who overcome problems and stay faithful to their mates through the trials of life become the kind of salt-of-the-earth people that society needs.

A lot of books are being written today about success, mostly from the earthly, human perspective, but true success is found in the realm of the Spirit. It is finding the will of God and doing it. Success is believing in Jesus and finding Him in there with you when tragedy strikes. Success is learning to respect your wife and maturing in un-conditional love for her. Success is taking all the maturity you've gained from your marriage into the marketplace, for the good of humanity.

How strong is your belief in heaven? Are you afraid to die? Do you know where you will spend eternity?

How strong is your belief in your marriage? Are you afraid to die to your self-will?

Good Marriages Build Good Character

A good marriage is on-the-job training for success in any career, any studies, or any leadership role in the Church or society. Good mar-riages build good character. A godly mate will break down your pride and show you all your immature characteristics that disqualify you for leadership, then build you up again in an atmosphere of uncondi-tional love. A godly mate who forces you to manage well your home finances and family affairs is doing you a favor by preparing you to manage a company.

Some people manage to avoid being responsible at home because they think they can get away with it. The only reason they perform better at work is because the company's accountability system im-poses negative consequences if they don't maintain a certain stan-dard. A man could hold the office of governor and still be cheating on his wife until he has reason to believe he might be exposed pub-licly. He doesn't have the character to be faithful, but the fear of negative consequences keeps him at a certain level.

At home the real you shows up. It may seem that you can be a difficult person at home and Mr. Friendly at the workplace, but you are the same person. It just takes another level of pressure to bring out the "real" you. That is a sign of immaturity. You can't be trusted. You have forgotten that God knows all about it.

You've got to get something from God to be able to handle chal-lenges. You've got to be like Him inside.

In any company, if you could get marriages in line, from the presi-dent all the way down to the janitor, you could cancel most of the "leadership training" programs. If you have heaven in your home, you're going to be a lot more capable of setting up the environment of heaven at your job or in your classroom—without ever having to call it "heaven."

Churches whose members had heaven in their homes would be so inviting to outsiders that they wouldn't be able to keep unbelievers away. As it is now, the division and striving for position in the Church, the workplace, and the university are just irrefutable evidence that the same kind of fighting is going on in the home.

Stephen R. Covey wrote this in his best-seller *The 7 Habits of Highly Successful People*: "Dag Hammarskjold, past Secretary-General of the United Nations, once made a profound, far-reaching statement: 'It is more noble to give yourself completely to one individual than to labor diligently for the salvation of the masses.' I take that to mean that I could devote eight, ten, or twelve hours a day, five, six, or seven days a week to the thousands of people and projects 'out there' and still not have a deep, meaningful relationship with my own spouse, with my own teenage son, with my closest working associate. And it would take more nobility of character—more humility, courage, and strength—to rebuild that one relationship than it would to continue putting in all those hours for all those people and causes."[14]

You have to see how your marketplace success relates to the conditions in your home. Your jurisdiction starts there. Just as Adam spoiled the Garden, you can spoil the garden of your home. When you have sin in your house, you never have real, God-given success out in the marketplace. You may be rich and famous, but in God's eyes you are "wretched, and miserable, and poor, and blind, and naked."[15]

Here are some practical examples of how improving your relationship with one person—your wife—will bring you success in the marketplace and the ministry and help you keep the events of your life—your real life—in the proper perspective.

HOW A GOOD MARRIAGE HELPS MAKE YOU SUCCESSFUL ANYWHERE

It's awesome! The character you develop as you build a great relationship with your wife will make you the kind of person every company wants and needs.

In the following examples, look at how the qualities of a godly husband we have been talking about in each chapter will prepare you to be successful in the marketplace or ministry.

From Chapter 1. Character qualities that result from *really loving your wife,* which will make you successful in the marketplace or ministry:
  · Bringing a happy attitude to work each day, not the pain of strife at home
  · Being in love, which makes every day look brighter and every task look easier
  · Promoting women whenever they deserve it, even if men always held those positions before
  · Helping other husbands to have good attitudes toward their wives: refusing to indulge their complaints and criticisms; advising them how to love their wives as Christ loves the Church
  · Respecting women in the office (no flirting or sexual harassment)
  · Dressing professional, never seductively

From Chapter 2. Character qualities that result from *becoming blended after being single* that will make you successful in the marketplace or ministry:
  · Helping single people to be responsible, virtuous, and mature
  · Providing good role models of a married couple for people who are not yet married
  · Maintaining good health habits, including diet, exercise, and rest
  · Able to adapt to change and to help others to adapt

From Chapter 3. Character qualities that result from *being a grown-up man,* which will make you successful in the marketplace or ministry:
  · Arriving at work early, taking only the allowed amount of time for breaks, not rushing out as soon as the clock hits quitting time
  · Respecting all those in authority over you, especially the owners
  · Saying the same things about those in authority when you are with them as you do when they are gone
  · Freedom from inner conflicts
  · Able to restrain anger, not losing your temper
  · Responsible

- Faithful with a few things so you can be promoted to handle many things
- Frugal with company expenses
- Careful with company property, never stealing even a pencil for personal use at home
- Looking for ways to save the company money
- Consistently doing all paperwork required
- Separating company time and personal time
- Not asking for special favors or bending the rules
- Not striving for advancement at others' expense
- Being content with your wages, asking for an increase only at proper times and with right attitude
- Studying company manuals to understand policies and procedures and interpret them for others
- Attending in-service education seminars and taking outside classes that will help you do your job better

From Chapter 4. Character qualities that result from *blowing your wife's mind,* which will make you successful in the marketplace or ministry:
- Generous
- Out-serving others
- Able to make purchases to benefit the company
- Being a blessing to your boss by your thoughtfulness
- Helping your boss learn how to blow his wife's mind
- Giving small, thoughtful gifts to others on staff to make their work easier
- Secret giving

From Chapter 5. Character qualities that result from having *the home-court advantage,* which will make you successful in the marketplace or ministry:
- Consistently friendly, cheerful, and pleasant
- Making it a point to get to know about other staff and their families (on your own time—breaks, before and after work, etc.)
- Conscious of keeping a pleasant atmosphere at work
- Coordinating with housekeeping staff to keep trash emptied, areas dusted, etc.
- Supportive of staff suggestions and creativity

- Able to integrate new employees and maintain pleasant environment
- Good interpersonal relations
- Strong communication system and memos
- Maintaining orderly desk and office filing system
- Overseeing supplies so that everyone has enough
- Not provoking people, and when they provoke you, refusing to get upset

From Chapter 6. Character qualities that result from *going low for your wife,* which will make you successful in the marketplace or ministry:
- Feeling no task is too lowly for you, even fixing coffee for others
- Maintaining servant attitude
- Dedicated
- Able to keep a job because you want to be a good provider
- Understand authority and submission in relating to those over you and under you
- Willing to learn new skills or be trained for a different position, even if you don't want to be moved to a different department
- Realizing that it's not having the position that's important but how faithful you are in that position
- Remembering you work for your employer, not yourself
- Looking at problems as opportunities to help people
- Having a servant's attitude toward the public, accepting and resolving complaints without striking back, even if they are personally directed at you

From Chapter 7. Character qualities that result from *respecting in-laws and parents,* which will make you successful in the marketplace or ministry:
- Respectful to those who are older and/or more experienced than you are
- Seeking wisdom and knowledge from experienced staff members
- Teaching other staff to respect their in-laws and parents as the occasion arises in off-time discussions

From Chapter 8. Character qualities that result from *loving your children and believing in them,* which will make you successful in the marketplace or ministry:

- Able to teach and train employees in a kind, thorough, fatherly way
- Encouraging people to increase their knowledge and skills so they can advance—on the job and in life
- Building people up to feel successful
- Bringing out the best in people
- Knowing how to be funny without telling off-color jokes
- Treating young people under you as you would want a boss to treat your children
- Training staff how to best meet your needs and the needs of your boss

From Chapter 9. Character qualities that result from *being a priest and prophet in your home,* which will make you successful in the marketplace or ministry:

- Praying for members of the staff during private devotional time at home
- Offering to pray for someone in need
- Sharing life-strengthening Scriptures with staff on your own time
- Inviting people to go to your church, telling them about free Vacation Bible School, etc., for their kids
- Visionary
- Innovative
- Willing to take risks, even to fail, if necessary, because you know you can pick yourself back up again
- Coming to work refreshed and ready to give 100 percent
- Honest, having integrity
- Never taking a bribe (money, promotion, merchandise, etc.) but doing what you see is right
- Not giving away company secrets to competitors
- Not ruled by money
- Being a serious thinker who comes up with better ways of doing things, which will be a benefit to everyone involved
- Taking time to plan ahead for the benefit of the company

A CHALLENGE TO CHURCHES, SCHOOLS, AND BUSINESSES

I would like to challenge churches, schools, and businesses to launch an all-out program to improve their companies by improving the marriages of their staff, using the principles in this book. If heaven is real, why wouldn't every church, school, and business want to promote an atmosphere of heaven there every day?

This is something that can be measured. After the seminars, evaluate the resulting change in productivity at your place of business. Find out how much things improve at work when husbands are blowing their wives' minds at home, giving them the home-court advantage, and going low in humility instead of raising up. These men and their wives can become awesome company presidents. They can be awesome at any place on the company totem pole. It's all the same. It's all the kingdom of God.

I'm telling you, try it out! See what God does in your church, school, or business when you hold these seminars and the homes of company employees, teachers, and church members start becoming like heaven on earth.

Christians as Real Assets

Jesus said, "Thy kingdom come. Thy will be done in earth, as it is in heaven."[16] Sometimes it seems as if the Church has lost the biblical concept of heaven—not only in the sense of dying and going to heaven but also of dying to self, of being faithful over a few things so Christ can make you ruler over many things. Christians should be the greatest experts at making every workplace on earth a type of heaven.

Instead, not many secular businesses are going to the Church for advice with personnel problems. It's just the opposite. Businessmen usually tell Christians to keep their faith to themselves and stop wasting company time with their proselytizing. That isn't always persecution. Sometimes it's just common sense.

If Christians were really contributing something to the companies—if the companies were not totally sold out to the devil, at least—their words would be welcomed, not ruled out of order. There is an economic value to true holiness. Holy people are valuable to companies, but holier-than-thou people are a detriment. Which are you?

Jesus sent the Holy Spirit to work on you from the inside out. Outwardly you can sound like a great Christian if you're talking to people on the job about Jesus, but inwardly you may remain unchanged. You may still be a rebel, and you're just using your "Christianese language" to look good to your wife or your church friends in defiance of your boss. That doesn't mean you never speak of your faith at work, but you do it in the spirit of meekness. You do it as if you were Jesus.

You can be a leader on your job. You can be the manager. Man may have given you awards, but God is still not giving you any rewards because your character is not like Jesus'. You may have authority, but do you have all kinds of trouble with the people under you? What's the problem? You're a rebel with authority. It's man-given authority, not God-given, because God has to release the power before you can flourish in anything you do on earth. And He judges you by your inner man.

You can have real power only when you are submitted to God, because all authority has been given to Jesus. All authority under Jesus is delegated authority. You may have position among men on earth, but you don't have true authority in the realm of eternity unless you are submitted. Don't you want it?

Daniel's Vision of God's Power

The prophet Daniel wrote about the awesome demonstration of God's power and authority that he saw in heaven. This power is something you and your wife can tap into, if you lead a holy lifestyle with God's purity inside. It serves God's purposes for holy people to have power.

Daniel wrote, "I watched till thrones were put in place, and the Ancient of Days was seated; His garment was white as snow, and the hair of His head was like pure wool. His throne was a fiery flame, its wheels a burning fire; A fiery stream issued and came forth from before Him. A thousand thousands ministered to Him; ten thousand times ten thousand stood before Him. The court was seated, and the books were opened. I watched then because of the sound of the pompous words which the horn was speaking; I watched till the beast was slain, and its body destroyed and given to the burning flame. As for the rest of the beasts, they had their dominion taken away, yet their lives were prolonged for season and a time."[17]

Daniel added, "I was watching in the night visions, and behold, One like the Son of Man, coming with the clouds of heaven! He came to the Ancient of Days, and they brought Him near before Him. Then to Him was given dominion and glory and a kingdom, that all peoples, nations, and languages should serve Him. His dominion is an everlasting dominion, which shall not pass away, and His kingdom the one which shall not be destroyed."[18]

Who is the Son of Man? Jesus! Who was the Ancient of Days? God the Father.

He's an eternal spirit.

He's an eternal God.

He's an eternal Son.

We have an eternal spirit, we have an eternal Word, and so certainly we should have eternal authority.

One of the major differences between Christianity and false religions is that we have real, intimate access to God through our relationship with Jesus. In the same way as Daniel saw Jesus in his night vision, approaching the Ancient of Days, you are able to come near to God when He approves you. You are to have dominion and a kingdom, but you become worthy only by the degree to which you develop inner attributes according to the image and likeness of God. You are saved by grace, but you have to become qualified to reign at that level.

The whole essence of what you're about has to do with whether or not God approves you. How does God show His approval? With His presence.

HOW TO BECOME "RULER OVER MANY THINGS" BY BEING "FAITHFUL OVER A FEW THINGS"

Jesus said, "Well done, good and faithful servant; you were faithful over a few things, I will make you ruler over many things. Enter into the joy of your lord."[19]

Keeping your word

- Spending time with your wife when you have made a commitment to her to do it
- Coming home for dinner when you said you would come
- Calling when you said you would
- Doing errands as promised
- Attending your children's games and recitals and not saying you have to work

Finishing a task
- Completing projects cluttering up the garage and yard
- Cooking dinner and cleaning up
- Taking care of your dirty clothes
- Helping your wife and children with their projects

Showing others how to do their jobs well
- Training your children to be faithful workers
- Overseeing your children's education
- Explaining to your wife the way you like certain foods fixed, clothes cleaned, etc.

Being a good steward of money
- Helping find bargains for grocery shopping
- Eating less expensive food items when necessary
- Purchasing without using credit cards and interest payments
- Budgeting
- Planning vacations
- Doing long-term financial planning
- Giving your children music and other lessons

Taking care of your possessions
- Servicing the car on time
- Keeping the car clean
- Doing or arranging for home maintenance
- Keeping up the yard or hiring and supervising help

Stewarding relationships
- Spending quantities of time with your wife and children daily and for all special events

Being a good provider
- Keeping a steady job
- Not expecting anyone else to provide for your family but you

Maintaining integrity
- Telling a store clerk if he makes a mistake in your favor while ringing up an order
- Being honest with everyone
- Asking forgiveness quickly

Mentoring others with the unselfish goal of making them more successful than you are
- Preparing your children so they can outdo your accomplishments in every area

Guarding your tongue
- Speaking highly of your wife and children to them and to others
- Being careful never to curse with criticism
- Building up your family with positives even while you correct the negatives
- Never gossiping

Keeping your word
- Keeping work commitments or explaining what hindered you
- Taking things in to work that you mentioned you had at home that would be helpful

Finishing a task
- Completing assigned projects by the deadlines

Showing others how to do their jobs well
- Instructing your staff patiently and repeatedly as necessary
- Dealing graciously with vendors

Being a good steward of money
- Valuing company money as if it were your own
- Giving more time than shows on the clock

Taking care of others' possessions
- Being careful with office equipment, furniture, and vehicles entrusted to you

Stewarding relationships
- Maintaining pleasant, respectful relationships with staff and with the public

Being a good provider
- Doing what is necessary to keep a job without compromising your convictions

Maintaining integrity
- Maintaining accurate records
- Always telling the truth, even if it hurts

Mentoring others with the unselfish goal of making them more successful than you are
- Training employees under you to be promoted over you if they have the skill and dedication

Guarding your tongue
- Commending other staff members in every way possible; looking for what they do right
- Correcting them in the spirit of Christ, who has shown you mercy
- Never gossiping

The Example of Johnny Johnson

A "disadvantaged" father's legacy to his son: Be faithful and you will be rewarded. Whatever hardships you endure as a family, you can always teach your children valuable lessons about life that they will never forget. Here's an example of a father whose attitudes in the home helped his son grow up to be successful in spite of every obstacle.

James E. "Johnny" Johnson, former U.S. assistant secretary of the navy, grew up during the Depression, the oldest of nine children of a black father and a Native-American mother. While he was still a child he got his first job picking up pieces of cardboard at a box-manufacturing firm in Chicago. Every night when he went to work he remembered his father's words: "Whenever your boss gives you a dollar to do a job, give him a dollar and a half's worth of work."[20] As a result, he advanced quickly on that job and on every other job he held, all the way to appointments by U.S. presidents. There were many times when he had to overcome racial prejudice, but his father would never let him use that as an excuse. Johnny's training from a father who was "faithful over a few things" would later propel Johnny into a lifetime of breaking through into numerous honors and careers previously closed to black men.

The senior Mr. Johnson was born in Mississippi in 1865 after the end of the Civil War. His only early education came from a white friend courageous enough to defy the taboo against teaching Negroes to read, write, and do mathematics. His textbook was the Bible. When he learned enough to catch the local store proprietor cheating him, as he had been doing to all the other local blacks, the store owner threw him out.

Mr. Johnson left the family farm at seventeen and went to work at the Blackfoot Indian Reservation in Oklahoma, where he impressed the chief with his skill and hard work. When he was thirty-seven, he decided to marry fifteen-year-old Veola, and paid her father a horse, two calves, and some blankets for the privilege. He taught her how to cook, sew, read, and write, and when he was forty he found a one-room school and enrolled with the children to try to improve his meager education. They let him stay only until they discovered that he was married with children, then forced him out.

With all the seeming disadvantages that this man had, he made the most of every opportunity to be faithful over a few things, and he trained his children to be the same. He refused to take handouts for his large family, even from the church, where he took his family every Sunday and taught them to know and trust the Lord.

"When men were laid off, he was always the last man to go." Johnny Johnson wrote:

> On most jobs Dad usually became straw boss. When men were laid off, he was always the last man to go, and every time he finished one job, he'd be recommended for another.

"Then I'd be the last one to leave, too," Dad would tell me. "I'd collect the tools and clean them and put them away. I was the last one. I'd lock up and hand the keys to the boss.

"Now, you don't tell me they aren't going to keep a fellow like me on. I believe I should give a boss every ounce of work he deserves, because when payday comes, I don't want him to cheat me out of one penny. That's why I give him a dollar and a half's worth of work."[21]

Earthly employers reward faithfulness, and so does God. Men like Mr. Johnson stand out from the crowd. They are the ones most likely to keep their jobs in crunch time. Most employees are always watching out for Number One. (So are the employers, but don't let that stop you from being the best employee they ever met.)

If earthly employers like to see faithfulness, don't you think God likes to see it even more? Every time you do what you're called on to do—at home or on the job—and you do even more besides, you earn more favor with your Father. Because you'll live on into eternity, the character qualities you are developing now are for the purpose of bringing the kingdom of heaven to earth and also for preparing you to rule and reign with Christ in His future kingdom. How you respond to your wife is a key part of your training for your future on earth and your future role in the kingdom of God. Your life is a seed life for eternity.

PREPARED FOR HEAVEN

What Will You Say on That Great Day?

What if the Lord said that the only understand that you're going to have in eternity is what you have gained on this earth? If the Lord required that you transfer only your present spiritual knowledge over into the next world, how much of your knowledge would actually be kingdom knowledge? Would you be spiritually retarded in the next world or a functional adolescent? What do you actually know of kingdom reality? That's why you need to forget what you're going through. Just say, "I want to be like Jesus in it. I don't just want to say that I heard this Word. I want to be the Word manifest before my family."

What if God were to seal you now in the state you're in and say that's the way you will be in heaven? Would you be satisfied? Would you expect rewards? Or would you like a little more time to improve your heaven-bound resume?

A lot of Christians will be crying and sobbing so seriously at the Judgment Seat because they didn't allow God to form them into everything that He wanted them to be. On that day, when you look back at what you could have done, there will be no time for all the excuses:

"I didn't have time."

"My wife didn't understand me. She wasn't like my momma."

"It wasn't my fault."

"I didn't have enough money."

Jesus is going to look right through you and show you all that you could have done and been regardless of your limitations. He's going to show you that your problems were there for your growth. He's going to show you the choices you made and all the times when you should have pressed through but you gave up and quit. He's going to show you every instance where you chose the path of least resistance and others were hurt as a result. You're going to be at the gate and on your way into heaven, but when you see what you could have done, even though it's going to be good to be there, you'll say, "I could have done so much more."

I don't want to be crying at the gates of heaven because I could have done so much more! I want to be rejoicing. Every day that I live, God is giving me another opportunity to show myself worthy of ruling in eternity. I don't want to miss a single opportunity in my home or out in the world. Every opportunity that I get to prove myself as a son before my Father, He can see that He can entrust me with real power. That should be our attitude—be faithful over a few things in our families, our careers, our education, and God can promote us when we get to heaven.

We Need a Vision of Eternity

We need a vision for the future to make us live better now. If we don't see that marriage is on-the-job training for the future, both in time and eternity, we'll try to squirm out of every trial. The Bible says that without a vision—or where there is no vision—the people perish.[22] The Lord wants to give us vision, both for ourselves and for our families, so that the destiny of God can be fulfilled, both on earth and in heaven.

Your earthly success is a factor in fulfilling other people's destiny on earth and in heaven. Your willingness to go down and be different is a key part of your wife's breakthrough into achieving God's vision for her life. Your godly fathering is going to make the difference in your children's success or failure. And what God sees will be credited to your account in heaven.

Be Faithful to the Vision

God will be faithful to guide you as you lead your family into their destiny. When God gives you a vision for what you can become, He also gives you a gradually unfolding road map that shows you how to get there. At each turn in the road, He says, "This is where I want you to go. Will you do it?"

God told Abram, " 'Leave your country, your people and your father's household and go to the land I will show you.' . . . So Abram left, as the Lord had told him. . . . He took his wife Sarai, his nephew Lot, all the possessions they had accumulated and the people they had acquired in Haran, and they set out for the land of Canaan."[23]

God wanted to teach Abram how to obey. He could have sent him anywhere. He was testing his obedience without giving him all the details. God was calling Abram into both obedience and dependence. His obedience in leaving his country proved his dependency on God. His disobedience in taking Lot with him and lying to Abimelech showed his independence. Abraham is a hero of the faith, but it took him a long time to obey God in everything. A lot of time and effort was wasted in the process. Sounds a lot like us.

Most people want to know what God wants them to do, but they aren't willing to sign a blank contract in advance telling Him that they will obey once they get His instructions. What good would it do to tell you to do something if you have proved you are not like the Lord in the area of obedience? Why should He invest His revelation in you if you are just going to reject it and go your own way without counting the cost in terms of your relationship with Him? God wants you to agree to obey Him in your relationship with your wife and kids. He'll give you the details later.

Jesus Delegated Authority to You to Lead People

We are called to be like Jesus. If we will be like Jesus, we will influence people, and if we influence people, then we become a role model for them for the future reality of the world to come. The first place we do this must be in our homes. When your home life is strong, it gives you the credibility and the confidence to make your mark out in the world.

We're not just trying to get people to live nice lives and not get into trouble in this world. We're trying to show them that this world is just on-the-job training for the next. The Bible says that the average life span is "threescore years and ten and if by reason of strength . . . fourscore."[24] That isn't but eighty years. Can God reproduce what is in your life that is from Him for the future, or is your life polluted with worldliness? Are you influenced in your daily life by the wrong father (the devil)? You have eternal life. You are going to live in eternity. The question is, what kind of rewards are you going to get?

The sixth foundational doctrine in Hebrews 6 is called eternal judgment, and the aspect of eternal judgment that God is dealing with is rewards. At the Great White Throne Judgment,[25] God rewards the wicked with eternal punishment. At the Judgment Seat of Christ,[26] He rewards the righteous.

The rewards of the wicked, the devil, and the fallen angels—all of them have a destined place in the lake of fire. All of the devil's people will spend time with the devil for eons and eons. All of almighty God's people will spend time with Him forever.

God Gave Adam His Own Inner Attributes

God gave Adam three abilities that made Him like God: He was made like God in his inner attributes, and he had the ability to choose and the ability to reason. Even though we fall short of God's glory, He still sees us as He ordained us to be.

Creating a man and then creating a woman to help him was God's idea. We were created with His attributes so we could carry out His purposes and carry His destiny within us. "How blessed is God! And what a blessing he is! Long before he laid down the earth's foundations, he had us in mind, had settled on us as the focus of his love, to be made whole and holy by his love."[27]

God wants us to be like Him on the inside so that we will have the ability to take dominion as He intended Adam to do. When Adam fell He lost the divine commission over the Garden and over the world. It is now restored to us through Christ.

The original dominion mandate was a corporate dominion to both man and woman. Inside the man, before the woman was visible, she was there. There was only one human being visible, but there were two in potential within that body. When God spoke out of His creative order in Genesis 1, He was addressing them both.

> Then God said, "Let Us make man in Our image, according to Our likeness; let them have dominion over the fish of the sea, over the birds of the air, and over the cattle, over all the earth and over every creeping thing that creeps on the earth."
>
> So God created man in His own image; in the image of God He created him; male and female He created them. Then God blessed them, and God said to them, "Be fruitful and multiply; fill the earth and subdue it; have dominion over the fish of the sea, over the birds of the air, and over every living thing that moves on the earth."
>
> And God said, "See, I have given you every herb that yields seed which is on the face of all the earth, and every tree whose fruit yields seed; to you it shall be for food. Also, to every beast of the earth, to every bird of the air, and to everything that creeps on the earth, in which there is life, I have given every green herb for food," and it was so.
>
> Then God saw everything that He had made, and indeed it was very good. So the evening and the morning were the sixth day.[28]

OUR MARRIAGE TO JESUS IS COMING

When you marry, you restore that oneness of body, soul, and spirit that existed when God blessed man with the woman still inside him. The two of you together become unified to fulfill His eternal plan, and your relationship to each other and to God is already established in heaven. There is a wholeness about you when you are called to be together, and you walk out that wholeness every day in sacrificial love.

When you are born again, you enter the espousal period for another marriage that brings an even greater level of wholeness to your life. This time you are preparing to marry Jesus. The Bible calls it the Marriage of the Lamb. This time the spotlight is not on the bride, as with all marriages now, but on the Groom, Jesus.

This is what the brothers call meddling, but I'm going to say it anyhow. Our present-day weddings should be changed to focus on the *bridegroom*, not the bride! That's one of the things that should distinguish a Christian marriage from the marriage of unbelievers, because the groom represents Jesus Christ in the coming Marriage Supper of the Lamb. Notice that it isn't called the "Marriage of the Bride."

God presented Adam with a wife who was created especially for him. Therefore it would be safe to say that his wedding was for the man. Adam had looked for a helper among the animals and could not find one. The entire setting and ceremony of God's provision of Adam's bride was arranged before the woman was created.

Women will have a hard time thinking of the wedding as an event designed to focus on the men and not on them! Can you imagine the bride letting the man handle all the details of the wedding, let alone the man wanting to do it? But that was the biblical model in the beginning and will be the same at the end.

In the beginning, Adam's marriage to Mrs. Adam (her name didn't become Eve until after the Fall) was arranged by God. Marriage has been the work of God from eternity to eternity. In the life to come, it is the Bride who makes herself ready, but it is the Lamb of God who has set everything in place for her to come. John heard the multitudes in Heaven saying, " 'Let us be glad and rejoice and give Him glory, for the marriage of the Lamb has come, and His wife has made herself ready.' And to her it was granted to be arrayed in fine linen, clean and bright, for the fine linen is the righteous acts of the saints."[29]

His wife has made herself ready. Are you ready to be the bride of Christ?

The Jewish Wedding Helps Us to Understand How Christians Marry Christ

The Middle Eastern Jewish wedding is described in both the Old and New Testaments. It includes three main stages of progression, leading to the consummation of the marriage. God uses the example of earthly things to help us understand heavenly things. He uses the example of the Jewish marriage on earth to help us understand the marriage of Christ and the Church in heaven.

The three stages of the Jewish wedding are (1) the betrothal, (2) the coming of the bridegroom for his bride, and (3) the actual ceremony, including the marriage supper and the physical consummation—the sealing of the blood covenant of marriage.

Here is the application of those three stages to the marriage of Christ and the Church.

1) *The betrothal* is the beginning of a legally binding covenant that comes when individual members of the body of Christ are saved.
2) *The coming of the Bridegroom for His Bride* is the rapture of the Church.
3) *The Marriage Supper of the Lamb* occurs in connection with the Second Coming of Christ to establish His millennial kingdom.

The Excitement of Getting Ready to Marry Christ

God enters into a covenant with you when you are born again. That begins your espousal period. From then on you should begin preparing to be the Bride of Christ.

When a woman knows she is going to be married on earth, doesn't she get excited? She gets seriously busy preparing herself. This is the most important day of her life! She goes out shopping for the most elegant dress she can find, the prettiest veil, the most beautiful flowers. And you know who she wants to please? Her groom. She dresses for him. She finds a style of dress that will have him standing with his mouth open when she walks down that aisle.

As a Christian, you should be paying lots of attention to your preparation to marry Jesus. Just as the bride dresses in white, you should dress yourself in righteousness. As she is constantly thinking about how she can please her groom, you should be always thinking about how you can please the Lord. You should be growing continuously into the kind of person Jesus would want to marry. Every day He should see by the excitement in your life that you are trying to honor

Him as Lord. Then, when the time comes for your Groom to appear and take you to His wedding, you'll be ready, and He'll be excited!

Do You Have a Heart for Jesus?

Jesus lived out His earthly life as a Jew. His parents' wedding and the weddings He attended were part of the Jewish culture. They helped foreshadow the coming Marriage Supper of the Lamb.

The following section describes the similarities between the traditional Jewish wedding—as described in both the Old Testament and the New Testament—and the marriage of Christ and the Church.

As you read, check out your heart.

Are you in love with Jesus? Is He your First Love?

Are you being faithful to Him during your espousal period?

Do you love, honor, and obey Him as His espoused Bride should do?

In a wedding on earth, only one person who comes to the wedding knows she is the bride. There is no doubt about it in her mind. Everyone else is a guest or a member of the wedding party, and they know it. Do you know it? Are you preparing yourself for that great day?

Examine Your Heart Toward Your Wife

Are you in love with and committed to your wife? Is she your first love on earth, or do you have more love for your job, your children, or your momma than you do for your wife?

Do you respect and honor your wife?

Are you seeking on a daily basis to be a better husband?

Can Jesus see from the way that you treat your wife that He would want to be married to you?

STAGES IN THE JEWISH WEDDING CEREMONY

Stage 1: The Man Leaves His Father's House to Find His Bride

Jewish marriage. The young man traveled from his father's house to the home of a prospective bride.

Example from Scripture—Old Testament:

"Then Isaac called Jacob and blessed him, and charged him, and said to him: 'You shall not take a wife from the daughters of Canaan. Arise, go to Padan Aram, to the house of Bethuel your mother's father; and take yourself a wife from there of the daughters of Laban your mother's brother. May God Almighty bless you, and make you fruitful and multiply you, that you may be an assembly of peoples; And give you the blessing of Abraham, to you and your descendants with you, that you may inherit the land in which you are a stranger, which God gave to Abraham.'

"So Isaac sent Jacob away, and went to Padan Aram, to Laban the son of Bethuel the Syrian, the brother of Rebekah, the mother of Jacob and Esau."[30]

Christ and the Church. Christ left His Father's house in heaven and came to earth to win His Bride, humbling Himself as the lowliest man.

Example from Scripture—New Testament:

"Let this mind be in you which was also in Christ Jesus, who, being in the form of God, did not consider it robbery to be equal with God, but made Himself of no reputation, taking the form of a bondservant, and coming in the likeness of men."[31]

Stage 2: The Groom Pays the Bride's Purchase Price

Jewish marriage. The groom negotiated with the father of his prospective bride to determine the price that must be paid to purchase his daughter. In so doing, the groom honored his future father-in-law for his role in raising his daughter, and also indicated his willingness to take financial responsibility for his bride.

Example from Scripture—Old Testament:

In the case of Jacob, Laban, the father of Rachel, exacted the price of seven years of labor before he would let him marry Rachel.

"Then Laban said to Jacob, 'Because you are my relative, should you therefore serve me for nothing? Tell me, what should your wages be?'

"Now Laban had two daughters: the name of the elder was Leah, and the name of the younger was Rachel. Leah's eyes were delicate, but Rachel was beautiful of form and appearance. Now Jacob loved Rachel; so he said, 'I will serve you seven years for Rachel your younger daughter.'

"And Laban said, 'It is better that I give her to you than that I should give her to another man. Stay with me.' So Jacob served seven years for Rachel, and they seemed only a few days to him because of the love he had for her."[32]

Christ and the Church. Christ paid the bridal price for us with His own blood.

Example from Scripture—New Testament:
"For you were bought at a price: therefore glorify God in your body and in your spirit, which are God's."[33]

Example from Scripture—New Testament:
"It cost God plenty to get you out of that dead-end, empty-headed life you grew up in. He paid with Christ's sacred blood, you know. He died like an unblemished, sacrificial lamb. And this was no afterthought. Even though it has only lately—at the end of the ages—become public knowledge, God always knew he was going to do this for you."[34]

Stage 3. The Marriage Covenant Is Sealed and the Bride Is Set Apart for the Groom

Jewish marriage. As soon as the bridegroom paid the purchase price, the marriage relationship was established. From then on, the espoused man and the woman were considered as husband and wife, even though no physical union had taken place.

Example from Scripture—Old Testament:
"If a young woman who is a virgin is betrothed to a husband, and a man finds her in the city and lies with her, then you shall bring them both out to the gate of that city, and you shall stone them to death with stones, the young woman because she did not cry out in the city, and the man because he humbled his neighbor's wife; so you shall put away the evil from among you.

"But if a man finds a betrothed young woman in the countryside, and the man forces her and lies with her, then only the man who lay with her shall die. But you shall do nothing to the young woman; there is in the young woman no sin deserving of death, for just as when a man rises against his neighbor and kills him, even so is this matter. For he found her in the countryside, and the betrothed young woman cried out, but there was no one to save her."[35]

Example from Scripture—New Testament:
"Now the birth of Jesus Christ was as follows: After His mother Mary was betrothed to Joseph, before they came together, she was found with child of the Holy Spirit. Then Joseph her husband, being a just man, and not wanting to make her a public example, was minded to put her away secretly."[36]

Christ and the Church. As soon as believers are born again, they are sanctified, or set apart, exclusively for Christ.

Example from Scripture—Old Testament:
God said to Israel, "Later, when I passed by and saw you again, you were old enough for marriage; and I wrapped my cloak around you to legally declare my marriage vow. I signed a covenant with you, and you became mine."[37]

Example from Scripture—New Testament:
"For I am jealous for you with godly jealousy. For I have betrothed you to one husband, that I may present you as a chaste virgin to Christ."[38]

Stage 4. The Groom and Bride Drink from the Cup of Betrothal

Jewish marriage. When the covenant was established, the groom and the bride drank from a cup over which the betrothal benediction had been pronounced.

Christ and the Church. At the Last Supper, Christ served a covenant cup of Communion to the apostles. They were the first representatives of His Bride, the Church.

Example from Scripture—New Testament:

"The Master, Jesus, on the night of his betrayal, took bread. Having given thanks, he broke it and said, 'This is my body, broken for you. Do this to remember me.'

After supper, he did the same thing with the cup: 'This cup is my blood, my new covenant with you. Each time you drink this cup, remember me.' "[39]

Stage 5. The Groom Returns Alone to His Father's House

Jewish marriage. After the marriage covenant was in effect, the groom left the home of the bride and returned to his father's house. He remained there for a period of twelve months separated from his bride.

Christ and the Church. After His resurrection, Christ returned to His Father's house. He had paid the purchase price for His Bride with His own blood on the cross. He remains there, awaiting the day when He will return for His Bride.

Example from Scripture—New Testament:

"As [the apostles] watched, [Jesus] was taken up and disappeared in a cloud. They stood there, staring into the empty sky. Suddenly two men appeared—in white robes! They said, 'You Galileans!— why do you just stand here looking up at an empty sky? This very Jesus who was taken up from among you to heaven will come as certainly—and mysteriously—as he left.' "[40]

Stage 6. The Groom Prepares a Place for the Bride

Jewish marriage. During this period of separation, the bride gathered her wardrobe and prepared for married life. The groom prepared living accommodations for his bride.

Christ and the Church. Christ is preparing a place for His Bride and is also sending pastors and teachers to perfect the Bride for the coming wedding.

Example from Scripture—New Testament:

"In my Father's house are many mansions: if it were not so, I would have told you. I go to prepare a place for you."[41]

Stage 7. The Groom and His Companions Return for the Bride

Jewish marriage. After this period of separation, the groom, the best man, and other male attendants met at the house of the groom's father, usually at night, and then walked together in a torch-lit procession to the home of the bride.

Christ and the Church. Christ will come from His Father's house in heaven accompanied by an angelic host.

Example from Scripture—New Testament:
   "And if I go and prepare a place for you, I will come again, and receive you unto myself; that where I am, there ye may be also."[42]

Stage 8. The Bride Knows the Groom Has Returned When She Hears a Shout

Jewish marriage. The bride was expecting her groom to come for her, but she did not know the exact time. Thus, the groom's arrival was preceded by a shout.

Example from Scripture—New Testament:
   "And at midnight there was a cry made, Behold, the bridegroom cometh; go ye out to meet him. Then all those virgins arose, and trimmed their lamps."[43]

Christ and the Church. Christ's return will be preceded by a shout. We expect His return, but we do not know the day or hour.

Example from Scripture—New Testament:
   "For the Lord himself shall descend from heaven with a shout, with the voice of the archangel, and with the trump of God: and the dead in Christ shall rise first."[44]

Stage 9. The Groom Takes Home the Bride

Jewish marriage. The groom received the well-prepared bride with her female attendants and returned to his father's house.

Example from Scripture—New Testament:

Jesus told this story: "Then the kingdom of heaven shall be likened to ten virgins who took their lamps and went out to meet the bridegroom. Now five of them were wise, and five were foolish. Those who were foolish took their lamps and took no oil with them, but the wise took oil in their vessels with their lamps. But while the bridegroom was delayed, they all slumbered and slept.

"And at midnight a cry was heard: 'Behold, the bridegroom is coming; go out to meet him!'

"Then all those virgins arose and trimmed their lamps. And the foolish said to the wise, 'Give us some of your oil, for our lamps are going out.'

"But the wise answered, saying, 'No, lest there should not be enough for us and you; but go rather to those who sell, and buy for yourselves.'

"And while they went to buy, the bridegroom came, and those who were ready went in with him to the wedding; and the door was shut. Afterward the other virgins came also, saying, 'Lord, Lord, open to us!'

"But he answered and said, 'Assuredly, I say to you, I do not know you.'

"Watch therefore, for you know neither the day nor the hour in which the Son of Man is coming."[45]

Christ and the Church. The bride will be caught up with the Lord to be with Him.

Example from Scripture—New Testament:

"And the dead in Christ will rise first. Then we who are alive and remain shall be caught up together with them in the clouds to meet the Lord in the air. And thus we shall always be with the Lord."[46]

Stage 10. The Bride and Groom Are Secluded for the Physical Consummation of the Marriage

Jewish marriage. The bride and groom entered the bridal chamber and privately entered into physical union for the first time, consummating the marriage. Sometimes this took place during the week-long marriage festivities while the guests were still celebrating. In the scriptural account, even though Laban tricked Jacob by giving him Leah instead of Rachel, once the marriage was consummated they were legally wed.

Example from Scripture—Old Testament:
   "So Jacob served seven years for Rachel, and they seemed only a few days to him because of the love he had for her. Then Jacob said to Laban, 'Give me my wife, for my days are fulfilled, that I may go in to her.' And Laban gathered together all the men of the place and made a feast.

   "Now it came to pass in the evening, that he took Leah his daughter and brought her to Jacob; and he went in to her. And Laban gave his maid Zilpah to his daughter Leah as a maid. So it came to pass in the morning, that behold, it was Leah. And he said to Laban, 'What is this you have done to me? Was it not for Rachel that I served you?' "[47]

Christ and the Church. Christ's union with the Church will take place in heaven for all eternity.

Example from Scripture—New Testament:
   "And after these things I heard a great voice of much people in heaven, saying, . . . Let us be glad and rejoice, and give honour to him: for the marriage of the Lamb is come, and his wife hath made herself ready.

   "And to her was granted that she should be arrayed in fine linen, clean and white: for the fine linen is the righteousness of saints.

   "And he saith unto me, Write, Blessed are they which are called unto the marriage supper of the Lamb."[48]

Are you blessed? You are if you're called to the Marriage Supper of the Lamb. Be blessed, and be a blessing to your wife. Get her ready and get yourself ready to be the Bride of Christ. Jesus is coming soon.

PRAYER FOR BECOMING LIKE JESUS

Father, thank You so much for the anointing of the Holy Spirit and for the Word of the Lord. You are breaking forth on the right hand

and on the left. Thank You that as You are teaching us and we are being trained for eternity, we can have joy unspeakable now.

Thank You that you are giving us the capacity to be joyful in the midst of trouble.

Thank You for the witness of the Scripture that You are training us to be like You, and someday we will be with You forever. Thank You for that awesome promise. Please help us to get ready.

In Jesus' name I pray. Amen.

SELAH

Create a plan where you can begin not only to implement what you have learned in this book, but also to teach it to others. Wouldn't an improvement in people's marriages make a difference in your neighborhood, your church, and your workplace? Don't you know people right now who are hurting because of their relationships with their wives, their children, or their in-laws?

In some foreign countries, missionaries who would ordinarily be forbidden to preach the Gospel are allowed to teach the Bible in the context of teaching the people the English language. Maybe a series of lessons from this book on marriage for your unsaved friends would break through that translation barrier you have been trying to cross to teach them about Jesus.

Think about it, pray about it, and come up with a plan. Then do it.

You're the one. God doesn't have to look for another.

$\mathscr{N}$OTES

PREFACE

[1]Revelation 3:20 KJV.
[2]Deuteronomy 4:29.
[3]Joshua 1:6–8 NIV. Emphasis added.
[4]1 Timothy 4, *The Message*.

CHAPTER 1. REALLY LOVE YOUR WIFE

[1]Romans 8:28–29.
[2]Proverbs 21:4 KJV.
[3]Matthew 11:29 KJV.
[4]Ephesians 5:25 NKJV.
[5]John 19:30.
[6]Isaiah 53:12.
[7]Matthew 19:19, 22:39; Mark 12:31, 33; Luke 10:27.
[8]Luke 9:23 NKJV. See also Matthew 16:24 and Mark 8:34.
[9]Luke 9:29 NKJV.
[10]Luke 9:35 NKJV.
[11]Luke 22:27.
[12]Mark 10:47 NKJV.
[13]Mark 10, *The Message*.
[14]2 Corinthians 3:18 NKJV.
[15]2 Corinthians 3:16 KJV.
[16]2 Corinthians 3:17 KJV.
[17]Romans 8:29.
[18]Ephesians 5:26–27 NKJV.
[19]Ephesians 5:28–30 NKJV.
[20]Ephesians 5:31–33 NKJV.
[21]Genesis 1:28 KJV.
[22]John 1:4.
[23]Luke 22:27.
[24]Luke 22:24–27 NKJV.
[25]Psalms 139:23–24 KJV.
[26]Galatians 4:19 KJV.
[27]Hebrews 12:1–2 KJV.
[28]Jude 1:22 KJV.
[29]Isaiah 66:7–9 KJV.
[30]Revelation 19, *The Message*.
[31]Genesis 13:14–15 NKJV.
[32]Ephesians 6:12 NKJV.
[33]Ephesians 6, *The Message*.
[34]Exodus 3:10–12 TLB.
[35]Philippians 2:13 KJV.
[36]2 Corinthians 3:6.
[37]Exodus 3:12.
[38]Galatians 5:20.

CHAPTER 2. BECOMING BLENDED:
MAKING THE TRANSITION FROM
BEING SINGLE TO BEING MARRIED

[1]Isaiah 54:5.
[2]1 Corinthians 7:5.
[3]Hebrews 10:25 TLB.
[4]Revelation 2, *The Message*.
[5]2 Timothy 2:15 KJV.
[6]Deuteronomy 24:5 NIV.
[7]Haggai 2:8 KJV.
[8]Jeremiah 17:5–8 TLB.
[9]John 8:29 NKJV.

[10]Galatians 6, *The Message.*
[11]1 John 2:16–17 KJV.
[12]Ephesians 1:6.
[13]1 John 4:8–12 TLB.
[14]Matthew 5, *The Message.*
[15]Matthew 5, *The Message.*
[16]Hebrews 13:5.
[17]Song of Solomon 2:15.
[18]John 3:16 KJV.
[19]John 15:12–13 KJV.
[20]Philippians 2:5–8 NKJV.
[21]Ephesians 5:21.
[22]James 4:10 NKJV.
[23]Kenneth W. Osbeck, *101 More Hymn Stories* (Grand Rapids, Michigan: Kregel Publications, 1985), p. 141.
[24]Ephesians 4:15.
[25]Matthew 5:7.
[26]James 2:13 NASB.
[27]2 Corinthians 2:14–15 KJV.
[28]John 5:41 KJV.
[29]Psalms 75:6–7 KJV.
[30]Romans 2:15.
[31]Isaiah 62:10 KJV.
[32]Ezekiel 33:6.
[33]Matthew 5:8 KJV.
[34]*Book of Common Prayer* (Episcopal) (New York: The Church Hymnal Corporation, 1979), p. 427.
[35]Deuteronomy 22:13–19 TLB.
[36]Deuteronomy 22:25 NKJV.
[37]1 Corinthians 3:16–17 NKJV.
[38]Hebrews 13:4 NKJV.
[39]Acts 20:35.
[40]Song of Solomon 2:10–12 TLB.
[41]Romans 1:18.
[42]Matthew 5:8.
[43]Romans 12:1 NASB.
[44]2 Corinthians 11:14 KJV.
[45]2 Corinthians 11, *The Message.*
[46]Joshua 3:5 KJV.
[47]Ezekiel 36:27.
[48]Matthew 5:6.

[49]Leviticus 11:44 KJV.
[50]Numbers 15:37–40.
[51]Matthew 6:14.
[52]James 4:7 KJV.
[53]James 4, *The Message.*
[54]Luke 8:46.
[55]Strong's number 1411 (Greek), *The Complete Word Study Dictionary: New Testament.* Revised Edition (Chattanooga, Tennessee: AMG Publishers, 1973).
[56]Matthew 5:28 NKJV.
[57]2 Corinthians 10:5.
[58]Matthew 5:8 KJV.
[59]Matthew 5:29 NKJV.
[60]Romans 1, *The Message.*
[61]1 Corinthians 6:18.
[62]Revelation 21:8.
[63]Galatians 6:9–10 NKJV.
[64]1 John 3:10 NKJV.
[65]Hebrews 6:6 TLB.
[66]1 John 1:7–9 NKJV.
[67]John 8:11.
[68]Ezekiel 33:6.
[69]Hebrews 12:2 KJV.
[70]Hebrews 12, *The Message.*
[71]John 14:2–3 KJV.
[72]Hebrews 7:25.
[73]Isaiah 65:24 NKJV.
[74]Romans 8:29 NKJV.
[75]Romans 8:30 NKJV.
[76]Romans 8, *The Message.*
[77]Ephesians 1:6.
[78]Romans 8:34 NKJV.
[79]Romans 8, *The Message.*
[80]See Leviticus 25 and Deuteronomy 15.

CHAPTER 3: WOMEN SHOULD MARRY ONLY GROWN-UP MEN

[1]Song of Solomon 2:4–5 TLB.
[2]*American Heritage Dictionary,* Second College Edition (Boston:

Houghton Mifflin Company, 1985).

[3]Hosea 1:2.

[4]Malachi 2:14–16 TLB.

[5]Matthew 12:31–32.

[6]1 Corinthians 13:4–8, 11 TLB.

[7]Ezekiel 33:17 NASB.

[8]Ezekiel 33:7–8 NASB.

[9]Romans 14:10.

[10]Luke 9:29.

[11]Proverbs 17:22 NKJV.

[12]James 4:10 KJV.

[13]Ephesians 4:15.

[14]Luke 16:12 NKJV.

CHAPTER 4: BLOW YOUR WIFE'S MIND

[1]Matthew 6, *The Message.*

[2]Matthew 6:4 NASB.

[3]1 Timothy 5:8 NKJV.

[4]Luke 17:10 NIV.

[5]Matthew 6:19–21 NKJV.

[6]Ezekiel 16:9–14 TLB.

[7]1 John 4, *The Message.*

[8]Romans 2:4.

[9]Ephesians 5:25 KJV.

[10]Genesis 2:21–23 KJV.

[11]Genesis 2:23 KJV.

[12]Genesis 2:24 KJV.

[13]Hosea 6:3.

[14]James 1:19 KJV.

[15]James 1, *The Message.*

[16]Acts 2:42 KJV.

[17]Craig S. Keener, *The IVP Bible Background Commentary, New Testament* (Downers Grove, Illinois: InterVarsity Press: 1993), p. 330.

[18]2 Corinthians 5:18–19.

[19]Leviticus 25 and Deuteronomy 15.

CHAPTER 5: HAVE THE HOME-COURT ADVANTAGE ALL THE TIME

[1]Matthew 7:16 NKJV.

[2]Genesis 1:31 NIV.

[3]Ephesians 5:25–26 KJV.

[4]Psalms 27:1 KJV.

[5]Genesis 2:21–25 TLB.

[6]Genesis 9:18–27.

[7]"The union of husband and wife in heart, body, and mind is intended by God for their mutual joy; for the help and comfort given one another in prosperity and adversity; and, when it is God's will, for the procreation of children and their nurture in the knowledge and love of the Lord. Therefore marriage is not to be entered into unadvisedly or lightly, but reverently, deliberately, and in accordance with the purposes for which it was instituted by God." *The Book of Common Prayer,* p. 423.

[8]Hebrews 13:5.

[9]2 Timothy 2:13 TLB.

[10]Revelation 12:11.

[11]Philippians 2:1–5, *The Message.*

[12]Romans 5:6–8 TLB.

[13]Ephesians 5, *The Message.*

[14]Pronounced *ek-klay-see' ah.* Strong's number 1577.

[15]James 3, *The Message.*

[16]James 3, *The Message.*

[17]1 Peter 3, *The Message.*

[18]1 Peter 3, *The Message.*

[19]Proverbs 18:21 NKJV.

[20]1 Corinthians 13:7 TLB adapted.

[21]Ephesians 5:27 KJV.

[22]2 Corinthians 6, *The Message.*

[23]2 Corinthians 6:3–7 NKJV.

[24]James 4:10 KJV.

[25]Isaiah 57:15 NKJV.

[26]1 Peter 3:4 KJV.

[27]Strong's number 4240 (Hebrew), *The Complete Word Study Dictionary: New Testament.* Revised Edition (Chattanooga, Tennessee: AMG Publishers, 1973).

[28]1 Peter 3, *The Message.*
[29]1 Corinthians 3, *The Message.*
[30]1 Corinthians 3, *The Message.*
[31]1 Chronicles 12:2.
[32]Titus 2, *The Message.*
[33]1 Chronicles 22:19 NIV.
[34]Proverbs 18:23 NKJV.
[35]Colossians 3, *The Message.*
[36]Colossians 3, *The Message.*
[37]Matthew 7, *The Message.*
[38]Matthew 20:26–28 KJV.
[39]Song of Solomon 2:10–13 NKJV.
[40]2 Corinthians 13, *The Message.*
[41]*The Book of Common Prayer.*
[42]Deuteronomy 11:18–21 KJV.
[43]Philippians 1:9–11 NKJV.

CHAPTER 6: HOW LOW WILL YOU GO
FOR YOUR WIFE?
[1]Proverbs 21:4.
[2]Isaiah 14:13–14 TLB.
[3]Isaiah 14:15–16 TLB.
[4]Luke 9:55.
[5]John 15:13 KJV.
[6]Revelation 12:10 KJV.
[7]1 John 2:16 KJV.
[8]Philippians 2, *The Message.*
[9]Ephesians 5:25 KJV.
[10]See Philippians 2:8–11.
[11]Revelation 12:10–11 NKJV.
[12]All quotes from *Uncle Tom's Cabin* by Harriet Beecher Stowe use the dialect and punctuation style of the author. It was first published in 1852.
[13]Matthew 5:5 KJV.
[14]John 12:24 NKJV.
[15]2 Corinthians 5:6–8 NKJV.
[16]From an unknown slave woman (1816). From a Stephen Hays tract, American Tract Society.

CHAPTER 7: IN-LAWS ARE NOT
OUTLAWS
[1]John 4, *The Message.*
[2]Read Genesis 29.

[3]Genesis 29:20 NIV.
[4]Read 1 Samuel 17 and 18.
[5]Read 2 Samuel 1.
[6]Exodus 20:12 KJV.
[7]*Kabad* or *kabed* is pronounced *kaw-bad* and is Strong's number 3513 (Hebrew).
[8]Exodus 4:18 TLB.
[9]Exodus 18:7 KJV.
[10]The Hebrew word *shachah* [pronounced *shaw-khaw'*], Strong's number 7812.
[11]Exodus 18:8–12 NIV.
[12]Exodus 18:13–26 NIV.
[13]Exodus 18:27 NIV.
[14]Matthew 15, *The Message.*
[15]Proverbs 23:24 NKJV.
[16]Proverbs 1:8–9 NKJV.
[17]Proverbs 30:11–13 TLB.
[18]Romans 12, *The Message.*
[19]Proverbs 28:13 TLB.
[20]Proverbs 23:22–23 TLB.
[21]Proverbs 11:30.
[22]Isaiah 58:7 NKJV.
[23]Isaiah 58:7 TLB.
[24]Song of Solomon 2:15 KJV.
[25]Romans 2:4 TLB.
[26]Proverbs 31:29–30 NKJV.
[27]Titus 2:7 TLB.
[28]Titus 2:2 TLB.
[29]Titus 2:3 TLB.
[30]Titus 2:4–5 TLB.
[31]Titus 2:8 TLB.
[32]Ephesians 6:4 TLB.
[33]Deuteronomy 22:18–19 TLB. See also verses 13–17.
[34]Ezekiel 3:17–19 NKJV.
[35]1 Corinthians 13:8 TLB.

CHAPTER 8: CHILDREN ARE A
BLESSING FROM THE LORD

[1]Luke 15, *The Message.*
[2]*Prodigals and Those Who Love Them* by Ruth Bell Graham

(Colorado Springs, Colorado: Focus on the Family Publishing, 1991).
3Romans 8:1 KJV.
4Luke 15, *The Message.*
5Romans 6:11 KJV.
6Proverbs 22:6 KJV.
7Romans 5, *The Message.*
8Romans 5:8.
9Mark 12, *The Message.*
10Mark 12:29–31 KJV.
11Galatians 5:22–23 TLB.
12Isaiah 28:10 KJV.
13Ephesians 5:1 KJV.
14Ephesians 5, *The Message.*
15Exodus 20:12.
16Matthew 8:5–13.
17John 14:28.
18Ephesians 5:22 NKJV.
191 Corinthians 2:9–10 KJV.
20James 3:13–18 NIV.
211 John 4, *The Message.*
221 John 4, *The Message.*
23Matthew 18:2–4 NIV.
24Matthew 12:34 KJV.
25Introduction to Philippians, *The Message,* p. 411.
26Frederick Douglass, "Letter to His Former Master," published in *The Liberator* (Boston), September 22, 1848.
27Matthew 7:24–27.
281 Corinthians 3:9–15.

CHAPTER 9: BE THE MAN OF GOD YOUR FAMILY NEEDS
1John H. Sammis (1846–1919), "Trust and Obey," Osbeck, *101 More Hymn Stories,* p. 92.
2Hebrews 3:1.
3Hebrews 7:24–25 NKJV.
4Matthew 21:13 KJV.
51 Peter 5:7 TLB.
6Exodus 28:11.
7Deuteronomy 18:15.

8Matthew 7, *The Message.*
9Hebrews 3:9–11.
10Hebrews 4, *The Message.*
11Exodus 20:8 NKJV.
122 Peter 1:19.
13Osbeck, *101 More Hymn Stories,* p. 92.
14Joshua 1:7 TLB.
15See, for example, the story of Samuel's conception in 1 Samuel, Chapters 1 and 2, and Isaac's conception in Genesis, Chapters 17 through 21.
16Matthew 7:13–14 TLB.
17John 14:18 KJV.
18Proverbs 24:16 KJV.
19Genesis 3:21.
20Psalm 139:23–24 KJV.
21Luke 1, *The Message.*
22Luke 1, *The Message.*
23Psalm 139:13–16.
24Luke 23:45–46 NKJV.
25John 14:6 KJV.
26John 1:29.
27Osbeck, *101 Hymn Stories,* p. 146.
28Osbeck, *101 Hymn Stories,* p. 147.
29John 1:29 KJV.
30Genesis 6:9 KJV.
31Genesis 6:8 KJV.
32Genesis 6:18 NKJV.
33Genesis 6:9 NASB, including marginal definitions.
34Genesis 6:22 NASB.
35Hebrews 11, *The Message.*
36Deuteronomy 13:1–3, 10, NIV. Emphasis added.
37Deuteronomy 18:20–22 TLB.
38Ephesians 1:17 NIV.
39Isaiah 10:27.
40Pronounced *khris-tee-an-os'.* Strong's number 5546 (Greek).
41Pronounced *khris-tos'.* Strong's number 5547 (Greek).

[42]Leviticus 21:10 KJV.
[43]Exodus 40:15 NASB.
[44]Luke 6:38 NKJV.
[45]John 7:24 KJV.
[46]Hebrews 11:6.
[47]Psalms 133:1–2 NKJV.
[48]1 Corinthians 6:19–20.
[49]Psalms 118:24.
[50]Exodus 28:1.
[51]1 Peter 2:9 KJV.
[52]Hebrews 2:17 KJV.
[53]Genesis 1:27.
[54]2 Peter 1:4 KJV.
[55]Romans 8, *The Message*.
[56]Colossians 1:26–27.
[57]Ephesians 3:20 NKJV. Emphasis added.

CHAPTER 10: MARRIAGE IS ON-THE-JOB TRAINING FOR THE FUTURE

[1]1 Corinthians 15:6.
[2]Revelation 11:15 NKJV.
[3]Luke 22:29.
[4]Luke 22:29 KJV.
[5]Luke 22:26 NIV.
[6]Isaiah 57:15 NIV.
[7]Matthew 25:21 NKJV.
[8]Ecclesiastes 3:11 NASB. Marginal renderings signified by brackets.
[9]Mark 4:19 KJV.
[10]Psalms 30:5 KJV.
[11]Details of the story are adapted from the book *Dam Break in Georgia* by K. Neill Foster with Eric Mills (Camp Hill, Pennsylvania: Horizon Books, 1978).
[12]Song of Solomon 8:7 KJV.
[13]1 Corinthians 13:8.
[14]Stephen R. Covey, *The 7 Habits of Highly Effective People* (New York: Simon and Schuster, 1989), p. 201.
[15]Relevation 3:17 KJV.
[16]Matthew 6:10 KJV.
[17]Daniel 7:9–12 NKJV.
[18]Daniel 7:13–14 NKJV.
[19]Matthew 25:21 NKJV.
[20]This story is adapted from the book *Beyond Defeat* by James E. Johnson with David W. Balsiger (1978).
[21]*Beyond Defeat,* p. 14.
[22]Proverbs 29:18.
[23]Genesis 12:1, 4–5 NIV.
[24]Psalms 90:10 KJV.
[25]Revelation 20:11–15.
[26]Romans 14:10–12, 2 Corinthians 5:10.
[27]Ephesians 1, *The Message*.
[28]Genesis 1:26–31 NKJV.
[29]Revelation 19:7–8 NKJV.
[30]Genesis 28:1–5 NKJV.
[31]Philippians 2:5–7 NKJV.
[32]Genesis 29:15–20 NKJV.
[33]1 Corinthians 6:20 NKJV.
[34]1 Peter 1, *The Message*.
[35]Deuteronomy 22:23–27 NKJV.
[36]Matthew 1:18–19 NKJV.
[37]Ezekiel 16:8 TLB.
[38]2 Corinthians 11:2 NKJV.
[39]1 Corinthians 11, *The Message*.
[40]Acts 1, *The Message*.
[41]John 14:2 KJV.
[42]John 14:3 KJV.
[43]Matthew 25:6–7 KJV.
[44]1 Thessalonians 4:16 KJV.
[45]Matthew 25:1–13 NKJV.
[46]1 Thessalonians 4:16–17 NKJV.
[47]Genesis 29:20–25 NKJV.
[48]Revelation 19:1, 7–9 KJV.